MW00636691

SACRED INNOCENCE

WENDY M. JOHNSON

Dear Sara + Jimmy,
I am so grateful for you
both. I absolutely love
Jonah, Dessa Rose + Grace. I
love your family + have been
so blessed + have you in my life.
love. Wendy

Living Legacy Publishing, Inc.
North Salt Lake, Utah

Editor: Gary Wright, Cheryl Call
Cover Designer: Nicole Jaussi
Back Photo: Busath Photographers
Front Photo: Joey Johnson
Printer: MC Printing, Provo, Utah

Living Legacy Publishing, Inc.

Copyright © 2007 by Wendy M. Johnson

All rights reserved. No part of this book may be reproduced
or transmitted in any form or by any means, electronic or
mechanical, including photocopying, recording, or by any
information storage and retrieval system, without permission
in writing from the publisher.

Published by Living Legacy Publishing, Inc.

Printed in the United States of America

Johnson, Wendy Michelle, 1967-
        Sacred Innocence : An inspiring story of one
mother's promise to provide a better life for her children by
finding the courage to confront her childhood abuse and
experiencing the healing powers of Jesus Christ.

Wendy M. Johnson
ISBN-13: 978-0-9791487-0-5
ISBN-8 98447-001007

Please visit www.Livinglegacypublishing.com

ACKNOWLEDGEMENTS

I would like to take this time to thank my husband, Joey T. Johnson for supporting my healing process. I am so grateful for his wisdom and spiritual counsel. We both desired a better life for our children and were willing to do whatever it would take to give them that life. The better life we strived for consisted of stopping the chain of abuse in both of our family lines. As converts to The Church of Jesus Christ of Latter-day Saints we feel we are pioneers and Joey has walked "a mile in my shoes" many times, always supporting me and at times carrying me. I am so grateful for him loving me during my darkest hours. I am grateful for the sealing powers of the temple and the eternal perspective it gave to our marriage.

I would like to acknowledge my five children. They constantly gave me the motivation to change and work through the most difficult times in my life. I am grateful for motherhood and motherly love. The greatest gift I can give my children is showing them that the gospel can heal pain and change lives. My life is a living testimony of the power of the gospel and I want them to know that I could not have found the courage to have gone through what I did to heal without them. They bring joy in my life that the gospel promises and I love them.

I would like to acknowledge the power of Jesus Christ. Upon joining the church in my early twenties I tapped into His gospel and my life changed forever. His gospel and teachings have enabled me to experience joy in this lifetime after so much heartache. I am eternally grateful for His gospel and being able to experience laughter, optimism and love.

Sacred Innocence

There is Life After Abuse

Wendy M. Johnson

Living Legacy Publishing, Inc.

North Salt Lake, Utah

5

TABLE OF CONTENTS

INTRODUCTION

This book was written with the sole purpose of talking about the subject of abuse and providing guidance on where to find answers to healing. I share quite openly about my journey in dealing with abuse and healing. My greatest desire and hope is that, by sharing my story, victims of abuse will come back to the Lord and learn to trust Him. A strong testimony that God does love us and has not forsaken us is the only way and assurance to healing.

I know it can be hard to believe, but healing from abuse is not only possible but obtainable in this lifetime. Finding the courage to confront our fears is possible with the aide of Jesus Christ. As a victim of abuse, you may have heard or been told that the abuse will stay with you forever; it will always be a part of you and you will always suffer from anxieties. I was told this time and time again and believed it for so long–*until* I decided to put the gospel to the test and see if the Lord could really heal the "brokenhearted."

What I found on my journey was that I was reachable, even though I was in the depths of depression, loneliness and doubt. My testimony was dangling by a thread. Although I went through the motions of day-to-day life, my heart ached underneath the surface. It was not until I made a conscious choice to see if I could really be healed that my life changed forever. I realized *healing is a conscious choice.* It is a goal one sets out to accomplish and it all starts with an earnest prayer to the Lord asking for guidance.

Many people who have not been abused will counsel to simply "get over it." They will question, "Why are you unable to move on?" When one's sacred innocence has been violated the pain from that experience or experiences confuse the victim about their very identity and worth. When a person's identity is at question, moving forward is difficult because that person questions the very essence of the gospel. They question the purpose of their existence. They question why Heavenly Father would let abuse happen.

These are serious questions that deserve valid answers. The most important principle I hope you learn as you read this book, is that there are answers to these questions. The void you feel inside can leave and you can be made whole as you learn to trust in the Lord.

You may attend church but only have a vague understanding of the power of the gospel of Jesus Christ. A strong testimony and true faith provide unconquerable power against all forces stopping you from healing. A strong testimony leads you to truths that no other form of information in this lifetime can bring you. It will become your sustaining power on your journey to healing.

I testify that the Lord loves you and has a path of success ready for you to tap into. You do not have to experience a lifetime of feeling worthless, damaged or flawed. Life does not have to be hard because of abuse. By confronting your abuse, your life can be transformed into a powerful testament that Jesus Christ has limitless power to help you to heal and enjoy a fulfilling life! As you set out on your own journey, let Him demonstrate His absolute power in your life and dispel your disbelief that healing can occur.

It is my hope as you read this book you will know you are not alone. Your feelings are shared by many others suffering from abuse. You may have suffered from physical, verbal, emotional or sexual abuse, or even rape. My story may be different from yours in some respects, but virtually all victims of violence experience many of the same feelings, have many of the same questions about healing, and share the same doubts you have. We have a lot in common. The most important commonality we share is that healing is possible for all of us. Just because you were abused, you were not robbed of your eternal possibilities and potential here on earth. Even though you were abused and may have made some wrong choices in life, the Lord still loves you in a very special way and you are worthy of His healing powers. Your journey will be different from mine. It may be shorter or longer. But never forget that Jesus Christ has a perfect love for you. Let Him into your life, and you will find peace from your trial and experience a life of fulfillment. You will find that there is life after abuse.

CHAPTER ONE

Past Feeling

It all started at a time in my life when I did not think much about the future. My life had consisted of many starts, but not many finishes. At times, when I thought of pursuing a dream, I could not follow through. I lived day by day.

I did know whenever I stepped out of my comfort zone I would get hurt. I did not want anymore pain. So I kept busy. I did not know what each new day would bring-only that if I did not keep busy, I would have to deal with reality. I had not dealt with it for a very long time. As a matter of fact, I had rarely faced it up to this point in my life.

As I reflect back on this time, I am amazed at how paralyzing my pain was. I hurt so badly that to do anything different would potentially cause more pain. Fear of the unknown was real to me as my past was filled with so many difficult experiences. Why move forward just to get hurt again? My life was a pattern of getting hurt. I got hurt at home, with friends, even with people I did not know. I decided to be cautious and to keep my guard up. I felt so alone in life and stopped trusting anyone. The thought of looking beyond my present situation rarely occurred. I was afraid of what something new would bring. Although I was tired of the hurting, pain had been with me since I can remember. Sometimes, I would try to wonder what life would be like without pain. Each time I would come up empty. I did not know what to replace the pain with.

I did not know of the journey that was before me. I just knew that to move past the pain, a miracle would be required. And, well, that is exactly what would happen.

I was 22 and still living at home with my parents. I had moved out for a short time with my ex-boyfriend and had recently moved back to their house. My parents were disappointed with me, but not for reasons you may think. They were not upset I lived with someone else. They were upset I left their house. It was not the first time.

My parents were uncomfortable with the thought of me growing up. They had a strong hold on me; however, I wanted to exercise freedom. I had rarely experienced it. The only time I had experienced freedom was when they did not know about it. It was either that way or I felt like a prisoner in their home.

I was not ready for real life. I was not ready to be an adult. I just knew I needed to get out of my parents' home. I had no-where else to go. Although I lived with my ex-boyfriend, it was not a first choice for both of us. He was helping me. We were on the verge of breaking up. I guess I was desperate. It was during this time I moved out that I could make my own choices. However bad they may have been, they were still my choices. My parents rarely talked with me and I rarely visited them.

On one of my rare visits I showed them my new car. I had bought it with my own money. They did not help at all. I was so proud of myself. I did something on my own without them. I felt like an adult should. My parents did not share the same excitement. They were not happy I was growing up. They saw something I did not even recognize at the time. They could see I was growing away from them and that made them angry. Most parents would be proud of their children buying their own automobile but mine saw it as an act of freedom. In my home freedom was only exercised behind their backs.

While I was away from home I started to have panic attacks. I would abruptly wake up in the middle of the night and it felt as if a heavy weight was on my chest and I could hardly breathe. Although I would wake up afraid that I could not breathe, I would be having a nightmare that I could not remember. I did not know what was happening to me. I was getting worried the affects of my drug use were catching up to me. During the day, I would notice a cut or bruise on my leg or arm and could not remember how I got it. It was as if I were *past feeling* and during my sleep something was trying to seep out.

Although my time away from home was short, I did grow. Going back to my parents' house was hard for me. The night I went back, my father was the only one home. There were no hugs welcoming me back. Instead, my father was raging. The house was a mess, as usual. Clothes were hanging all over the stair banisters and mail was scattered all over the staircase. I could hardly see the kitchen counters and he was upset that the house was like that. I fell right back into place. Fear set in and I hurried to help clean what I could. He felt it was important to clean out the home office which my mother also kept as her closet. I could not see the floor. He wanted me to clean it. It would take hours before I could see the floor as I hung up all her clothes and tried putting the papers back in random piles. It was not until I was exhausted, that I stopped and took my suitcase up to my room and went to bed.

I was upset at myself for having to move back to my parents' house. I could not make it on my own. In their house going to bed was difficult for me. During the day I would forget about my intense fear at night. Fear would set in. I did not understand why. As I would get into bed I would start to pray to someone, hoping I would be heard. I always prayed to sleep well and to not be so afraid. I was afraid I would be attacked by someone. I thought someone would walk right into my room and hurt me. As I got older my prayers became more like wishes, random thoughts of a better life. I lived in a home where my father was an atheist and my mother taught me that Jesus Christ and the stories in the *Holy Bible* were myths. Beyond me, there was no one. Only the hope that maybe, just maybe, there was more out there. I knew the environment I grew up in was somehow not right. Something inside of me told me it was wrong. But I knew nothing different. I saw nothing different. How could I believe any differently? It seemed when I was around my parents I would forget there was any hope. At night when I would pray, something inside of me told me I was worth a lot more than how my parents treated me. I did not know what to do about it because I always seemed to come back to believing I was lazy and wouldn't amount to much in life. I was told this from the time I was a little girl.

As a 22 year old, I felt as if my life were heading in a downward spiral. I had recently dropped out of college before receiving my Bachelor of Arts. I had received my Associate of Arts but could not stay committed. My addictions were taking a toll on my life. As a young adult my life had become so confusing. How did I get to this point? The first memory I have of dramatically reaching out was in high school.

In high school I should have been diagnosed with anorexia/bulimia. I would binge on food only to get sick in the bathroom shortly thereafter. I wore layered clothing to hide my excessive weight loss. I did not do this because I thought I was overweight. I just wanted something to control in my life, although I did not understand why I was doing it at the time.

High school memories are difficult to express. I was afraid of everything and everyone. I was lonely. I did not have many friends and was often ridiculed-perhaps for my clothes, my lack of personal hygiene or my immaturity. I could not control the hurtful comments. I could control what I did with food.

I had an older sister and although we lived in the same house, we lived two separate lives. We were both in survival mode. We had a distant relationship. We rarely communicated or discussed the family problems together, and I did not even know she knew about my binges.

One day when I was getting sick in the bathroom after a binge, my sister told my mother what I was doing. My mother came running up the stairs and banged on the bathroom door, screaming, "Don't you dare waste my food!" "Don't you dare waste my money!" I did not open the door. I remember leaning against the bathroom wall and slowly sliding down to the floor crying after my mother's screaming session. I cried for a long time. For my mother to scream like she did was a surprise, as she would rarely yell.

I wanted someone to hold me and tell me they loved me. I wanted someone to tell me I was alright and that I would be safe. In my parents' house, I did not feel loved or safe, and those were the two things I longed for most in life. Ironically, I did not want just *anyone* to hug me, *I wanted my mother to.* I had seen such affection from my friends' mothers before. But my mother rarely hugged me, and my father was all too willing.

My mother never asked me why I was throwing up or ever discussed it with me from that time forth. She knew it was deliberate, but it was just another example of her emotional absence. For all she knew, I could have continued it for

17

years. She made it clear that she was more concerned about the food I was wasting than my problem. I was sent a clear message that I was not worth her bother. *If I were not worth much to my own mother, to whom was I worth anything?*

Dating in my teenage years was a new experience for me. I was getting older and my parents did not know what to do. They had used fear to keep me home alone after school. I was one of those kids they now refer to as a "latch key" kid. I came home to no one. I started this at age nine. I was not allowed to have anyone over, nor was I allowed to visit anyone after school. I was not even allowed to talk to the neighbors. If anything bad happened to me, I was on my own. There were many times I wanted to call my mother at work, but sometimes I would forget the phone number. It was not written anywhere for me. My parents were not around to raise me, so they used fear to keep me home. Watching television for hours a day was not enough for me in my teenage years as it had been when I was younger.

When I started dating, often times, after getting ready for the date, my father would tell me I could not go. The person I was going on a date with would show up and I had to tell him that my parents changed their minds and that I could not go. I would be upset and embarrassed. I could not depend on my parents' words.   .

My day–to–day life would depend on my parents' moods. What they would say was okay one day, whether it involved other people or not, would not be okay the next. They had little regard for commitment and others' feelings. Unfortunately, I would have to be the bearer of the news. They would not talk to other parents. Perhaps they did not want to have to explain their actions to another adult.

One time there was a dance where the girls asked the boys. This event would change the course of my life. It would actually confirm the lack of control I had in my life and my own nothingness. My parents said I could go. I asked a young man on whom I had a crush for a long time. He accepted. The dress code was to wear cowboy and cowgirl clothing. I was so excited. I remember I wanted to look as pretty as possible and had an idea of the outfit I wanted to wear. I described what I wanted to wear and asked my mother to help me put it together. I wanted to wear a denim skirt, a ruffled shirt and a bandana around my neck. My mother was not interested in helping. This was my first high school dance where a young man would actually pick me up and I wanted to look good. I remember crying and being so confused as to why she would not help me find something. This was a big deal for me. The young man came from a good family. He carried himself confidently and compassionately. He was nice to me. I wanted to impress him.

The night of the dance, still with nothing to wear and very nervous, I pulled on a pair of jeans and a t-shirt. I went to my closet to find some shoes but my tennis shoes had holes in them and my laces were broken off. I was sure he would be disappointed. I was ashamed. My mother would not help me with my hair or makeup, but I tried to look the best I could.

A short time before the young man was supposed to pick me up my father said I could not go. He had decided that he did not like the idea. This young man was a year older than I and my father said he had thought about it and did not want me to go with him. I remember him telling me so coldly, not caring about the boy's feelings or mine. I was devastated. It was as if my parents never intended for me to go. My mother agreed so I had to call my date and tell him my parents had changed their minds. The young man was so upset he made me talk to his mother. I was humiliated and embarrassed as I tried to explain my parents' actions. His mother wanted to speak to my parents, but they would not come to the phone. She explained her son could have gone with someone else if my family would have told him sooner. She explained there are only a few dances in the teenage years and that each one was special.

I felt so badly I cried myself to sleep. He came from a good family and was a respectful young man. He barely spoke to me after that, and it quickly got around school. I was so confused by my parents' actions, once again. Before, their unpredictable behavior affected only me, but as I was getting older it was affecting other people. I did not know where I could go for answers. I just knew something was wrong with this behavior. I felt judged for my parents' actions and I did not like the affect it had on me. I was the one treated badly by other people because they thought my family was odd.

From that time on, I realized I was not good enough for people like him. I remember the distinct impression that I was just what my father always told me. Although he would only say it when he was mad, which seemed everyday, I finally believed him. I was pathetic. I was lazy and not deserving of much in life. I realized he had been right the whole time.

With acknowledging the real state of my life, I changed. I became angry. I quit the high school track team. My parents never came to watch me anyway. I changed my friends and found other people who seemed to know the truth about their pathetic lives also.

I also changed my clothing and only wore black. I cut my hair, dyed it dark auburn and started associating with people some would consider less desirable. The crowd I chose was a mixture of backgrounds, but we all had several things in common–lack of parental supervision, emotional absence from our parents and no role models. Each of us wanted more from life, but did not know what to do about it nor did we know where to find the answers.

I decided to date without telling my parents. My parents had not taught me about morality, so I learned it from the youthful examples I saw. I remember thinking that whatever meant a lot to me, was always put down or somehow ruined by my parents. I decided to stop telling them anything. I did not trust them any longer. I do not know if I ever really did. I do know in my teenage years, my mistrust became a conscious thought. I put my guard up and would not let anyone in.

After school it would take me longer to get home or I would not go home like I was supposed to. My parents did not know. They did not discuss dating with me. I did not know the rules. I just knew the "rules" changed day to day depending on how my father felt.

Dating was liberating for me. I could be alone with someone without my parents around to stifle my freedom. They could not stop what we did away from them. But, I lacked social skills and often treated the boys I dated the same way I was treated at home–horribly. I was not given any advice on dating by my parents. I did not get any guidelines from them. The only guidelines I adopted came from the people with whom I hung around. I was yearning for love. So often my relationships turned into short, mock marriages. They became serious fast and went too far.

My parents' examples were deeply engrained in me. I had learned from my father that it is okay for a man to indulge in pornography. I had also learned from him it was acceptable to be unfaithful to your partner. My father had cheated on my mother several times. So my loyalty to a single person was low. On the other hand, my mother's life evolved around her and her problems. So, I too became self-absorbed and emotionally absent in my relationships.

I had become hardened—protecting myself with an impenetrable shell. I was not going to let another person hurt me again. Although I was still ridiculed and put down, I drowned out my feelings of shame. I did not care much about anyone's feelings since I had become so numb myself. I had little respect for other people or life. As I look back now, how I wish I had been taught or counseled about dating!

By the time I was sixteen, I was learning a lot from my new friends. I remember being at a park where I was introduced to alcohol. It provided me with a new means of escape. It took my mind off the present and made me feel like a new person. Alcohol became a more satisfying therapy than binging, so I stopped my eating binges. I could drink without denying myself of food. It made me happy. As I reflect back on my teenage years in high school, it seems sad that alcohol was the only solution I could come up with to seek happiness in my life. I was always trying to find something that would dissipate my pain. The closest I came to happiness at that time in my life was when I drank alcohol. I never liked the taste of it, though. I did not drink for the taste. I drank with a specific purpose in mind—to try and be happy again. Usually, I would take it too far and black out, not remembering what happened the night before. It did not bother me. The less I remembered the better.

My father also knew I was drinking a lot. My friends would come over with alcohol and he would let us drink before we left the house. He would comment that my eyes were red and would often ask my friends were I okay. They, of course, would tell him I was fine. It was a game he played. He would not have done anything had they said yes. He used the fact that I was "out of it" to his advantage. He knew I had an alcohol problem. He knew before I did. He also knew he was the cause. He knew I could handle his parenting if my mind was not focused on reality. As a young father he too was an alcoholic. He stopped after my mother told him she would leave him. I did not know then that addiction to alcohol is a clear indication a person is running from something, especially a teenager.

Shortly thereafter, I was introduced to drugs. I can honestly say where there is alcohol there is drugs. It's hard to go to a party where alcohol is and not have drugs. As I reflect back as an adult on my teenage years I am surprised at how many parents knew their children had substance problems. Many parents introduced it to their own children. I remember time and time again, parents drinking at the parties with their own children. At the time, I thought it was "cool," but as an adult, now, it is a sad thought. It was confusing to me as a teenager to see an adult use drugs or sell them to teenagers. I was already confused about life and remember thinking that if an adult is doing this, maybe, it is okay. Although it was against the law, having adults around participating in this behavior somehow made it okay. I could talk with these adults about it and it somehow was glorified and deceptive at the same time. It made me feel good and it was something I could keep from my parents who were not "cool."

There finally came a time when I became addicted and could not wait until the weekend to participate. I brought it into my parents' house. Soon, thereafter, came the harsh reality that both of my parents knew I did drugs as a teenager and young adult. But their response was not "cool." My mother would

23

often come into my bedroom and see them on my dresser, but she always acted like she had not seen anything. As I look back now, I had purposefully been careless. A part of me wanted a mother to take care of me, to help me, to ask what was wrong. It did not happen. Instead, my mother would continue her conversation and act as if she had not seen anything. As I reflect, now, this was her role. She did not respond to the bad in our lives. Her indifference was just more evidence to me that I was not worth much. I was not worth helping or worth her time. My mother's emotional absence from the home was devastating. She did not care that my father hurt me and she did not care that I did drugs. She did not care about the consequences her emotional absence had on me. It was a sad reality I had to deal with everyday. How hard this would be to overcome in the future! The more careless I became, the more she ignored my situation and turned the other way.

My mother never addressed these problems. To do so would mean she, too, would have to deal with reality. She would have to ask herself why she was comfortable with this way of life. While one can never actually be okay with this way of life, one can run from it or deal with it and try to change it somehow. She chose to run. Perhaps not dealing with reality and running from life were the only two things we had in common at that time. I ran from life through binges, drugs, alcohol and promiscuity. My mother ran from life by overeating and sleeping. Although my mother and I coped with life differently, we were still running from the reality of our day-to-day life.

As I look back, my parents deliberately did not want me to deal with reality. Otherwise, they would have tried to get me help or try to counsel me from doing regretful things. To get such help would mean their way of life might be exposed. It was better to encourage my addictions than to expose themselves. They did not answer to anyone. They worked too hard to keep the family facade from crumbling.

By the age of 22 my life still had no meaning. I had to move back to my parents' home and I was disappointed I could not make it on my own. I woke up in the mornings, got dressed and went through the motions of the day. I had tried to quit my drug addictions but failed each time. I did not do them as often, but I still did them. I still blacked out when I drank. I was not drinking everyday but several times a week. Although I questioned where I was at in my life, I still did not believe in myself.

CHAPTER TWO

My Soul Delighteth

And my soul delighteth in the covenants of the Lord which he hath made to our fathers; yea, my soul delighteth in his grace, and in his justice, and power, and mercy in the great and eternal plan of deliverance from death. (2 Nephi 11:5-7)

Drinking was not a casual thing for me. It had a specific purpose. When I drank, I could handle my father raging and screaming uncontrollably at me. I never knew what to expect from him. I could also handle my mother letting him rage. I did not question why she let him do this. I could even handle it when he felt like hitting me for no reason. He would often come up to me and slap me on the side of my head. If he was in a mean mood he would tease me by pushing me a little then as I got upset he would slap me as if he were upset that I got mad at him for bullying me. My mother would not say anything. He had done this my whole life.

I was in my 20's now and something inside of me knew this was wrong. Something inside of me was finally outraged by his behavior. Legally, I was an adult now, but in my parents house I was still treated like a ten-year-old. I never felt I had emotionally matured past this age. Although more privileges were given to me, inside I still felt like a little girl. It was never verbalized, but I felt that my father did not want me to grow older, and he was angry that he could not control my natural development. He was also learning that he could not control me as much. Deep inside, I felt I was not the little girl he could bully anymore, and yet, I did not know how to stop him. I was paralyzed with fear. Fear was his way of keeping us all from growing and doing things that could have been good for us. He used fear to motivate us to do things we did not want to do. This was our way of life at home. I realized at a very young age that life was mentally, physically and emotionally hard.

When I dared to confront my parents' behavior from time to time, it was a bad day for me. I learned at a young age that I would be blamed for the family problems. I internalized this as a belief that something was wrong with me. I was everyones' scapegoat. I could be gone all day, and when I came home I was blamed for my father's rageful outbursts. I grew up in fear. He terrified me. I was scared because no one protected me from him. I thought my mother would or *should*, but I was left to my own defenses. Often his rages had nothing to do with me. I was just a figure or a target to hit or verbally abuse. So, not surprisingly, drugs and alcohol became my allies and shielded me from my painful reality.

For the past four to five years, my addictions had imprisoned me. I could not grow. This way of life had become a habit, a bad one. Yet, deep inside, I wanted out. I did not know what to do, how to stop it or to whom to turn. I would attend parties and always feel alone. I find it interesting to be surrounded by many people and yet feel so alone. I would keep drinking, hoping I would feel better, but I never did. Addictions have a way of making you believe that you will feel better. I believed that they made me more comfortable in public. But as the years went on I had to overindulge to get the same feeling as when I first started.

At this time, I did not feel I had any meaningful relationships with anyone. I felt I was on a merry-go-round and could not stop. But, unexpectedly, amidst this unhappiness, I met someone. After a month of seeing each other, he informed me he had to leave for two years. He explained he was a member of The Church of Jesus Christ of Latter-day Saints. I had never heard of them. Then he explained they are also known as "Mormons" and I recognized that name. He told me he was going on a mission to preach the word of God.

I was interested as to why he would go on a mission for God. Jesus was not real-or so I had been taught my whole life. But, my friend bore testimony that Jesus *is* real and informed me he would be leaving for a mission soon. I thought going on a mission would take a lot of courage. He would be leaving his parents' home and going to another state without them. I wanted that kind of freedom. He also told me he was not getting paid and was actually paying to go. I thought this was responsible and amazing. Being so dependent on my family I craved the independence he possessed. I also thought Jesus Christ was a myth and that my friend was leaving to convince people He was real. I decided I wanted to know exactly what he would be preaching.

My new friend started sharing with me what a missionary teaches. I found it fascinating. I had never heard of the things he was sharing. When he mentioned he believed in the *Book of Mormon,* I thought it was great. I was never taught the *Holy Bible,* so having two testaments of Jesus Christ sounded good to me. It also made me question, could it be true? Is there really a God? Not just stories motivating a person to be better. At that point in time, motivational speakers were everywhere, teaching that only "you" can make things happen. They would teach that no one can make you do great things-only you. To me, it seemed such a heavy weight to bear. I had felt alone my whole life. On the other hand, some said the Bible was just a crutch and that only the weak relied on it. I did not want to be labeled as weak.

I remember a conversation my mother and I had concerning the Bible. We were discussing Jesus Christ. I was about 21. I had asked her opinion of the Bible. We did not own one, nor had I ever read a verse in one. She said the stories were myths. I believed her. I believed there was no God, no higher power. How could there be? The home in which I grew up was a testimony that there was nothing else. I was raised believing that whatever I could do on my own was it. There was no other help. In my parents' house, Jesus Christ was an expression of anger–that was the only time He was mentioned. I thought the *Holy Bible* was made up of fictional stories. I did not even know Jesus Christ had lived on the earth. Saying this now sounds so sad, but it is true. I never knew about His birth, His life or His purpose.

I was invited to my friend's missionary farewell. It was held in someones' backyard during the day. I was not used to going to parties during the day but I was thinking it would be just like any other party. I was in for a big surprise. There was absolutely no alcohol at that party. Everyone was dressed conservatively. I was impressed at how everyone came up to me and wanted to know who I was and they were happy I could be there. Never in my life had I experienced such a warm reception from strangers! I had never felt these feelings of acceptance before. They were truly interested in who I was.

Families were together at the party. I was surprised. They were all enjoying each other. It was an amazing observation. It touched a deep part of me. A part of me had dreamed that maybe families could love each other or even just like each other. I was witnessing living proof of mothers laughing with daughters and a father holding a baby. My most memorable surprise was a man asking a woman how her baby was doing. It could have been sick or a newborn. I do not know. But I was astounded that a man would be interested in the well-being of a child that was not his. That experience had a great affect on me.

The next thing I knew, my friend was on a mission and my life went back to what I called "normal." I remember meeting with one of his friends who had nothing good to say about the church, nor did he care about the Mormon lifestyle. I remember thinking it was a lifestyle that interested me. At the time I did not know it, but my Lord and Savior was preparing me for a new life. Had Mormon missionaries come to my parents' house and knocked on the door, I would have turned them away. But my successful introduction to the church came about through a friend.

Without thinking, I stopped going out with my other friends. For a whole month I did not go to a party. When my friends called, I said no. When I wanted to go out, no one was home. During this period of time, I did not drink, nor did I do drugs. I could not explain what I was doing. While many people get professional help of some sort to overcome substance abuse, I stayed home. I spent most of the time in my room, on my bed. My body was not handling my withdrawal from my addictions very well. Something deep inside of me had the strength to do this. It seemed being away from my old friends and away from the environment in which we would gather gave me strength and a new perspective. I longed to go to another party like the church farewell I attended. It seemed a whole new world was opened up to me. There was an inner strength with which I had never been acquainted. Nor had I experienced it before. I had no intention of changing my life. Even though I did not know what the future held, I had no purpose in doing this. I was not doing it consciously. I can only say that there was a power stronger than me helping me overcome my substance abuse. This power was stronger than anything I had ever experienced. It was as if all my temptations were gone.

At the same time I was doing this, it was getting harder to deal with my family. The violence in our home was extreme and seemed more evident. With no place to which I could escape, the hitting, screaming and belittling seemed to increase. In reality, nothing had changed-except me. The violence was more intense because I had nothing to hide behind. Yet, something inside of me carried me through this time, as well.

I received a letter from my missionary friend. He boldly told me to get baptized so I could go through the temple. I knew this meant one thing–a conscious change in my life. Although my life was changing, I did not feel it was conscious. I could see things differently at this time, but it seemed no matter how much I longed for a different life, being told I needed to change put up another barrier. There were so many things I would have to give up for a whole new way of life. I felt uncomfortable with his request. After all, what was wrong with the way I was? This was a sensitive subject to me. I always felt something was wrong with me and now it seemed to be confirmed. Why would I have to change to get baptized? What was the temple? He even told me to contact the missionaries to discuss this issue. I wrote him back stating that I was not ready for that kind of change in my life.

My friends had stopped calling almost completely. Why should they call? I was not fun anymore. It had been almost a whole month since I last saw them. They could not stick around and wait forever. That is just what friends did–at least the friends I hung out with. If I did not party, I had nothing in common with them. I was starting to feel rejected–again. I was lonely.

It seemed that my only link to the outside world was my friend on a mission. His letters urged me to contact the missionaries. He did not understand that it was hard for me to accept his request. My self-esteem was so low that I felt confused. I was also mad that someone would actually tell me I needed to change. Pride sheltered the fact that I knew deep inside, my life needed to change. I wanted answers, but I was afraid of what stepping out of my bubble would bring. On the surface, I was adamant that I was okay. My whole life, I had been made to believe that something was wrong with me. I was given the message I was not good enough. But I needed to appear to be okay to everyone else.

Keeping the family facade in place was something with which I was comfortable and something I had learned to do well. It was something my parents had taught me. We never discussed our problems or the events in our home with anyone. Their threats were clear and I believed them. They did not have friends over and I was not allowed to have friends over until I was in my late teens. I had to be okay just the way I was. It was survival. But a part of me did not want to live this lie anymore. And yet, I was too afraid to learn what else was out there.

I was actually feeling for the first time in my life. I was feeling the pain of my family life and the pain of my friendships. I felt so alone in the world. I had to deal with reality. It was not easy. As a matter of fact, reality hurt very much. In the past, when reality would spill into my life accidentally, I did not recall this much pain because I would remedy it immediately. I was feeling it now with no escape. A new feeling was emerging that I had never experienced before. It was a strength within me to know that I was capable of doing something right. For how much I was hurting, I was growing with inner strength. I did not like what I saw in my family or my life, but I also knew I needed to see it.

I realized that truth has strength of its own. It can carry a person from one way of life to another. Truth can set one free from a former way to a better way. I was starting to deal with the truth–just a little. I was starting to see that I could deal with the pain in my life. I was starting to see things as they really were, not how I wanted to see them. In the very near future, truth would become the most important guide in my life. It would be my driving force. It would give me strength to deal with the past and what the future had in store.

Then, on a beautiful sunny morning, I was off to run an errand. As I was entering my car, there they were. Two young men. Riding their bikes with long black pants, short-sleeved white shirts with ties and, of course, helmets. Fourteen years ago, helmets and ties meant only one thing–Mormon missionaries. I was actually amazed. I called to them to come over. I could not believe it. I asked them what they were doing on my street. I had not seen them before. They informed me that the counselors in the singles ward lived on this street and they often came here to have dinner and meetings. I had lived on my street for almost 15 years and had never seen a missionary ride by.

They informed me the bishop of the singles ward lived in the same development. I told the missionaries I would like to talk with them. We agreed they would call me at the end of that week. I had heard how missionaries would just show up unannounced. At my home, no one came unannounced. I went on with my day and decided to go to the movies with my parents that night. Going to the movies with them was safe. There was usually no arguing and we could sit together for two hours and enjoy the entertainment. As I was entering the theater, my inactive Mormon friend from high school was there. We hugged each other. It had been some time since we had seen each other. I immediately began to tell her about the missionaries. She informed me that she was attending church again–the singles ward. She invited me to come the next Sunday.

The Missionaries did call Friday at noon. I told them I was going to the singles ward. They informed me the couple on my street they were visiting were also counselors in the ward I was going to attend. On Sunday morning, I picked up my friend and off we went. I remember the day like it was yesterday. I was sitting on the back center pew. I was amazed at all the young people there–attending church without their parents. They were going on their own to learn about God. On Sunday mornings, I was usually sleeping until noon. By that time, these young adults had already been in church for three hours. It was amazing.

On that very special day, the bishop was speaking. His name was Bishop Jones. I will always remember him and his talk. He was speaking about morality, virtue and dating. It was to be the most beautiful words I had ever heard. He was counseling these young adults to be chaste, telling them that their bodies are a temple and to treat them with respect. He talked about loving ourselves as we are and always striving to be a better person by serving others. He talked about getting married in the temple for time and all eternity. I had never been taught this or heard such wonderful things.

My parents did not discuss with me how to date or how to respect myself or my body. My father made it clear what a woman's body was for. He would leer at me. I remember constantly telling him to stop looking at me as if he were my date. My mother would not say anything. I would say, "Mom, tell him to stop looking at me that way!" I would say this in front of my father. She would not respond, as if to encourage my father's behavior. As the bishop spoke of temple marriage, I could not imagine wanting to be with one person for eternity. I saw my parents' failing marriage and did not think that was a good idea. Nevertheless, I desired to know more about this new type of marriage.

As I sat there on that back pew, something changed in my heart. For the first time in my life, my soul felt full. I guess a part of me always wanted guidelines. A part of me wanted to be part of a greater plan than what I had. The bishop was talking about an eternal plan and my soul delighted in his words and counsel. I had longed for a different life than the one to which I was accustomed. I had always hoped there was a better way of life. For the first time, I was hearing that we were created by a God and that Jesus Christ was real and had lived on this very earth. The thought of getting baptized entered my mind, but I quickly dismissed it. I barely knew anything about the Mormon church. I only know that something inside of me was testifying that these teachings came from the Lord Himself. I had never had such a feeling come over me. It was real. It touched my soul. A soul that had been dormant for as long as I could remember.

I remember being flooded with thoughts of my childhood and my parents' relationship. It was a lot different from what was being said. I sat back in the back thinking about respect in a relationship. I had not experienced it or seen much of it at home. I could hear my mother's voice saying, "Respect is earned. Nobody gets it until they have proven themselves." Apparently, I hadn't proven myself to her. And yet, as Bishop Jones spoke, somehow those memories stopped for a moment and my soul was filled with hope rather than pain. The hope I had held onto my whole life that there was more out there and that I was not alone. I was suddenly overwhelmed with emotion. I would soon discover that I had been touched by the Holy Spirit. That feeling would be my guide to the truths in my life. The feeling of the Holy Spirit would give me strength to make life-changing decisions in the future.

Another realization I had on that very special day was the bishop was not just speaking to the members of his ward, he was speaking to me! He was telling me that Heavenly Father loved me–unconditionally. I was overwhelmed with all these feelings. Unconditional was not a word in the vocabulary of my life. It was a word about which I would desire to know more.

The next thing I knew, I was telling my friend I needed to meet with the bishop that very day. He did meet with me. I was nervous and had some serious questions. He was so full of life, happiness, and love. He answered some of my questions and set me up with the missionaries. I asked if we could meet at the church building since my parents were not Mormon and I did not know how they would respond. At the end of the meeting, I had begun to believe there was more out there. I was pondering if the feeling I had deep inside my whole life was right. Could there really be more out there? Could there really be a God? I could not wait for the missionaries' first discussion with me.

CHAPTER THREE

Renew a Right Spirit Within Me

"Behold, thou desirest truth in the inward parts: and in the hidden part thou shalt make me to know wisdom. Purge me with hyssop, and I shall be clean: wash me, and I shall be whiter than snow. Make me to hear joy and gladness; that the bones which thou hast broken may rejoice. Hide thy face from my sins, and blot out all mine iniquities. Create in me a clean heart, O God; and renew a right spirit within me. Cast me not away from thy presence; and take not thy holy spirit from me. Restore unto me the joy of thy salvation; and uphold me with thy free spirit." (Psalms 51:6-12)

It was an evening after work that I met with the missionaries at the church building. They were two young men. Although I was barely 23, they were only 19 and 20. I retrieved my pad of paper that was filled with many questions. Prior to my first discussion, my mother and I sat down and discussed what I should ask them. She helped me with my list of questions. I found this interesting since she never spoke of God or His teachings. Apparently, she wanted to know some things, too.

I was eager and started asking questions to the missionaries. One of the elders stopped me and asked if we could have a prayer first. I remember feeling uncomfortable. I did not know how to pray. At least, not out loud like the missionaries prayed. The missionaries folded their arms, closed their eyes and started with, "Dear Heavenly Father." They ended, "In the name of Jesus Christ, Amen." In between, they were actually talking with Heavenly Father about our discussion and used my name in the prayer. I was used to hearing about how people memorized their prayers, not actually conversing with Heavenly Father. I was touched.

After seeing my pages of questions, I'm sure the missionaries thought I was a handful. I wanted to lead the discussion and the missionaries would patiently listen. After I was done talking they would re-direct me back to the intended lesson. As they were teaching, I found my mind drifting as that feeling I had sitting in the rear, center pew came back. I had several pages of questions, but for just a moment the answers would not have mattered. The thought that I would get baptized was there again. These feelings were overwhelming. At the time I could not explain them. I only know they comforted me.

On our second meeting, the missionaries noticed I did not know how to pray on my own. They stopped the discussion and taught me. I felt, and still feel, being taught how to pray was the greatest blessing in my life. They taught me how to converse with Heavenly Father. Praying made Him seem real. I did not understand why kneeling or closing my eyes were so important. The missionaries quickly taught me that it is done out of respect for our Heavenly Father. Folding our arms and bowing our heads shows reverence. Respect and reverence were two words I did not use often. At first, when they asked me to say a prayer, I would get embarrassed and tell them I was not ready. They were so patient with me.

The missionaries taught me there is an open line of communication with Heavenly Father, even though I had been told the Heavens are closed and miracles do not occur. I remember thinking it was a miracle I was learning to pray. I thought it was a miracle I was even searching for a God or contemplating if a Heavenly Father really created me. I never thought of how I was created. I was in survival mode for as long as I could remember. Survival mode kept me focused on myself and not on the world around me. Survival mode kept me in control and led me to be very cautious of people because they always let me down. As far as I was concerned, to reach out and learn about God was a miracle.

The missionaries taught me I had to be sincere in my prayers. I had to be honest. I was taught Heavenly Father knows my real thoughts and intentions. This meant I was accountable for my actions and thoughts. Accountability was not part of my life. I had grown up in an environment where fear and belittling were the motivating factors to get me to do something. Society had taught me, if you do not hurt others first, they will hurt you. Society had taught me to say whatever was on my mind just because I felt like it. Society had taught me there were no limits. Not only was it okay to do whatever I wanted, I had a right to do it! The words of the missionaries had a great impact on my conscience. I had never heard these teachings before. I took them seriously.

When I would kneel down to pray, it was hard. I did not know what to say. I imagined being in the Lord's presence and asking for help, but I could not do it. I felt so unworthy. To hold a conversation with Him about my feelings–well, I never discussed my feelings. I held them in. They were always just in my thoughts. I did not share them. To share my thoughts would be a betrayal of the life in which I had been raised. No one discussed his or her feelings in my home.

The missionaries told me to just talk with the Lord like I would anyone else. The problem was I was superficial. My conversations were light and hardly ever deep. This was something I had to admit to myself as I tried to pray on my own. I rarely, if ever, shared my true feelings with people or even myself. I was hardened on the outside. To be honest with God would mean that I would have to be honest with myself. I was afraid of where this might lead me. Whenever I expressed my true feelings, I usually got hurt by friends or in a lot of trouble at home. The picture I had been looking at my whole life was starting to get bigger. Maybe there really was more than just me.

I would kneel down to pray and just freeze with a blank mind for a long time. I did not know what to say. I did not even know I could or should share my feelings about attending church that first day. I did not know how to thank God for that experience. I did not know I could share with Him my feelings of pain inside, or how much I wanted them to go away. I did not talk about my pain, not to anyone. Every once in a while my friends would make comments about my family that were usually not good. I would just blank those comments out and change the subject. But now, maybe I could talk about things to Him.

In personal prayer, no one would know but Heavenly Father. When I would confide in my friends at times, my words would get around, or my mother would tell my father things that I thought were just between us. Often, when she was not around, I would get into trouble with my father for telling her things. So sharing my true feelings usually had a negative consequence. I rarely did it. It would take me a while before I learned to be comfortable praying on a daily basis. Prayer would be the beginning of letting out many feelings I had stored up my whole life. Prayer would change the course of my life by allowing me to admit things I never thought of admitting, or had been too afraid to confess. How could anyone know what I confided to Heavenly Father?

As the discussions continued, my mother became very interested in what I was being taught. She would have me ask questions for her. I thought this was wonderful. It seemed she liked the teachings and longed for a different way of life, just as I did. I was amazed when she would open up to me about God. For the first time, we really discussed her relationship with my father. She did not love him. She did not know if she ever had. I already knew this. I grew up knowing my parents did not love each other, but this time it was different. This time she really seemed to want out of the marriage. She told me of her dream situation in life. But, as I pondered what she shared, it did not include my father, my sister or me. Nevertheless, it explained her depression.

Growing up in a home where parents did not love each other was hard. The whole family was affected. There was no role model of a loving relationship with anyone. It was hard to have family unity with parents who did not love each other. It was hard for my sister and I to know how to love each other and others. For the first time in my life, my mother and I were starting to bond and have deep conversations. This closeness would only last for a little while, but it showed me that she *could* be loving and communicative.

At that time, I was still doing things with people at my work. I felt we were pretty close. I would share what I was learning and feeling during the missionary discussions. My life was changing and I thought they supported me. Maybe they felt the same way I did. They would ask questions and I would find out the answers. They were not argumentative-at first.

I had lost contact with most of my other friends. Every once in a while I would go out with them, but I wouldn't drink. It was at these times that I saw things as they really were. I used to think I could not have a conversation with anyone unless I had a few drinks. But this was not so. I was starting to see just what I had been like for years. I did not like it. I was uncomfortable with the surroundings. The temptation to drink was strong, but the feeling inside of me to see the truth was stronger. Still, I did not like the temptations and it was hard to have a conversation with someone who was intoxicated.

43

I looked more and more anxiously to my meetings with the missionaries. After the tithing discussion, I started to question some things. I just did not understand the principal. I was concerned because of the way other churches used their money. I had never heard how the Mormon Church accounted for its money. I wanted a guarantee of where my money was going. Then they pulled out a tithing slip. It allocated where the money went to. They explained each of the categories and at the end of the year I got a tax sheet for the donations. I liked this system. I just was not sold on it yet. They asked if I was willing to pay tithing. I said, "No," but I would think about it. I had never given anything away unconditionally. Why would I want to give my money away?

The fact is, I was a taker. I was self-consumed. I did not know why at the time, but after living in the home I did for so long, I *had* to take care of myself. Self-preservation became the mentality I lived by. I was always cautious of how a situation would benefit me.

During the missionary discussions, I needed some things explained to me. Some of my friends still believed that the doors of Heaven were closed and that He did not speak to His children anymore. This explained why my prayers were never answered. Although I did not pray to Heavenly Father technically, I was praying to someone. If He loves all of His children, why was I left out? The missionaries did not know what I was praying for exactly, and I was too embarrassed to confide in them that I wanted protection and for the bad feelings to stop within me. They did say, perhaps, the Lord was waiting to answer my prayers when I was at an age where I could act on my own. That comment had a huge impact on me. I felt empowered that I *was* at an age where I could act on my own.

My work friends also told me that the Lord had said all He needed to and that is what the *Holy Bible* was for. They made that clear to me that there were no more scriptures than the *Holy Bible*. Anything else was not of God. I began to question the *Book of Mormon*. I was starting to feel the pressure at work. At first they did not say anything when I shared the gospel with them, but after a while they were very strong about their opinions. My mother was also starting to look in other directions. I did not understand. So to appease them, I really tried to understand some of the myths out there. Although I did not realize it at the time, in trying to keep peace in my relationships, I had to study deeper to understand the gospel.

I was also making new friends who had been raised in the Mormon Church. Their outlook on life was very different from mine. I felt somewhat of an outsider. I felt unworthy to hang out with them. The feelings I had as a teenager came back to me. I had tried to hang out with respectful people, but I was always rejected or my parents somehow embarrassed me by their unpredictable actions. I was just waiting to say the wrong thing and have these new Mormon friends not want to be around me.

I'm sure I was a handful, and yet they were patient with me. If I would mess up somehow, they overlooked it. I was truly longing for this. These people really knew how to love. They were young and I really looked up to them. I strived to be a better person so I could feel comfortable around them. But something deep inside of me quietly told me I was not worth their love and acceptance. Their lifestyle was too good for me. Deep inside I was reminded that I would probably say something wrong or do something offensive, or that if they had really known all the things I had done in my past, they wouldn't want to associate with me. I was stepping out of my comfort zone once again with the hope that I could truly make friends. Their example of unconditional acceptance was something I will always remember.

Eventually, I began to feel a lot of pressure from people at work that I was doing the wrong thing. They were constantly confronting me and belittling my efforts to change my life. They would tell me I was making an "eternal mistake." They stopped going out with me. I was hurt on the surface, but deep inside I was used to being rejected. This time it was different. As I was rejected, I was being filled with something else. It was something good that involved new friends and a new life. I was willing to let go of my old lifestyle, rejection and all. I did not like how I was being treated but I yearned for a better life.

At home my mother and father told me they were happy I was changing. They had grown to respect the church and the things that I was being taught. Somehow the fear that had paralyzed me for so long was set aside, making room for something new. But the fear did not just disappear. It would linger, reminding me that I was not worth much. Nevertheless, something else inside of me was growing. A feeling I had never felt before. The feeling that maybe I was doing something right. For the first time I had the support of my parents. I actually felt their support, and it was different. They did not support me nor did they stand by my decisions before. This time they did.

My father was traveling a lot at this time and, honestly, we were all glad. When he would leave on his trips there was a unified sigh of relief. We knew there would be no yelling, and I always felt safer. My father had shared, he had learned about the church years earlier. He knew all about Joseph Smith and actually had great respect for him. He had learned about the modern prophet in college. I had never known this.

So this was a good time in our home, even if it were only for a short while.

As the discussions were drawing to an end, I was asked if I would be baptized. My first response was "No." I certainly was not ready for that. Then the missionaries started coming over to my parents' house for dinner and dessert. I will never forget the feelings they brought with them. My mother never let people come over for dinner. As a matter of fact, I have no recollection of any friends coming over for dinner. When we were little children, people did come over, but I could not have been older than seven. My mother had no friends.

When she said the missionaries could come over, it was a big deal. She loved them. She engaged in conversations with them. She did not talk to my friends. Those missionaries brought such a sweet spirit into our home that even the horrible truths of our lives were suspended for the time they were there. I loved having them over. And mostly I liked seeing my mother being friendly. They opened a side of her I would only see temporarily. I will always be grateful and it was this side of her that I would try to remember in the future.

Then an event happened that would change the course of my life again. I was invited by my friends at work to go to a Halloween party. I had not done anything with them for a while. I felt I should go to try to rekindle our friendship. The party was on a boat. I knew there would be drinking. Of course, where there is alcohol, there are usually drugs, too. As we arrived at the boat, I had mixed feelings. Many people had too many drinks. Then my friends bought me a drink. They bought me a hard drink. I took it to not offend them, but was reluctant to drink it. I had not tasted alcohol for so long–at least it *seemed* like a long time to me. It was probably only about a month and a half, but a lot had happened during that time.

After watching everyone and feeling like an outsider for a while, I started to rationalize that one drink could not hurt me. Everyone was laughing and seemed to be having a great time. I was just a bystander. Watching their pleasure did not fulfill my insecurities. Perhaps one drink would. But, I did not handle my one drink well. I got intoxicated quickly. Soon I was laughing with everyone like old times. My friends and I were enjoying ourselves. I do not remember how many drinks I had that night, but I blacked out again. I only remember having one. Obviously, I had more.

During the party I thought about what I had given up. I was suddenly having a good time. Alcohol always seemed to come through for me. Nothing else in life gave me pleasure. The last few weeks, life had become so serious! My guilt for even considering my first drink that night was gone. I started to question, "What have I been thinking these last few weeks?" I had always experienced fear on a daily basis in my home, and now, by not drinking, it was magnified. I had given up the one thing that brought me some type of happiness or pleasure in life. I had forgotten how alcohol made me feel around other people. I felt accepted. The last month and a half were too intense for me. I did not really want to feel or see what I saw in my home. I remember thinking my quest for a better life was just a facade.

Then the next morning came. I remember sitting up in bed in shock at what had happened the night before. What had I done? As I sat there I decided I was too tired to go to church. My head hurt. So I decided that I wouldn't go. I was also consumed with extreme guilt. I was plagued with thoughts that I can never follow through on anything! I was so disappointed with myself. I had learned from the past that when I felt this way, I needed to escape. Escape at this time meant going back to sleep and missing church. But then something marvelous happened. It was a very special experience. As I laid my head back on my pillow in shame, I was half way asleep and the thought of getting baptized was so strong. I sat up for a moment to think about the thoughts and then tried to go back to sleep. Again, the thought came back so strong. I knew I had to go to church and tell the missionaries I would get baptized. The next thing I knew, I jumped out of bed and got ready for church.

As I was rushing to get ready, I remember being on fire with the Holy Spirit. It was burning in me like nothing ever had before. Just the previous night, I could not believe I had given up drugs and alcohol. I thought I was a fool. Now I wanted to be baptized! I was consumed with many feelings all at once. I was determined to repent and do whatever it would take to get baptized. I knew that having an experience like this was a miracle, unlike anything I had ever experienced before. No drug or alcohol could even compare to the feeling. I felt as if so much information were put into my mind at once. I uncovered several realizations about my life. I realized that drugs and alcohol were no longer my allies–only an escape from life. I also realized that my new allies were the Holy Spirit, Jesus Christ and Heavenly Father.

As I entered the church building, barely making it in time, I looked for the missionaries. I wanted to share my decision with them right then! As I started to make my way down the row, I stepped on a few toes and I don't remember if I excused myself or not. I was just fixated on the missionaries. As I squeezed next to them, I told them I had made a decision. One elder kept telling me to talk a little lower. But, I was on fire! I told them that I was ready to be baptized. They looked at me with unbelief. I had given them a hard time at our last meeting about my insecurities. I reiterated that, yes, I wanted to get baptized and that I was ready. A huge smile came across both of their faces and I started to be consumed with guilt. As I looked at their smiles, I knew I had to tell them what happened the night before. I motioned to the elder sitting next to me that I had to whisper something in his ear. I told him that I had kind of messed up the night before with a few drinks, but that I was not going to do that anymore. I was done with that way of life. Although nothing could wipe the smile from my face, his was quickly dashed as he looked down and said a loud, "No!" At the time, I was hopeful that no one heard him, but reflecting back, I'm sure they did. I promised him I was serious. I was done with that way of life and wanted to set a date for baptism.

After the meeting, the missionaries told me I would have to talk with the bishop about my baptism. They were excited for me, but I could tell they were a little disappointed. I guess I was disappointed as well. Giving into the old ways was easier than not. I think if I had not faltered the night before, I would have stumbled in the future if left on my own without inspiration from the Holy Spirit. How loving Heavenly Father was! He saw me fall and immediately provided a way for me to come back to Him. I realized that the Savior can inspire us, but if we do not act on it, we are left to ourselves. How grateful I was to be carried by Him! I realized my decision to be baptized rested on my shoulders. Jesus Christ inspired me and I had to act.

When I told my parents of my decision, things changed. Things did not change very often in my home. I was happy. I was really happy. I wanted to get baptized immediately, but because of my fathers trips I would have to wait over a month. This was not easy for me. I now understand why, once the decision to get baptized is made, it is important to

50

do it immediately. I was definitely tested during my waiting period to get baptized and it seemed like a lifetime.

During this month, my mother, though she liked the activities and teachings of the church and loved the missionaries, would not look any further. She was my first experience of someone feeling the Holy Spirit and denying it. I was amazed. I felt like a new person was emerging within me. My whole perspective on life was changing. She had been with me from the beginning. I thought she might want to get baptized also. But she found another church immediately. I almost felt as if she wouldn't come with me because *I* had found the church. I saw her interest, and yet she was hesitating.

At that time in my life, I was also thinking of going to law school. This was something my mother had also starting pursuing. After being encouraged by the attorney I worked for, I wanted to pursue this field. She was mad at me for pursuing her same goal. She did not want me to be an attorney. I was planning on taking the entrance exam, the LSAT, in January or February of the next year. She blatantly told me to pursue being a psychologist. After not being under the influence of anything but reality the last few months, her jealously was evident. I thought I had found something I would love to pursue and she adamantly demanded that I do something else.

For some reason she saw me as competition. And so it was with the church. Pride led her to a different one. I asked her to take the discussions but she felt she would be following me. That was not her way. Tensions in the home were growing again. My father was gone a lot and that was good, but a side of my mother was coming out that was not accepting of me *again*. She did not support my decisions to go to law school or join the church. She said she would go to the baptism and that she still liked the missionaries, but she refused to ever attend a service with me. It was as if she were afraid. She was unsupportive of what I had to do to get baptized. She would not help with my special day at all.

Before I got baptized I would have to repent of all my sins. I would have to face them. This would be hard for me in the near future. Repenting would be hard because deep inside I knew I had to acknowledge my wrong doings. That is not easy for other people and it was not for me. My desire to get baptized was much more powerful than my fear of admitting my wrong doings.

At work my co-workers blatantly told me not to get baptized, and our friendships changed forever. I had dealt with rejection my whole life, but this was different. I had never been persecuted for believing in God. I finally believed, but it just so happened to not be in their God. Their arguments would have me believe there were two Gods–mine and theirs. The things they said were wrong. They had never taken the discussions. They had never attended a service or met with a bishop or the missionaries of the Mormon faith. They were preaching something else. I would take their myths to the missionaries and they would explain the truth. This really bothered me. I remember asking one of my friends where she got her information and she had informed me at her church they held classes on Mormonism. Obviously, these classes were not taught by a member of the Mormon Church. This also bothered me.

One of the reasons I loved the Mormon church so much was that they did not preach about other religions, just about Jesus Christ. They were focused on getting people to return to Heavenly Father rather than teaching what other churches believe. There was a peace I can not explain. An understanding I had longed for my whole life. I was always judged by others, so joining a church that did not judge others in their teachings brought a level of comfort to me. I would receive a confirmation that God lives and loves all of us. That was another blessing I would learn. It would carry me through the hardest times in my life. Going to work was uncomfortable. The literature my co-workers were bringing were inappropriate and wrong, and they refused to go to my baptism. I knew I would have to look for a new job soon. I was hurt. I was being rejected from every direction.

Although I had basically lost all the friends with which I had hung out for years, the Lord replaced them with new friendships. I always felt inferior and not quite good enough around these new friends, but I was happy. I loved what I was learning.

CHAPTER FOUR

White As Snow

Come now, and let us reason together, saith the Lord: though your sins be as scarlet, they shall be as white as snow; though they be red like crimson, they shall be as wool. (Isaiah 1:18-19)

Prior to my baptism, the bishop announced my baptism to the whole ward three Sundays in advance. Two nights before the service, I was with my new friends at a gathering. I did not know it at the time, but that special night I would meet my future eternal companion. I asked him if he were going to my baptism. He said he would be there. I had never met him before, nor had I seen him, but I thought he was handsome and invited him.

I had to meet with the bishop before I was baptized. I was nervous because he had already announced my baptismal date to the ward. Deep inside, I thought that, once he heard about my life before the gospel, he would not let me get baptized. It was on a Sunday after the three-hour block of meetings when I had my meeting with the bishop. I was nervous. He said to me that we were just clearing the slate. He explained we could discuss anything I felt we needed to talk about. At this point, having been sober for two months, I had a lot on my conscience.

After having been taught the standards of the church and its way of life, I internalized all my mistakes as a barrier to God. I was confused. I was mad at my parents for not discussing any of this with me and upset that I did not know any better. I admitted my substance abuse and remember not being able to explain why I got so heavily involved. I could not explain why I started. Expressing how I felt inside was not a strength of mine. All I could say was that I did use drugs and did not know why.

Then I shamefully admitted my promiscuity. I wanted to explain that was my way of life. Everyone I knew had intimate relations before they were married. Love was a physical thing between a man and a woman. Words to me meant nothing. My father told me he loved me but would constantly hit me or scream at me and tell me I was worth nothing. The things he yelled were devastating to my self-esteem and my very soul. Year after year of this treatment it affected me in deep, negative ways. He would make me do things against my will and tried to control my every move. I had learned that, just because someone was in a good mood and said they loved me, it did not mean they really did because their true feelings always came out later. I shared with the bishop that I thought I had loved people in my life, but deep inside I did not think I really did. I tried to explain that my relationships had resembled a short marriage. I wanted to be loved so badly that, maybe if I got serious with someone for a long time, I would really fall in love. It never happened up to this point.

I had to confess what my greatest barrier to the Lord was. I learned at a young age that, having gone so far with sexual relations, I was dealing with a force I could not explain or control. Having experimented with sexual relations at a young age, I got pregnant–twice. Both times I had an abortion. I had been brought up in a home where life did not mean much and I certainly could not run to my parents for help. I had to keep the abortions a secret.

I explained to the bishop, in the life I had before I was taught the gospel, I was taught it was a blessing to be brought up in a world where a woman has a right to choose an abortion.

But I was a teenager, not a woman. The abortion choice was too big of a decision for a teenager like me to make alone. I was on my own and believed what I had heard. I believed that life did not start until late in pregnancy anyway. Actually, I never thought about when life started. I was so young. I was too focused on not feeling pain, so pondering the great questions of life did not occur.

Having a law protecting a woman's right to choose was so confusing. It was as confusing as being around adults who indulged in drug use and glamorized it. If it was a liberating choice for a woman, and a law women should be proud of, why did I feel I needed to keep my choice a secret? I guess I believed what the media was saying. It was a personal choice and one I deserved to make. It was no one's business but my own. I understood that the people trying to protect my rights to have an abortion as a teenager were trying to protect me from a medical stand point. In my own little teenage mind I really believed I was doing myself and the future baby a service anyway–why bring a baby into this cruel world? Life hurt too much. I could not take care of it. I was brought up in a world that gave teenagers the right to abort a life without consent from their parents. The legal system defended my right for this choice. I had made bad decisions before, but I usually got caught by my parents and suffered serious consequences. With this decision, however, they did not have to know and my records would be kept confidential. I was told this was a good thing. *But, if it were such a good thing, why did I feel so bad?*

Amidst all of the confusion, something deep inside of me knew this was all wrong. But that part of me rarely came out. It was that part of me that would come out every once in a while to let me know that my life was not right. But I would rationalize that the law made everything okay. It protected my choice. I was desperate and afraid. I was young. I tried to convince myself that a law passed to protect my choice to abort a baby must be a good thing. I would think that, perhaps when I was older, I would appreciate what a blessing this law was.

I remember wanting sound advice during the crises of these abortions, but I had no one to whom I could turn. My parents had alienated us from other people and other members of our family, so I relied on other teenagers for support. All I could think about was how to make the situation go away. One would think that parents are the best protectors of their children's welfare. But in my case, telling my parents would expose me to violence.

I remember walking into the clinic. There were anti-abortion demonstrators throwing pamphlets at me and giving me graphic pictures. One lady was pleading with me, saying, "Please don't do this, young lady, please!" But she did not understand–I had no other choice. No one could know. I was afraid of what my parents would do. She did not understand what happened in my home if we did something wrong. My parents might kick me out and I would have no place to live. I had already run away twice. I knew what it was like to have no home. Being homeless seemed worse then putting up with the abuse. The fear of what would happen to me if my parents found out was worse than having the abortion itself. The demonstrators' pictures scared me. It is all I could remember about her. I would have loved to have heard her tell me there were other choices I could make instead of handing me graphic pictures I did not want to look at. Instead of scaring me, I would have loved to have heard that there are other places I could go to talk about this issue and handed me a number to call.

As I sat in the waiting room I was surrounded by other teenage girls. Some had their mothers with them. At the time, I longed for that. It would not be so bad if my mother were there with me. Today, how sad this thought is to me!

When they finally called my name, I entered the room just before surgery and began to cry. I was all alone. This was a common feeling for me, but this time it was different. A big decision was being made and I was afraid. I remember shaking with fear about the choice I had made and being afraid if I were going to be okay. I could only hope that I would feel better after the procedure. How I wish I had an adult with me, someone to comfort me and give me guidance. When the nurse came in, she explained the procedures and counseled me on the pain I would experience from the shot. But I was never counseled on the pain I would hold within me for the next twenty years of my life.

The next thing I remember was waking up in a recovery room with other girls about my age. I began to cry. What had I done? It seemed that a choice that was such a blessing did not seem like a blessing at all. At the time, I did not think about whether an abortion was right or wrong, I was just thinking about survival. But now, as an adult, I realized I had to take responsibility for my actions, even when I was a teenager. How I wish the abortion clinic provided non-biased counseling on other alternatives and contacts for me. I do not know of the decisions I would have made if I would have received advice. But, how I wish I could have talked to another adult about my problem. I went under a major medical procedure without my parents consent. As a mother now, I could not imagine my children not being able to come to me regarding their concerns and problems.

I also had to admit another issue. At twenty-one years of age, I was pulled over for drunk driving. This was not the first time I had driven under the influence, just the first time I got caught. It had become a habit. It was important that I "black out" before I got home. I never knew what to expect. Although I did not do this consciously, I did it often. I had little regard for life—mine or others! Spending a night in jail did not change a thing. As I reflect back, maybe it could have made a difference, but my parents did not get mad at me for drinking. At the time, deep inside, I found this odd. It was acceptable to them that I drank and did drugs! I internalized their behavior as condoning my behavior. It helped me rationalize my decisions.

My father did not rage on me for driving drunk and spending the night in jail. But if I played the piano too long, my father would rage and scream at me to stop. He could never just ask. He was always at a boiling point. If I dropped a spoon and it made too loud of a sound, he screamed at me. If he had a bad day which had nothing to do with me, he took it out on me. Naturally, I was confused when he said nothing about spending the night in jail.

Talking about my drinking did not hurt quite as bad as talking about the abortions. I began to cry. I had not cried like that regarding my decision. I had been accountable to only me for those decisions. Having to be accountable to God and the bishop was overwhelming. I had been numb for so long that just talking about it hurt so bad. I felt so unworthy and could not even look at the bishop.

As I kept my head down in shame, my eyes filled with tears. Then, in a peaceful, loving voice, the bishop said, "Wendy, do you not understand what baptism is about?" I nodded, yes, in silence, but deep inside I thought, no. I would do anything to join the Lord's church, no matter how long it took. He called my name again. "Wendy, please look at me." With tears streaming down my face and feelings of unworthiness and sorrow consuming me, our eyes met. He

60

said, "Wendy, you will be made pure again, as a virgin. All your sins prior to your baptism will be gone. The Lord Himself will forget." He continued expressing that the Lord is a merciful God and that He understands all things, including the decisions I had made. He repeated again, "You are pure and right before the Lord. You are white as snow."

I was shocked that the bishop did not reprimand me strongly. I had never met a person who showed me so much love and forgiveness and acceptance as I experienced that day. Surely, he was a servant of the Lord. I could not believe the feelings I was experiencing. It was as if a great weight had been lifted. I had always felt a heavy, dark feeling inside. Now, for the first time, I felt light and full of love. For the first time in my life, I was realizing that love is a feeling, not just a physical experience. For a moment I was feeling a force greater than me. I imagined Heavenly Father's arms wrapped around me, consoling my very soul, telling me that I was worth His time and unconditional love and that I could trust His teachings. His teachings wouldn't change from day to day. It was okay to feel loved and to feel that He really cared. And, most importantly, He forgave me and would forget the horrible deeds of my past life. I was overwhelmed. I always held grudges, even for the pettiest things. But He, Heavenly Father, would forgive me for the greatest of offenses!

To my surprise, I could still be baptized! I had to give up an old way of life to live a new way. How willing I was to live a new way! Having received mercy for the sins I committed, changed me. Even from that very moment, I experienced a freedom and a weight lifted from me that I had not experienced before. After our discussion, I felt the love of the bishop and my Heavenly Father. I felt an unconditional love I had never felt before.

As the days passed, time would be my greatest challenge. For just as quickly as I felt the power of repentance, mercy, and Heavenly Father's love, my old thought patterns of self-doubt emerged. Self-doubt seemed to always be lingering in the back of my mind, and showed up unexpectedly. It was no different the night before my baptismal service.

I was going to call the missionaries and tell them I had made a big mistake. I was so embarrassed and felt I had been on a roller coaster ride. I just could not do it. What was wrong with my life before? It was as if all the things I had been taught these last few months suddenly went out the door. All I could see was my past and the way things were. I had lost a lot of friends. My mother was being cold and my co-workers wouldn't even come to support my decision. What did they see that I could not? This was the biggest decision in my life and I was confused at the last minute. What seemed so sure earlier seemed like a big mistake. As I was experiencing doubt, one of the missionaries called. I expressed how I was feeling. All he said was to get on my knees and pray and that he would call back in a few moments to talk.

I kneeled down to pray. I sat there for some time with no thoughts coming to mind. I got up and walked around until I could communicate with the Lord. I came back and prayed. The only thing I said was that I know I am not supposed to ask for a sign but I need something. I was still getting to know Heavenly Father and still getting accustomed to our relationship. I was hesitant at times, but sincere. I told Him I felt like a fool and was so confused.

Just as I got up from my prayer, I had another phone call. It was my Mormon friend I had known since high school who had become reactivated. She was calling to tell me she was proud of my decision. She had known me during my roughest times and knew this was not an easy change for me.

She had friendshipped me during the missionary discussions and was helping with my baptismal arrangements. As I talked with her, another call came through. It was a new friend I had met. She was going to sing at my baptism. She was a dear new friend who was so accepting of me that, at times, I felt uncomfortable. She was calling to bare her testimony about my baptism. I started to cry. I told her about my doubtful feelings and my prayer. As she was comforting me, another call came through! It was another dear friend I had just met. She was excited about my baptism and was letting me know just how good of friends we were. I got off the phone with a most reassuring confirmation that I would be there the next day for my baptism. Within minutes the missionaries called me back and asked one thing. "Did you get your answer?" I said, "yes," and that I would see them the next day.

The day of my baptism was a day I will always remember. As I entered the room where we gathered, there was standing room only. I was overwhelmed with the support of all these people I did not even know. My family was there and only about two friends from my previous life.

At the time of the actual baptism, I felt a feeling of peace. I could not forget the feelings and confirmations I had while confessing to the bishop. I could not deny the power of the Holy Spirit. However, the doubt I felt the night before my baptism would be an experience I would draw upon in the future. I realized that, although I was touched deeply by the Holy Spirit, I would still be capable of potentially making wrong decisions. I compared this experience to Laman and Lemuel, who were brothers in the Book of Mormon, who saw an angel and later denied it. I would have to be careful to not let the wrong influence overpower me.

As I was immersed into the water, I had no doubt that I was on the right path. My old self was entering the cleansing water and a new person emerged. My baptism was beautiful and I finally received the gift my soul had longed for, the gift of the Holy Spirit. It was amazing to think that I would have it as a constant companion. The Holy Spirit had always been good to me, even though I was still getting to know Heavenly Father. The Holy Spirit taught me to trust my inner feelings and to listen to a conscience that had been buried by pain for so long. The Holy Spirit guided me to make the most important decision in my life–accepting Jesus Christ in my heart. I felt like a new person. I really did feel "white as snow." I also felt prompted to bare my testimony. I would consider my baptism to be the start of my new life. Everything would change-dating, friendships, morals and even eventually having to quit my job. But most importantly, I felt pure and cleansed. Not physically, but spiritually. I knew without a doubt there was more than just me. Although my testimony was new, I had no doubt there was a God and that He was merciful and loved me unconditionally.

CHAPTER FIVE

My Eyes Were Opened

"By the power of the Spirit our eyes were opened and our understandings were enlightened so as to understand the things of God." D&C 76:12

After being baptized, Christmas came in two weeks. It had a whole new meaning to me. My family did not have any Christmas traditions except buying a lot of presents for each other and eating breakfast together. I wanted to find some new traditions for my family. As I asked my new friends about their family traditions, Jesus Christ was at the center of them. When I went to my new friend's home, there was a peaceful spirit. In my parents' house there seemed to be a dark, heavy feeling. I did not know how to bring the gospel into my home without criticism from my family.

My family Christmas was about how many presents were given. It seemed a time to attempt to make up for the bad life we all had. If we had a lot of presents, somehow that would make up for all the problems. It could be predicted that Christmas resulted in some type of disappointment. We learned early on that if you did not like a gift that was given, the other family members always knew. They knew from disappointed looks and how we treated the gift. There were a lot of nonverbal messages in my home. Christmas was no exception.

Buying presents for my mother was especially hard. She would grimace if she did not like the gift or if she had not received enough. We learned to do the same. We would usually like the majority of the gifts but there was always something we disliked and made it known. It seemed our dislike for the one present became the most memorable part of the whole present-opening ceremony. Gratitude was not shared.

I wanted this Christmas to be different. I wanted my family to be different. After my baptism I thought I could help them change for the better. I did not want to spend so much money on presents or spend money I did not have, which had often been the case. I had learned the meaning of Christmas was to reflect on Jesus Christ. I wanted to do that. But, my family attitude, Christmas tree, and presents would be a reminder that I could not. I would have to go through the motions as I had all other Christmases. There would be at least 25 to 30 presents under the tree for each of us. I wanted to buy simple journals so my family could start recording their lives. They did not mention their childhood much, only that there was a lot of pain.

I woke up Christmas morning with an empty feeling. I had felt the Holy Spirit by my side almost everyday for the last two weeks, but not that morning. With it gone, life felt as empty as it had my whole life. I felt the pressure of the Christmas season to overspend and got lost in the buying frenzy as I had every Christmas before. I knew the expectations of my family. Nevertheless, I would still buy the journals as a special present for each member of my family. That Christmas morning would take so long to open all the Christmas presents. Of course, someone was always disappointed.

Eating together as a family was another Christmas tradition. It was a special tradition because we rarely ate together. My mother would cook a Christmas breakfast and dinner for us. That morning, as my mother was in the kitchen preparing breakfast with my sister, I asked my father if he would talk with me. I wanted to give him my special gift. My whole family knew I had bought special gifts for them and that I did not want to give them while opening all the other presents.

My father and I sat down. As he was opening his gift, I explained that genealogy was a big part of the Mormon Church. I felt so good inside as I shared this information with him. I explained I wanted to know his history. I had always wanted to know. I knew very little. I knew he was raised in a Catholic orphanage only to be taken home by his real mother years later. Although it was rare that he mentioned his childhood, I had seen tears come to his eyes on occasion. But, I did not really know the details. I was excited to give him my special gift. I asked him to accept it and to write his life story.

As our eyes met, I had a smile on my face which was quickly removed because of his disappointed look. It seemed as I was sharing the church with him, I felt the Holy Spirit, but for only a moment. His look erased any trace I felt. Fear set in. All I kept thinking was, "What did I do wrong? This conversation could turn really bad if I am not careful." I got scared when he got that look. My stomach would tighten and I would clinch my teeth in hopes that he would not start screaming at me–or worse, hit me. He looked at the journal, then at me and said harshly, "So this is your special present to me?" With my face expressionless, I cautiously explained my gift. I said I wanted to know about his childhood and his life. He said, "I'm not going to write about my childhood. The past is the past. Now leave it there, Wendy." He gave me back the journal and walked away. I remember sitting in the chair staring into space, thankful he had not "lost it" on me. I did not know what I had done. My "special gift" for each member of my family meant nothing to me now. I did not give my sister or mother the journals I had bought them. I would not risk their disappointment, also. My father was

67

raging inside, but perhaps because it was Christmas he held back from what usually would have been a violent situation.

I went and got dressed upstairs, waiting for breakfast to be ready and for my friend to come over. I sat in my room alone. It was better than engaging in conversation with my family. I never knew when the conversation would turn against me.

I remember as I came down the stairs for breakfast, my father was waiting for me at the end of the staircase. It was uncomfortable. My whole body tensed up. I remember the look he gave me. It was eerie. I was starting to get really uncomfortable with the way my father would look at me. He checked my body up and down, stared at my chest and said, "Honey, let's eat." As he touched me, I felt violated. I immediately pulled away and told him I would come in a moment. I ran upstairs and changed my shirt to a baggy one so I would not feel violated. Then I realized, he did not only scare me, he was uncomfortable to be around. He had so many different moods. This particular mood was common. It was as if he lusted after me. It was a common occurrence, a common feeling. In the past, I would dismiss it and run away from my thoughts. But this time, I acknowledged my uncomfortable feelings, not understanding what to do with the information. When my father was around, I often changed clothes and wore layered clothing. It was an unconscious act. This Christmas, I caught myself purposefully hiding my body from my father by wearing baggy clothing.

At breakfast, I felt like a bystander. My mind was racing. Although my father seemed to be somewhat over the situation with the journal, I was still scared. He did not rage or hit me, but I was still traumatized.

As everyone was talking, I seemed to drown them out with my thoughts. I was so confused about life. I was starting to question why I felt such a bad feeling in my home and why I would go to church and feel peaceful. My daily work and routines took me out of the house, and that was where I felt the Holy Spirit. I felt it away from home. That Christmas I realized that something was really wrong with my family. I should not have to fear that my father was going to hit me for asking him to tell me about his childhood. But, I did.

After breakfast I left with my new friend from church. I wanted my first Christmas after joining The Church of Jesus Christ of Latter-day Saints to be a spiritual one. I thought I would experience feelings similar to what I had on my baptismal day. Rather, I felt a heavy weight from the realization that just because I joined the church, my whole life would not change overnight. It was not as I had hoped.

After the Christmas holidays, I asked for my patriarchal blessing. I did not really understand what it was. I did know I wanted to get it. I remember going to the church alone and meeting with a man tall in stature with white hair and eyes that put me at ease immediately. He carried a strong spirit with him. I told him I was nervous about the blessing. I thought it would be similar to my very own horoscope. He quickly changed the term from "horoscope" to "personal blessing" and "communication with Heavenly Father directly to me." He told me a horoscope is for many people, but the patriarchal blessing was only for me. It was not meant for anyone else. I told him a lot had changed in my life the last few months and I did not know what the future held. I was nervous. I was not used to so much change. He had an aura about him that was calm and peaceful, patient and understanding. He took the time to listen to my feelings. I had no fear of criticism.

When he explained Heavenly Father communicated directly through him about my mission on earth, the Holy Spirit was strong. So strong that the room seemed to get warm and all my fears subsided. After we talked for what seemed like a long while, he asked if I were ready to receive my special blessing. After talking with him, I felt prepared to receive it. During the blessing, tears rolled down my face as the words he was saying meant so much to me. It seemed he was not describing me. I felt he was talking about someone else. He did go into some detail regarding me as a parent. I remember thinking that parenting was not so important and did not understand why he would even mention it. It would not be until the future that the guidance I received about being a parent would have a great impact on me. When he finally finished, a peace settled within me. As I shook his hand and thanked him, I was sad our meeting was over. His peaceful countenance would leave a strong impression on me.

During my first few months in the church, I had many overwhelming feelings and thoughts come to me. As a new convert, my mind was constantly on God and His gospel. I would be driving and thoughts of the gospel would overwhelm me. I was confused about why I had not been told God before. Why did I have to be 23 to finally have God in my life? I felt love and acceptance from my new friends at church. The Holy Spirit testified to me that God loved me, too. Then again, I was not just overwhelmed because of how I was feeling inside; I was overwhelmed because I was gaining courage to actually question my life. For the first time, I was feeling love. I understood that my life really *did* have a purpose. I was beginning to understand that I, too, had a special mission here on earth. We all do. I felt special for the first time in my life. Since I had a unique mission here on earth that meant maybe I could contribute to something. Maybe I was worth something more than I had felt my whole life.

After being a member of the church for a few months, my first spiritual challenge came-general conference. I felt I had been converted by the Holy Spirit and could not deny a force so strong. It had cut through all my addictions and once baptized I never felt tempted to drink or do drugs again. My temptations were gone. As a matter of fact, after only being a member a few months it was hard to imagine ever going back to that way of life.

In the singles ward, I remember the most wonderful posters in the hallway asking the questions, "What is my purpose here on earth?" "Where did I come from?" I had felt so alone before. It seemed many others were wondering the same things I had wondered as well. I had finally come to understand that I was not alone in this world. There were others who felt the same way. I did not have evidence God was real, but the Holy Spirit testified He was. I had not experienced a power like that in my life before. I had been so numb. For something to awaken my dormant soul, it had to be real.

General Conference was different. Other religions believed there were no prophets or apostles in modern times. It seemed having faith in Jesus Christ and Heavenly Father was easier than believing that a man could actually be a prophet. I was invited to go to General Conference. I was invited to attend the Tabernacle in Salt Lake City, Utah.

I was told twice a year the prophet spoke via broadcast, as well as the apostles. I had not seen the meetings and I did not know what to expect. I can honestly say I had doubts about the prophet. What would he say that would convince me he was a prophet? What would the apostles say that would convince me they were Disciples of Christ?

Beforehand, I had attended my mother's new church several times in an attempt to appease my family. I was used to professional singers with the best sound equipment. Everything was a production. The building was spectacular. The same speaker spoke each week. He seemed to be on an emotional high, and when I left, I often felt the same. Although I did not experience this at The Church of Jesus Christ of Latter-day Saints, I thought maybe General Conference would be similar to my mother's worship service. I was anxious so see what the production would be like.

Upon seeing the Salt Lake Temple for the first time I was touched by the beauty and splendor of the building. There were stores all around its gated setting in the middle of the city. As my friend and I crossed the street to enter the temple grounds, a most remarkable experience happened. There were protestors outside the gates waving their posters and warning us of what we would find within the gates. It was a bit overwhelming. But as we passed them and entered the sacred grounds, my anxiety left. I was not nervous anymore. The temple grounds were immaculate with the most beautiful spring blooms of all different colors. It seemed the grass was a deep green and cut to perfection. It was truly the most beautiful place I had ever seen. There were many people on the temple grounds, but they were not loud like on the streets. Everyone was in their church clothes and there seemed to be a certain reverence within the gates.

In addition to the beautiful landscape, the sight of the temple was pleasing to my eyes. I remember just staring at it for a long time. The gray granite building stood tall, as the blue sky was its background. I did not know what went on inside, I just knew I wanted to go in it as soon as possible. It was the most beautiful building I had ever seen.

As we entered the Tabernacle where the conference would be held, I could not believe how big the organ was. I thought General Conference would be a big production like my mother's church. As we found our seats, we were on the main level to the right side of the building. Not too far from the center. I could see the pulpit clearly. It was at that spot I would find out if there were a true prophet who lived as a man.

Everyone was sitting down and waiting for the meeting to begin. There was a rumble of voices that was to be expected in such a large building filled with so many people. I looked around. There were still many outside waiting to listen to the meeting from the outside speakers. Many of them could not get in. I was amazed that people came from all over the world just to be a part of this meeting, even if they could only listen outside. As I observed the crowd, I started to get a little nervous, but also felt I was supposed to be where I was.

Then, in the corner of my eye, I saw him. I saw an older man being helped onto the speaking area. I did not know who he was at first. I had not seen him before. I kept looking to see who he was. The meeting had not started and all the speakers' seats were not filled. Then everyone else started to stand up and whisper, "There he is, that's him." I looked at my friend next to me to ask her who he was and noticed she had tears in her eyes. As I looked back at him, I realized without asking it was a prophet of the Lord, carrying with him a spirit so strong that I knew who he was without being told. I recognized that special feeling. I knew without a doubt that this man was a living prophet. I did not have anyone explain to me his life or who he was. The Holy Spirit testified to me, again. I trusted that feeling. It had helped to change my life for the better, and when it came, it was strong. I stared at the prophet as others started their conversations again when he sat down. It seemed I could not take my eyes off him.

As the meeting proceeded, I could not believe the words which I had heard. The speakers were so calm and their words inspired. The music was beautiful and peaceful. The big production I had been expecting was superseded by a marvelous spiritual outpouring. The warning I received from the protestors outside the gates earlier was wrong. Gratitude filled my heart and the inspired words set new guidelines for my life. Later, I would learn that it was the last General Conference the prophet Ezra Taft Benson attended. How grateful I was for that experience! How grateful I was to have the beginnings of a testimony of a true and living prophet!

During that trip, we visited a home I will not forget. Upon entering the house, I immediately felt peace. There were three sisters enjoying one another. One of them was getting married in a temple in the near future. The others were huddled all together talking with excitement for their sister. We were all looking at the fabric she had picked out for her bridesmaids' dresses. Her mother was beaming and sharing how she had put the whole thing together while her daughter and fiancé were in school. She did not seem to mind or feel that preparing for a wedding was a burden. Each family member seemed to have a part in preparing for the special occasion. As a matter of fact, the whole family was beaming with excitement for the bride.

The sisters shared the same friends. I could not believe it. My sister and I had lived in the same house for 23 years and I barely knew her. When I turned 21, we started doing more together, but only to drink alcohol together. If we were not drinking, it was uncomfortable to be around one another. Our friends would not have been in the same room together.

Later, as I walked into the kitchen, the father was playing the guitar and two of the daughters were singing together. I thought families like this were only in movies. I would not do that with my father. I did not hang out with him. He was so uncomfortable to be around. Even if we were having a good time, he would somehow always find a way to get mad about something. He was such a bully. The father playing the guitar was gentle, kind and friendly to all his children's friends. He even knew them by name. I did not feel uncomfortable around him. He did not give me looks like my father did. This gathering would have a great impact on me. I was seeing living proof that life could be different in a home. I was witnessing that a home could be a safe haven and a place of peace and refuge.

My home was unpredictable and I often felt more nervous being in my own home than I did outside of it. I did not know what was going to hit me-my father's hand or his rages. He was either too nice or really mad. There was no in-between. He seemed to try and keep my family from bonding with each other. He would often lie to my mother right in front of me. He would tell me the truth, or I knew it anyway, and he would blatantly lie to her. He could be justifying why he was acting so crazy or had to hit me–not that she inquired often. It was as if he were trying to send a message that I was under his power and that he could lie and do whatever he wanted in his home. It was as if he wanted to make sure I always knew my place.

He talked so badly about my mother, his wife. He would complain that he was not attracted to her or that he did not love her, and he constantly complained at how sloppy she was in the home. He would tell me their intimate details. If there was one thing my father valued, it was a woman's body. He would often comment to me on how other women looked–to the point that, when I saw a woman, I knew if my father found her attractive. This was normal life. I would feel so sorry for him–almost guilty that my mother was so cold to him. As if I, somehow, had a responsibility to please him.

On the other hand, my mother would talk of her dream man. As a matter of fact, she had kept a picture of a man she had truly loved and had showed me his picture from time to time. At one time, she wanted to marry this other man. I asked her why she did not marry him, but she would not explain. I felt sorry for her. To not marry the man you truly loved seemed a tragedy. At the same time, my parents' actions sent me confusing messages. Both wanted to be with other people.

I dreaded going home after my Utah trip. I would yearn for the comfortable atmosphere and peace I felt there. I would yearn for a family that loved to be with each other. It is not that the family I visited did not argue. I am sure they had their share of arguments, but there was a genuine respect they had for each other. The warmth and spirit I felt there were something I would keep deep inside of me, just hoping that I would be so blessed as to find a gentle man who would lead our home with respect rather than anger.

Mother's Day was coming up. All of my former Mother's Days had been about presents and how much we could spend just like Christmas. My mother taught me that holidays were times when a lot of money was to be spent, whether you had it or not. As usual, the present count was important. Just like Christmas I wanted to do something different. I was not going to overspend like I did on Christmas. I would make sure my participation would be different.

My father was out of town and, as usual, that was a relief. My sister made my mother a gourmet meal. She spent hours cooking and spent a lot of money on the food and decorations. The meal was to be my sister's gift to my mother. I, on the other hand, knew that my mother really liked the dairy cows that had become a big hit as kitchen decorations. I bought her a basket set with towels and hot mitts and other decorative items matching the theme. I remember the three of us getting ready to sit at the table when a disgusted look came across my mother's face. She was disappointed.

As we ate, the conversation was between my sister and me. My mother sat quietly, but obviously she was upset and we were going to hear about it. I remember saying a prayer. I prayed that my mother would enjoy her afternoon with us and that she would be happy. I did not feel the need to give so much anymore. I guess I thought that, because I had changed, perhaps she had to. But, I was wrong.

In the middle of the meal I gave her my present. She opened it and liked it but set it aside and immediately asked where the rest of the presents were, knowing there were no more. My father had not bought her a gift himself and she was mad. She went on to complain that, if Dad had been there, she would have gotten a piece of jewelry and more presents. I remember my sister trying to defend herself, explaining how much time and money she spent on dinner and the decorations. I was just watching them interact with one another. Although such conversations happened at almost all holidays, I was watching from a distance. Going into debt for the present count was more important to my mother than appreciating our efforts. She was mad that, although my present was a basket full of gifts, it was not enough. My sister's cooking time was not enough.

Without even thinking about it, I raised my voice telling her she was wrong. I felt so beaten down by her! I was sick of it. I told her she was so ungrateful. Could not she see what my sister had done for her? Why was not my present enough for her? I stuck up for my sister and defended myself. I hardly ever stuck up for myself and sister before my mother. With my father I hardly ever stuck up for myself because of the physical consequences. With my mother I feared more of an emotional distance. My mother was shocked. There was an uncomfortable silence. Without finishing my meal, I left the table and went up to my room. It was my only escape. It was not until a few hours later that she picked up her basket of gifts and put them away in the kitchen, saying she liked them. But she had ruined the afternoon. I was seeing a change in me, but not in my family. She had been attending another church, yet her heart had not changed.

CHAPTER SIX

Above All Things

"Wherefore, the blessings which I give unto you are above all things." (D&C 18:45)

After being a new member for a few months, I was getting to know a very special man in the singles ward. We would see each other at gatherings and end up socializing with each other. We seemed to gravitate towards one another. We were dating different people at that time, but would find ourselves engaged in deep conversation. We could open up to each other. For the first time in my life, I could really open up to someone of a different gender. I would often think in the back of my mind that I wished I could date someone just like him. He was so peaceful and comfortable to be around. But, he was dating someone else, and so was I.

At that time in my life, although I was dating, I was still nervous. I did not feel good enough for my new friends and my new life. I was afraid I would mess everything up as I dated. I was so insecure. I constantly worried about what other people thought of me. My past relations became too serious and the level of respect was low on both sides. As a matter of fact, I realized that, not only did I have bad boyfriends, I was a bad girlfriend. It was hard to admit. I dated people who had been disloyal to me and I still wanted to be with them. I felt so badly about myself that I would take any "love" thrown my way. The wisdom of the world would have me believe that cheating on a partner was just a part of any relationship. It was not normal for a man to be with just one woman. There were so many from which to choose. Loyalty seemed so far away and unrealistic.

My father would say it was a shame to be "stuck" with one woman for a lifetime. I saw how cold and bitter my mother had become because of his infidelities. My parents never talked about it until I was much older. My mother shared with me how he had cheated on her so many times with all of her friends. As I reflect back on my dating years, it is not surprising how many unhappy relationships I had. I was not taught how to treat my boyfriends. I just mimicked how I had been treated at home.

I had a tendency toward finding and staying in relationships where I was constantly rejected. I find that interesting since rejection was one of my biggest fears. I was constantly rejected at home and in my relationships. After having relationships like this many times, I started becoming disloyal myself. It was better to hurt them before they hurt me. This would be my mentality in relationships for a long time.

When I joined the church and learned its moral standards, I felt out of my league. The last thing I wanted to do was to repeat my old ways. I had changed my life tremendously and could not bear doing anything that would jeopardize my new life. Deep inside, when I heard that a disloyal man most likely would be excommunicated, I felt that maybe my husband of the future would think twice before participating in that type of activity in this church. I had seen how cheating had affected my mother. Instead of leaving my father and dealing with the situation, she drew inward and became unapproachable.

When I was young, I did not know what was wrong with my mother. Only that she withdrew from my hugs and my love as if she were upset that she had had children. I felt like such a burden to her. I rarely saw her hug my father without grimacing. As a matter of fact, she would look straight at my sister and me and roll her eyes. We all felt the discomfort when he hugged her. So I learned to be the same.

When I was with my new friend at church, I was not nervous about being a new member around him nor did I feel I had to try to impress him. I could just be me. I was rough around the edges and he still wanted to talk with me. I had not felt like this with anyone before. He had a peace about him that helped lower my guard. He was someone in the ward who had respect from others. Thinking of dating him was out of the question. High school memories still haunted me when I tried to date "respectful" young men. Although my parents did not control who I dated now, the fear of how they would treat anyone I dated in the church scared me. Their actions were still unpredictable. I did not want to be embarrassed by their actions. I could initially only handle being friends.

Then, one Saturday afternoon, my friend called me to go to lunch with him. I remember being caught off guard, but happy just the same. He asked if he could stop by in thirty minutes. I do not think I ever got ready so fast. We ended up spending five hours together. We talked about spiritual things and genealogy. And mostly, I just enjoyed listening to him talk and being with him. We were friends, but I was falling in love with him on our first lunch date. I had not experienced feelings like that before. I felt at peace with him.

Throughout all my years of dating, I did not think of marriage. I was afraid of it deep inside. But out of no where, I was having thoughts that he was the one. He was so gentle and kind. Although I had not been on an official date with him, there was that feeling again. The feeling that I was doing the right thing and that being with him was a good thing. It was unexpected.

The next two weeks we spent time getting to know each other. I suspected he liked me because he was calling and we were doing things together, but he would not hold my hand. I had to ask a friend about the dating standards of the church. They were quite different from what I was used to. I did not want to make a mistake. He was such a good person. I was still a new member and it seemed, just when I thought I was starting to get the lifestyle under control, a new situation would come up, like dating. I also carried a lot of shame from my previous ways. We talked about many things but I always avoided getting too detailed about my past. I was embarrassed. Although I had been baptized and cleansed in the sight of Heavenly Father and had changed my ways, I knew others would judge me.

There was a part of me that loved the spiritual growth I was experiencing and another part, an old part that felt unworthy of it. I worked hard at living the standards of the church and became cautious as our relationship grew serious.

I was used to relationships where talking was limited and physical intimacy was the focal part of the relationship. I had also been under the influence of drugs and alcohol in all my previous relationships. I had never had a sober relationship. I had never been *friends* with those I dated. But, he was different and, more importantly, I felt different around him. I decided I would try hard to not take any of my old dating ways with me into this relationship. I had a lot of respect for a man whose main objective was to get to know me first.

I felt we had a special bond. I could open up to him about things I never shared with anyone. After being sober for six months, my life looked a lot different than it had previously. I was able to start sharing things about my family and my life. I remember being uncomfortable when talking about my family, but I felt I needed to anyway. He was attending a personal growth class and working on his own family issues. I admired him for being able to look at himself and his life and consciously strive to make changes.

After two weeks of seeing each other every day, I asked him on an official date. I needed to know just how much he liked me. Of course, he liked this idea, but he wanted to go to a movie theater the night before our big, official date. I sought some counsel from another young man on just what the dating standards of the church were. He was well pleased with my special friend because he had been respectful to me and was living the standards of the church. I figured if he was calling and we were doing things everyday that meant he liked me. I just wished he would have said something more about his feelings for me.

As we walked to the movie theater, we were lost in conversation. The next thing I knew, he had to let go of my hand to open the door for me. I did not even realize he had taken my hand. For all I knew, I had taken his hand. It just seemed so natural. Upon entering the theater, I experienced a feeling of peace. I guess he liked me after all.

My special friend's name was Joey and I think I loved him from our first lunch date. He had a calm disposition and an inner strength that I admired. But, I mostly admired a man with a firm testimony of the gospel.

On our official date the next night, I took him out to a restaurant on the harbor. The waters were calm with a slight cool breeze. He took my hand again and there was a sense of innocence. He had a testimony of Jesus Christ and made His teachings an integral part of our relationship. I had never experienced this before. I worked so hard to be a good match for him. I worked hard at being a better person.

For the next few weeks we spent a lot of time together–almost everyday. Each night we would end with prayer. Joey was adamant that, although we were attracted to each other and considered each other boyfriend and girlfriend, we would never take our physical relationship beyond an innocent good-bye kiss. I had not experienced this before. We were serious about each other, but the physical part of the relationship was only a minimal part. This type of dating was so different from what I had been taught! I loved every moment of it. I felt respected for the first time in my life. That was a big deal. No one had ever respected me before. My parents sure did not, nor did my past boyfriends. So what did Joey see that they did not? I would ask myself this question over and over. I was starting to feel really blessed. Joey made me want to be the best I could be, even though deep inside I still felt unworthy of him.

Remembering our first kiss brings a smile to my face, even now. That kiss meant a lot to me. How grateful I was for the church standards! I started understanding the sacredness of dating. I was starting to understand the impact my actions would have on my future. Joey's goal was to marry in the temple–he taught me that a man could have restraint. He taught me that a man could actually do what was right. Up to this point in my life, I do not think I had ever met someone with so much integrity and honor.

We were on a date and drove to a planetarium. The season was late spring and the night was cool. It had a balcony surrounding it. We were overlooking the city lights and enjoying the view. Our conversation was put on hold as we enjoyed the moment. Then unexpectedly Joey leaned over and looked into my eyes, and said, "You are so beautiful" and gently kissed me. It was so precious. Never in my life had I ever been told I was beautiful. I believed he meant it as he looked into my eyes.

I had been scarred by cruel comments people had made to me as a child and young adult. I remember being told I was ugly on many occasions. And believe me, being told as a young girl I was ugly was devastating! Not only did I feel ugly inside, other people confirmed I was on the outside. No one I ever dated had told me I was beautiful. What did Joey see that others did not? Why was he so kind to me? After our first kiss, our relationship seemed to become more serious. We were in love. I had not experienced this before and Jesus Christ and the gospel were the foundation of our relationship.

I found that Joey and I had a lot in common. I had an Associate's degree in psychology and he was attending personal growth classes. We would talk frequently about psychology. Joey would open up to me about his childhood. He was a convert who came from two alcoholic parents. They divorced when he was seven. He felt he had raised himself on his own. When he finally left his home at age fourteen, he went to live with his father, who he thought had sobered up. But he quickly learned this was not the case.

At the age of eight he already had a job as a paper boy. He told me stories of how he would have to brave the Minnesota winters to deliver the papers. I thought he was amazing. Most people who shared stories of walking through the snow with no shoes were in their seventies. But Joey was only in his twenties. He had joined the church at age nineteen and had dreams of becoming a professional tennis player. But tennis scholarships would keep him from going on the professional tour for another four years. Wisely, he finished school at the age of 23. Although older than most, he had planned to make his break and go on the professional tour. But the promptings of the Holy Spirit were too strong to deny, so two years later he had successfully served a mission in Johannesburg, South Africa. He returned home at the age of twenty-six, too old to start a professional tennis career. I asked him if he had any regrets about going on a mission. Although his dream from childhood was stifled, he shared with me that no tennis title could be as satisfying and fulfilling as serving the Lord. No trophy or tournament won could satisfy the soul as to bringing someone to Jesus Christ. That was Joey.

My family story was very different from his. When I would talk about my family, I would protect them. It always surfaced when I was quizzed about them. I told Joey my best friends were my parents. I told him that my father would describe us as a "perfect family." My father would tell people that he had everything he wanted in life. Somewhere deep inside of me, I wanted to believe it too. I had learned to put on a facade in public and defend them to other people. Although I knew it was not true, I wanted people to think we had a good family. I did not do this consciously. After seeing my father lie about it for so many years, I believed that was the correct answer to give to people.

Joey knew a little about my past. I did not share all of the details of the things I had done. He did know that I recently quit my addictions. With a drug and alcohol problem, he knew I was running from something. He just did not know exactly what, but he had his own suspicions. When I would put my father on a pedestal as I described him, Joey would be confused. I guess I only described the way I wished my father was. I would not verbalize his rages or cruel comments. I never did. Nor would I ever describe the times he would hit me, or my mother's emotional absence.

After meeting my family, Joey felt there was something wrong. He felt uncomfortable in my home and with my strong defense of my father. He had never met a "perfect" father before. I used those words to describe my father. Joey blatantly told me he thought my description of my family was fantasy-like. I had not had anyone talk to me like this before. He thought I might be out of touch with my relationship with my family. But I continued to defend them. It is not that Joey would talk badly about my family, he just did not think my description of our relationship had an ounce of reality in it. At the time, he suspected something was going on in my home, but only shared it with me later.

After two months of dating, I knew without a doubt that he was the one. But tensions in my home were getting worse. My father and I had a horrible argument and I finally shared it with Joey. I told him my father had a tendency to be very mean at times. It was the first time I opened up to him about some of the horrible truths of my family. I felt I could confide in him. At the same time, I felt awful because I had never betrayed my family's facade before.

The next day Joey called my father, but not for the reasons I thought. My mother knew about the argument and came into my room to tell me that Joey was trying to get a hold of my father. She was worried that he was going to confront him. No one outside the family had ever done that. Apparently, she thought I had told Joey about our family dynamics, even though in my own family we never talked about it. It was as if she was ready to cover-up the problems and wanted to make sure I was by her side to do it. I was afraid of what my father might say to him and do to me. He could be so violent. I drove down to my father's work place.

When I arrived, my father told me that Joey had gotten a hold of him and wanted to talk and have lunch with him. He looked so mad at me and asked "So what do you think he wants to talk to me about?" I did not know at first. Then my father said that Joey wanted to ask him a question. I suddenly realized that Joey was going to ask my father for permission to marry me. I do not know how, I just knew. I begged my father to be nice to him and accept the invitation. I told him how much I loved Joey and asked him to please not do anything that could jeopardize my relationship with him. I remember saying I was sorry for our argument. I remember apologizing for getting him so mad. Just like I was forced to do since I was a little girl. In reality, he had just felt like raging and, as usual, I was the target. I remember being so nervous. I was worried about what my father might do or say. I was afraid he would mess things up for me as he had done so many times before. When he got mad, he did not care about anyone's feelings. He just did whatever he felt.

When my father came home from his lunch meeting with Joey, he told me that Joey was going to propose to me that night. Joey had asked him not to tell me. But, of course, my father did. I do not think I had been so nervous in my entire life. I had fallen in love and had found someone I thought was the greatest blessing in my life, and was afraid that it all could go away because of my father. He never liked anyone I dated, and let it be known. Although he did like Joey, he was mad at me. When he was mad at me, he did bad things to hurt me without care for the consequences. He finally told me that he had given his consent to Joey.

My father was not a man of integrity. But I was relieved he told me because I would have worried that he did something to ruin my relationship with Joey. So, of course, knowing that my true love was going to propose to me, I went out and bought a dress for the occasion. I still have it to this very day, although it does not fit as well as it did so long ago.

That very night Joey picked me up and took me to the beach where we would always go. It looked like it was going to rain and he was so nervous! He did not know that I knew what he was trying to do. I just had a smile on my face the whole drive. I knew he had special plans for the evening. I did not know what, but knew he had mapped out the whole night. That's just the sort of thing he did. Every minute was planned in his life. You never saw Joey without his planner.

He was so nervous about the weather that he kept wondering if we should go another night. As we got closer to our destination, the weather was clear. We walked down to our favorite spot and sat upon the rocks. They overlooked the beach and we could hear the waves breaking on the rocks. He had brought a little picnic for us. It was so romantic. He thought of everything. After a nice conversation, he abruptly got on one knee and shared his favorite scripture with me. After he shared his love for me, I started to cry. Then he asked the sweetest question I had ever been asked. "Will you marry me?" Before he got to the word "me," I said "Yes!" I could not wait. As we embraced each other, it was the happiest moment of my life. We just hugged for the longest time. Holding Joey was magical. I could not hold him without tears streaming down my face. Perhaps I just felt empty before, but with him, I felt full.

When we got to the car, Joey opened the door for me, as usual, and surprised me with a beautiful bouquet of flowers. I had tears in my eyes with disbelief that I was actually going to get married to a man I loved. I could not believe that he loved me too. I felt so unworthy of his love, but the Holy Spirit was telling me it was okay to be happy. It was okay to accept his love. Joey informed me there was more. For the final surprise, he took me to a harbor and we went on a gondola ride. As we glided through the harbor, Joey wanted to know when we should get married. We both agreed to do so as soon as possible. I had not been a member for a year yet, so we contemplated having a civil wedding to let our families be a part of it and then go to the temple, when I would be eligible for a temple recommend. No one else was a member of the church in our families except for Joey's brother.

After meeting with our bishop, we decided to set the marriage to be a civil wedding. Although this is not what the church would usually recommend, we followed the wisdom and inspiration of our bishop. One can never predict what the future may hold. I did not realize what was in store for me in the coming months.

We invited people we did not know but who were my father's friends from many years before. My mother did not invite anyone and no one from her side of the family came. I felt lonely preparing for my wedding. My mother wouldn't help with anything and my sister told me her life could not be put on hold for my wedding. It was such a different picture in my home than the one I had experienced in Utah. No one was beaming with excitement and I had no help. My father paid for it, but besides that I was on my own. Even the morning of my wedding I was lonely. Nobody helped me except my hairdresser.

Unfortunately, the night before our wedding, Joey and I got into a huge argument. He saw a side of me he had never seen before. I raged on him. I did have such a temper, like my father, but I would internalize it in my home and express it to people outside of my home. Joey had seen the total cost of the wedding and was overwhelmed with how much my father had spent. He wanted to change our plans the night before and have it at the church. I explained I could not return the cake, flowers, reception reservations or food.

I was also overwhelmed from having no experience in hosting anything. I did not know how to help all the guests coming from out of town. My mother sure did not know either. The guests were mostly Joey's friends and family. I had hardly any friends coming. I was just overwhelmed. We had not yelled at each other before. We went back to the condo where we would live after we were married and talked till the early morning hours. We agreed to walk down the aisle the next morning and work through these issues later.

The next morning I awoke in a hotel room, where my sister and I had stayed together. We both got ready for the big day. As I look back, everyone seemed to be fending for him or herself. There was no real order to that morning. However, my hairdresser did a good job and, as I was about to pay her, she told me this was her gift to me. There were no strings attached. She came early in the morning to help this day be special for me. I will always remember that. That was a good part of the morning for me. Amidst all the chaos, I still recognized her generosity of time and sweetness.

Just before the wedding, as everyone lined up, I was so nervous! Our argument the night before was still with me. But, as I turned the corner to walk down the aisle, I could only see Joey. There were two sides of guests but I could only see Joey and all my fears went away. I knew without a doubt that I was doing the right thing. All I could think about was how blessed I was to be able to marry him. I felt at peace. I knew the Lord had put us together. Our wedding day truly was the happiest day of my life.

There were only two times in my life when I could say I felt beautiful. The first was when Joey told me I was beautiful and the second was the day of my wedding. All my fears and doubts were gone. For so many years, I had been plagued with thoughts of being ugly on the outside. I was not taught how to groom myself or take care of my appearance. I had to learn that on my own. I had tried so hard to look pretty on the outside, hoping that would somehow make me feel pretty on the inside. But it never worked. However, at least for one day-my wedding day-I felt beautiful.

The next day we left on our honeymoon. As we boarded the plane, I felt so happy inside. For the first time in my life, I felt safe. As we arrived on the east coast, I felt like a weight had been lifted from me. I never knew just how heavy I had felt emotionally. Joey and I had all kinds of sightseeing plans, but we detoured and went to church history sights instead. We learned a lot of history and solidified our new marriage in the gospel.

CHAPTER SEVEN

By the Power of the Holy Ghost

"And by the power of the Holy Ghost ye may know the truth of all things." (Moroni 10:5)

When it was time to return home from our honeymoon, I felt a sick feeling in my stomach. I did not want to go back. I was not sure why, I just knew I did not want to go home. For the first time in my life, I was sleeping the whole night not worrying that anyone was going to attack me. I felt safe being far away. I felt safe with Joey. I did not know what the root of my feelings were. I shared with Joey that I was sad to leave and go back to everyday life. Joey and I had our own condo and it was to be the beginning of our new life together.

Shortly after we returned, I started having chest pains, again. The chest pains came at night when I was in a deep sleep. I would abruptly wake up gasping for air. I felt a weight on my chest. I feared I was going to have a heart attack. I did not know what was wrong with me.

By this time, I had started working for my father. Working at the attorney's office after my baptism was too hard. It was the longest I had ever held a job, but I felt the treatment from my co-workers was cruel. Their disappointment of my baptism was evident with every conversation. I felt judged and did not understand their Christian perspectives. As I shared this with my father, he kept asking me to work with him. I was not living at home anymore and this would give us time to be together.

My father had offered to have me work for him as his accountant. I told him what I was making and that he would need to at least match what I was being paid. He agreed. But, after working for two weeks, he told me he had changed his mind. He did not think I should be paid so much. After I quit my other job and started working with him, he just changed his mind as he had always done. As a little girl I had no choice and could only put up with his moods. But, as an adult independent of him, I was outraged. He talked "big," only to fill me with disappointment. I was getting disgusted with his dishonesty. I was starting to see things as they really were. Joey was starting to see just how irregular and drastic my father's moods could be. He agreed with me that it was not right. Nevertheless, I continued to work for my father until new arrangements could be made.

My first year in the church was a hard one. I had changed my life dramatically and had started to see just how many insecurities I had. I felt I was watching my life from the side lines. I had changed externally and internally, but my family and former friends had not. Every once in a while I would run into one of my old friends. Life seemed the same for them, including their addictions. I felt I was observing life that first year. Taking in the good and trying to understand the bad. I felt like a sponge with the gospel, and after moving out of my parents' home, I felt safe. Safe to see things how they really were.

Being sober for over a year and having the gift of the Holy Ghost made it easy to see what was really going on with my father. His inappropriate discussions with me about my mother and their intimate life were getting uncomfortable to listen to. Although I had grown up with this kind of conversation about my mother, it was now harder to listen to him because I did not think they were appropriate topics for a father to discuss with his daughter. My father had a way of making me feel sorry for him because my mother rejected him. Although I resented him, I also felt sorry for him. Now

I was disappointed with the man he was. Joey and I had been married less than one month. Although I only had my parents' example of how to act in a marriage, I certainly was not going to discuss with my children our intimate details. I felt, if a married couple saw weaknesses in each other, they should discuss them in a private conversation and not involve the whole family–especially, intimate details. My father, on the other hand, talked badly about my sister and my mother. He saw them both as weak and he abused his power over them. He talked poorly about me to them. It is just what he did. He had no loyalty to anyone.

My sister also worked for my father. He paid her so little she could not even pay her own bills. I could not stand the dynamics of our family anymore. I would hear the lies and see the blatant mistreatment. My father felt he could still rage at me after being married. I started to dread going to work and my chest pains kept getting worse. I did not know what was wrong with me.

I talked with my medical doctor about my chest pains. He said they were stress related. When I was told I was experiencing stress and having anxiety attacks, I dismissed it. Growing up in constant chaos, I had become numb. After leaving my parents' home, the anxiety attacks were seeping through and I could not control them.

I was getting to a point where I could actually think about my family life without fear that I would get into trouble for my thoughts. After being sober for over a year, I was feeling and questioning the realities I was starting to see on a daily basis. What I saw was making me feel awful inside. I could not have stress. I did not understand it. I was so out of touch with my feelings. Although deep inside I did question the treatment I had received from my parents. I also pretended to have the perfect life. Pretending kept me away from seeing reality. When I joined the church and saw families eating together on Sundays and observed other family interactions, I knew my so called "perfect life" was a lie. I just was not ready to deal with it. I did not know how to deal with it.

Joey and I were getting ready to go to the temple two months after our civil marriage. We were attending temple classes and I was reading whatever I could to prepare for the temple. But I was breaking down. I felt safe with Joey in our new home, but when I went to work, I would feel sick to my stomach all day. I did not know what was wrong with me. My anxiety attacks were waking me up almost every night now.

As Joey and I were preparing for our temple marriage, our bishop was teaching classes on family dynamics. He was preparing several young adults for married life. Joey wanted us to attend the classes to strengthen our new marriage. He had attended the classes before I had met him and thought we would benefit from the bishop's teachings.

At our first meeting, I learned about communication. I was not very good at it. I wanted to learn how to communicate better with my husband. I learned about yelling and rage. Although I had never heard it put that way, I realized my father was out of control. He did not ask, he took-violently, if necessary. He had no boundaries and did not care about other peoples' boundaries. He could not have a nice conversation with me. He seemed to end up yelling or belittling or screaming at the top of his lungs. This is called verbal abuse.

I did not realize yelling to this degree was abusive. I just thought it was a way of life. I did not like it, but I did not know it had a name. I was not allowed to be around other families, so I did not know it was not right. The bishop was talking about the effects of verbal abuse and how name calling can stick with a person forever. He said that belittling can mold a person to have low self-esteem. I was amazed by this meeting. It was unlocking some pain I had buried. I knew my father's behavior was wrong, but I did not know what to call it. My father was the only one allowed to get mad in the house. When I did, I was out of control just like him. I would hold it in until I exploded. The only thing I understood about anger was that it hurt every time it was expressed, whether verbally, physically or emotionally.

When Joey and I attended the bishop's next class he talked about pushing, shoving, slapping or kicking to get someone to do something, or scaring them to motivate or punish them. This I learned, was called physical abuse. Again, I sat in my chair mesmerized. I was stunned. I did not know what to do with this information. My father hit me for as long as I could remember. He would whip me with a belt. He would make me pull my pants down and whip me. If I refused to pull my pants down, he would scream and yell and push and shove until I obeyed. It was as if he enjoyed doing this to me. He would do it even when I was in my late teens. It was so inappropriate, yet my mother would just watch. She actually let him do this. I did not just feel the pain of being whipped by my father, I felt violated as well. This violated feeling was common, but I did not know how to verbalize it until this meeting. During the class, anger towards my father came out. I did not live with him anymore and I was mad. It was now safe to be mad.

Just before hearing about the church, my father had thrown me to the floor and kicked me in the stomach three times. Then he told me to get up and he smacked me. Again, my mother just watched. After he hit me in the face, she told him to stop. This was probably one of the only times I remember her telling him to stop. I was overwhelmed with many memories like this during that class. I remembered when he was hitting me, I would go numb. It was like pulling out a home video and watching it with no emotions. I had become so numb that, although I did not like being hit, I had no emotion linked to it anymore. It had happened so often that every time I was hit I would immediately change my thoughts to other things. I disassociated myself from what had just happened.

I remember leaving the meeting and talking to Joey about my feelings. I was afraid to verbalize all my memories to him. I thought he would leave me if he knew from what type of home I came. He set such a good example for me. He was so gentle, even during our arguments. He never hit or screamed at the top of his lungs. He just wanted to work things out.

Before our third class, I went to work again. My father was talking to me. He had that look on his face. It was a familiar look. I had not really addressed it or given it a name. He was not looking at my eyes as he spoke, he was looking at my chest area. I felt violated. I felt sick inside. I was so disappointed with my father. I remember this feeling at Christmas time after my baptism. There were many times when I would tell my mother to make my father stop looking at me like that. She would not respond. It was as if she just let him do whatever he wanted, no matter how wrong or inappropriate it was.

Standing in my father's office that day, our eyes met and, for a split second, it was a moment of truth. Pure truth. It seemed he always looked at me this way. He was trying to look into my very soul to see if I remembered anything– anything he had done to me. I had been "out of it" for so many years, it was as if he were just checking to make sure I was still "out of it." I could not remember details right then, but I knew. I knew something was wrong with our relationship. I did not know exactly what it was right then, but something inside of me opened up that very moment and caught my father lusting after me. I could feel it in the air. The weight of that realization was heavy. I felt sick to my stomach. I was scared. I thought my own father was going to attack me right then. I thought he was going to rape me. Why was I thinking these thoughts? Fearing what would happen to me, I felt prompted to leave immediately. I went home. I did not know how to deal with it. Just why was my father looking at me like that? What did I really unlock at that moment?

As I shared this experience with Joey, he shared with me that many people have been sexually abused and do not remember it. The betrayal and acts are so horrible the mind literally shuts them out. I remember him saying that I could have been abused and did not even know about it consciously. I remember crying. This experience unlocked something within me. It unlocked a feeling that something had been taken from me. It unlocked a feeling that something was just not right with me. I was tapping into a part of me that had been lost.

I was concerned about what Joey and I had talked about. I had no memory of someone sexually abusing me. Sexual abuse to me meant full intercourse with a child. I was starting to realize, because of the classes I was attending, that there were some serious issues within my parents' home. But sexual abuse was different. That was against the law. Sexual abusers were only on the news, not in my home.

My mother invited Joey and me over for dinner. We had not been to my parents' house for some time and she thought it would be nice to get together. My sister would be there and having my mother cook a meal was a big deal. After we all visited for a while, we began to eat. The things I had been learning were weighing heavily on my mind. The thought of labeling my father a physical and verbal abuser was hard, even though he had done everything that defined one. I was not ready to deal with it.

During the meal with my family I started asking about our old home. I stated that I did not have many memories of it. I never thought about the fact that I did not have a lot of memories of my early childhood. My questions just sort of blurted out. I asked them if they thought that was odd. My mother's response was that life is so busy, how can you remember everything? I started sharing with them that I think I had blocked something out. Something horrible that had happened in my life. Everyone seemed to be trying to find an answer to my question. Then, without even thinking about it, I asked my family if I had ever been sexually abused by someone. Silence came over the room. Everyone stopped chewing their food. My mother quickly remarked that the neighborhood boys could have done something to me. I asked her, "What neighborhood boys?" She quickly responded, "Wendy, you were so little, you probably wouldn't remember." I remember feeling like she knew something but was not telling me. I told her, "Look, if you know something, tell me. I have a right to know. Besides, when was I ever allowed to play with other children?"

I hardly remembered the old house and my babysitter. It was a lady who took care of many children. I did remember not being allowed to go over to anyone's house. I remembered one occasion when I was allowed to have a friend over. But, that was it. I told them I was not alone with anyone but Dad. He would often come home early and it would be just him and me in the house. Then I looked at my father. He was looking down and would not even look at me. He mumbled, "I don't know what you're talking about." He looked sheepish. He looked uncomfortable. I admit, it is not a question one asks at every dinner, but the responses were confusing. I felt as if my mother was lying and had been ready to respond to the question as if she knew it would come up someday. I felt my father was not ready for the question at all. He looked nervous. I did not know what to make of it. I remember Joey and me looking at each other and both feeling uncomfortable with their responses.

After Joey and I went home, we discussed it further. I thought that, if nothing really happened to me, they would have been adamant. My mother immediately blamed some neighborhood boys and my father looked like he was caught off guard. I felt my mother was keeping something from me. I believed she knew something that she was not telling me. I was confused by her response and did not know what to do.

The possibility that I may have been sexually abused seemed unthinkable. So, I decided not to think about it. When I was a little girl, I would get lost in make believe with my dolls and pretend I was in another place. As a teenager and early adult, I chose substances to help numb me. But now, with the Holy Spirit as my constant companion, it was hard to hide from the truth. However, I would try for a while. I would try very hard.

Joey and I continued our classes with the bishop. He defined two words that had me perplexed about my past–sexual abuse. As he explained what they meant, I had tears in my eyes. I guess I was ready to hear the truth. I had hot flashes and body memories. I felt disgusted with these overwhelming feelings. I could not explain them and they would not go away. I did not know what was going on with me. I was burning up in the room. The class seemed to end so quickly. I felt like an opened wound that had been scarred over for some time and was suddenly re-opened. As Joey and I were driving home, I started to cry. I could not stop. It was a heavy cry. It was as if every pain I had ever felt in my life were in that cry. Joey had to pull the car over to console me.

I could not even talk. I could not verbalize what I was thinking or feeling. My mind was racing and overwhelmed with so many thoughts. I remember fighting internally that I could not have been sexually abused. I remember trying to convince myself that it just was not true.

I remember entering our home and running to the bed and kneeling in prayer and crying to the Lord. I was begging Him to please not let this be my trial. I had no memories at that moment. But, I knew it was true–I knew my father had molested me as a little girl. I begged the Lord to not let this be my trial. I would take anything but this. I would take the verbal and physical abuse. I would admit those. I would admit anything but this. I felt so much shame. All my past truths were in this cry. They seemed too much to bear. At that moment, it seemed like my numbness melted into bitter feelings, and they hurt so badly! Now I know why I had done everything possible to stop feeling!

I had just joined the church and invited Jesus Christ into my life. I had done what was right by getting baptized. I thought this was not fair. I even thought I would put up with my father's lustful looks at me. And yet, all I could do was cry because the truth would not go away. I felt ashamed.

Joey came into the room to console me. I had to officially admit it to him. I had to say it out loud. It was so hard to say those awful words! It seemed easier to push the truth aside. I wanted to, but could not. When I looked at him, his eyes had tears also. I said it out loud for the first time in my life. "I was abused as a child. I was sexually abused…" It seemed so hard to finish that sentence but I whispered "…by my father." I could barely get the words out, I was crying so hard. Saying the words out loud, I somehow felt afraid. My body was trembling. All I could think was, "What if Joey left me?" I remember thinking I was not good enough for him. I was somehow damaged. I felt there was something wrong with me.

As I was reflecting and sorting things out, being abused made sense to me. It explained why I felt so bad inside and so worthless. I felt so unworthy of Joey's love. I remember praying to the Lord and begging Him to not let Joey leave me. I could not bear it. It would be too much. I remember falling asleep in Joey's arms. He held me that whole night.

The morning after I awoke, I felt a deep pit in my stomach. My eyes were swollen. Depression had already set in. I felt heavy. This feeling would not leave me for years to come. My first thought was, "How am I going to tell my mother and sister?" They could not possibly know about this. I was worried about them. I did not want him to hurt them. I felt I needed to talk with them when he was not around.

As the day went on, I started thinking about things I had remembered but never verbalized. Things my own sister did to me when we were little. She would tell our parents that we were going to take a shower together. In the shower, she would have me play a game with her. She would act as the parent figure and make me do things to her or she would touch me all over. We were so young, just little girls. But, this went on for years. It started when I was about four years old and continued until I was eight. I always wanted to talk with her about this, but I was too afraid. I wondered why she did these things to me. Where did she learn them? I had to talk with her. I just did not know how or when. I was afraid to face this information. The anxiety attacks were easier to deal with than the truth of my past. The truth was that my father and sister had violated and sexually abused me.

That week I had a doctor's visit scheduled. I wanted to stop by the bookstore and find out more on sexual abuse. I picked up a book written by a psychologist on the subject. I was early for my doctor's visit, so I sat in the car reading pages at random. I stopped on a page that gave a physical description of someone who had been sexually abused. It described me. Anxiety attacks were one of the symptoms. I realized there was nothing wrong with me physically. There was nothing wrong with my heart. I was just afraid of dealing with reality.

After I married Joey and knew I did not have to go back home, I felt safe. That is why I was having the attacks. I was in a safe environment. The truth had been suppressed by the fear I constantly felt in my parents' house. My addictions added extra protection and were a back up just in case anything tried to seep out. Now, I was safe and sober and could not run from the truth. My attacks came at night. Perhaps that is when my father came into my childhood room.

I wanted to cancel my doctor's visit. But, I went anyway. During the visit they did all kinds of tests on my heart, but I knew what the problem was now. I knew I needed help, but it would not be anything a medical doctor could do for me. I needed to find a therapist. I was so overwhelmed. Joey and I had a temple marriage coming up in a less than two weeks. I was on overload.

It seems odd but I did not know what to do with this information. A part of me went into denial and a part of me was devastated. I knew my father was mean and a bully, but to have to admit that he was also a child molester was very hard. To have to admit that I was the victim was even harder. It was devastating. I was trying to fit the pieces together of a puzzle with no picture. I had no real memories of him actually doing anything to me. At least none I was ready to verbalize at the time. Although it was out in the open between Joey and me, I still had much to do before I could heal. I could not really deal with the weight of this trial. I had to look for another job to get away from my father. I had to tell my mother and sister, then find a therapist. The pain was so intense. The shock was unbearable.

I was remembering many things, but was too afraid to deal with them. Not new things, just memories I had never addressed. I was still afraid of my father. For some reason, I really thought he would kill me for talking about this. Fortunately, I felt the Holy Spirit draw closer to me at this time in my life. It gave me a glimpse of what I would deal with in the future, but I felt prompted to stay focused on my temple marriage. I could have easily found excuses not to go. My old fears of being with someone eternally seemed to be completely gone. I felt carried during this time. I needed to be. I was starting to get very depressed.

As I was preparing for the temple marriage, I was learning about eternal marriage and eternal families. Before the reality of my past hit, I had collected genealogies from both sides of my family. I had done this during my first year as a member. I also started observing other families in our ward. I needed to believe that family life could be better than the one from which I had come. I saw many examples of wonderful couples in our new family ward. Husbands and wives talking about their issues, making their family the first priority with family home evenings and keeping the Sabbath Day holy. I saw them praying together. I saw these couples really put in time and effort in their relationships. I saw healthy relationships between fathers and daughters. I saw healthy relationships between mothers and daughters, respecting each other. I even saw extended families in the same ward loving and accepting each other. I am sure there were tensions at times, but they always worked them out.

These examples made me want to be a good wife. I wanted to be sealed for time and all eternity to Joey. I could not imagine it with anyone else. I had never been in love before. Not like this. Our relationship's foundation was based on the gospel of Jesus Christ. We prayed together and blessed the food together. We read the scriptures together and talked of bettering our lives. Our civil marriage had been "until death do you part," as if there were not anything more out there. But there is! I was preparing for that and was ready to accept it.

Our sealing was not as big a production as our civil wedding. We invited our new friends from the ward. I had lost all my old friends when I joined the church, and had started to lose contact with new ones I had made when I joined. It seemed that change in my life was becoming constant.

So much had happened in the first two months of our marriage. I believe that, if our bishop had not encouraged us to get married civilly first, we would never have gotten sealed in the temple or married for that matter. Too much had gone on. Too much had happened. Joey and I had to be united at this time. The type of unity only a husband and wife can experience. I am certain that if we had only been dating, we would not have been sealed in the temple. We had to help each other through this time. It seemed the forces of darkness were trying desperately to break us apart. But, what Joey and I had, could not be broken so easily. With the foundation of our relationship based firmly in the gospel of Jesus Christ, we were firm in our conviction to each other. The fact was-I loved him. I would have done anything for him. I felt the reality of my abuse would weigh heavily on our marriage, but I wanted him to know I would grow and do everything I could to work through it. I would prove I was not damaged goods. I would pray that the Lord would protect what we had.

The day I received my endowment in the temple was one year exactly from the day I had been baptized in the church. We went with an older couple, the same couple who lived on my parents' street. I wanted to go through the temple more than anything. So much had happened. I was feeling confused about life. So confused about why, after all these years, I had just found out I had been sexually abused.

As we entered the temple I felt a peace I had never felt before. It was like coming home, to my *real* home. Something inside of me awoke that day. Something that had been dormant all those years. It was special to me because I was the only one going through for my own endowment. I remember sitting alone in a waiting room, not quite knowing what to expect. I prayed to Heavenly Father, thanking Him that, amidst all the adversity with which I would have to deal in the near future, I now had a place to come and find solace. I prayed that He would help me to remember everything I experienced in the temple that very special day. As the temple sisters entered the room, they greeted me with smiles and hugs. All the troubles I carried with me on the drive up to the temple were gone. I was surrounded by the love of these sisters who made me feel so special. I do not know who they were, but I was grateful for the unconditional love they shared with me.

The day of our temple sealing was a blessed day. I was worried that something bad would happen. I was eager to enter the temple with Joey. The temple was not a place for a big production wedding. It was a time to truly reflect on our purpose here in life. It was a time of reverence, beauty and awe of the creation of the world. True celestial feelings had come over me. True peace of mind and a new eternal perspective would make this experience one of the most beautiful days of my life. We were connected by God. We were sealed for time and all eternity, and all the children we would have would be born in the covenant. I had done something right. There was nothing greater than knowing that I was doing something right. Something pleasing to the Lord. My new perspective would help me understand that this life is a time of personal growth. It is a time to get closer to Heavenly Father. In the future, it would help me through my trial of dealing with the sexual abuse.

Upon leaving the temple, my parents and sister showed up. This would be one of our last meetings as a family. Joey was very patient with me. He was not in denial, but I was. He was so respectful to my family and never confronted them himself. Although he wanted to, he left that for me. Even though I knew I had been abused, I had still invited them. I was just going through the motions. Within a few weeks, I would start dealing with these issues again. I would find no escape from the truths in my life.

CHAPTER EIGHT

Blinded

"Otherwise Satan seeketh to turn their hearts away from the truth, that they become blinded and understand not the things which are prepared for them." (D&C 78:10)

It would be some time before I talked with my sister about my sexual abuse. I was having anxiety just thinking about talking with her. I had rarely discussed family issues before and on those occasions that I did, it was because I had to explain things. It could have been because my father made my girlfriends feel uncomfortable, or I would be crying and had to explain myself to other people. My sister and I rarely discussed the family dynamics, so part of me was glad to be able to finally do this. I naively thought she and I could heal together.

My sister was at work when I came to talk with her. After she got off the phone, I went into her office. An office she and my father shared. He was out of town. I told her I had something very important to talk about and that she may already know about it. By this time, I felt I had a little more inner strength than I did before. I still felt ashamed, but felt it was time to confront my family. I also suspected that what had happened to me may have happened to her.

Before I could begin, I started to cry. I cried before she even knew why I was crying. After a deep breath, I was finally able say, "Dad raped me as a child." This was so uncomfortable to verbalize! I had only verbalized it to Joey. She was speechless. I told her about my body memories. Maybe she had them too. I told her about the anxiety attacks in the middle of the night. I described my symptoms because maybe she experienced them also. She did not respond.

I asked her the questions I had always wanted to ask her. "Why did you touch me as you did when we were little girls? Where did you learn that game from?" She was silent with tears in her eyes, embarrassed and shocked at the same time. I had a very strong feeling the tears she had were not for me. I had a feeling she was not concerned about what she had done to me. I felt the tears were for her, perhaps for her own pain. She looked nervous like a little girl who had been caught doing something bad. It was as if she could not believe I was actually asking her to explain herself. She said that she did remember what she had done to me. She did not remember why she had made me do things to her or why she did things to me.

I repeated what our father had done to me. I was thinking that perhaps she felt just as scared as I did for finally verbalizing the family secret. I told her that, if this happened to me, perhaps it happened to her. Maybe she learned the "game" from our father. She was young and the things we were doing were so grown-up. I believed she was just repeating his actions. How could I have been the only one he violated? I wanted her to tell me from where she learned it. I wanted to hear it from her mouth. I guess I already had my suspicions, but I needed her to admit it to me. I did not want to be alone.

She said she could not remember where she learned to do those things. The look on her face was one I will never forget. She was lying. I always knew when she was lying because she would always scratch the side of her nose and rub it. She would not give eye contact. She had done this since she was a little girl. Perhaps in her heart she knew someday this would come out in the open. Her look told a story of its own. She was quiet and seemed unsure of how to handle the situation. She could not believe the things I was saying. Maybe not so much *what* I was saying, but perhaps just that I was saying them. No one in the family had ever verbalized it before. We were not allowed to. This was her moment of truth, but she did not have the Holy Spirit with her. She could deny it. She had denied it her whole life just as I had done.

I talked about all of the different types of abuse we went through and still she sat there quietly, saying nothing. She did not know what to say. Then she blurted out, "I work for him and still live at home, Wendy." I was shocked at this statement. Living at home did not change the fact of the abuse. She was not consoling me as I had imagined she would. She was worried about her finances and where she lived. She was not concerned that her father was a child molester and had abused me. She was concerned about herself.

Again, I repeated what abuse was and how we had been abused verbally, physically and sexually. Perhaps she did not realize just what abuse was or she just could not handle it. I had just learned about it myself. She would not say anything. She did not ask when it happened or for how long. She just sat there. She had a choice to make at that very moment and she chose to do what she had always done–nothing. She did not hug me or try to help my tears go away. She did not give me advice or anything.

I guess I was as stunned as she was. There was silence. Not an uncomfortable silence. We were both taking in what I had said. I was waiting for a response. A response I never got. I finally said, "I can not work here anymore. I will never come back to this office." She still did not say a word. I just looked at her, amazed. I asked her to please call me after she had time to think about all of this and to not share it with our mother or father. I would do that later. All she said was,

111

"Good-bye." No hug, no "I'm sorry to hear this." She just had tears in her eyes and did not get out of her seat.

I realize this was devastating information regarding our family. I could not have been the only one questioning my father's actions. But questioning something is different from confronting or dealing with it. Questioning is safer because no action is taken. By admitting and verbalizing the violence in our home and starting to take some sort of action I realized the whole family would be shaken up. I just did not expect my sister's reaction. I felt it was distant and cold. She was not outraged and did not seem to care that I was devastated by it.

Then again, shame was a personality trait in our family. It helped keep our "perfect family" facade alive and thriving. I was experiencing shame more intensely at this time, but it did not bind me like it had my whole life, previously. The lies had to stop. I know my sister must have been surprised and caught off guard, but her emotionally absent response seemed all too familiar. It is just the sort of thing my mother would have done.

I was embarrassed that I would now be labeled as someone who came from an abusive home. I was ashamed and confused as to why I had never told anyone and why no one did anything to help me. Abuse was everyday life for me. Did not my mother know what this was called? She was the adult. She saw it happen almost every day. She must have known what was going on. But my sister–maybe she was like me. Maybe she did not remember either.

I remembered what happened when we told my father he was crazy or out of control. We would get hurt. I knew what happened when we would stick up for ourselves or for each other. We would get hurt. Often I stuck up for my sister and my mother. My father could be so violent and crazy. He bullied who he wanted, when he wanted. He would do things to all of us in front of each other and no one would say anything to him except me. It was as if he wanted to show us all who was in control of the family. Maybe my sister could not admit it because she was afraid. But she was older than I. I guess I expected more from her. But my father could still hurt her. Maybe she feared for her life like I did. Maybe it occurred to her, like it did to me, that this man was capable of major harm. I still did not understand why she would not share those feelings with me.

Joey and I lived down the street from my parents, a full five minutes away. Although I still had a lot of fear, I was safer than my sister. My father would have to trespass into our gated community to get me, to hurt me. Still, she was an adult and could have gotten all of her belongings and left. He was out of town.

Our meeting hurt me. It actually crushed me. We were never really close, but I thought this was something we could work through together and use to build our relationship. I was sad that we did not have a relationship like the ones I had witnessed lately. Still, I did love her. She was my *sister* after all. We both experienced much of the same harshness and abuse. She was more sensitive than I. She could put up with more by not saying anything and holding it in. I would always say something. I probably got hit and yelled at more throughout the years because I had no respect for him and he knew it. He thought he could beat it into me, but with each smack, kick or spanking, I hated him more.
I could not just admit that I was abused and leave it at that. I needed help–professional help. My sister could not handle it. As I thought about our discussion, I realized it was not the actual abuse she could not handle. We had all handled it throughout our lives. What she could not handle was

113

admitting that we grew up in an abusive, neglectful home. She could not handle the fact that I was exposing the family secret. My father had groomed us to fear life. I now knew why I used drugs and alcohol. It was to escape from feeling the pain of being raised in an abusive home. As an adult no longer under his thumb, I realized the magnitude of what he did and I was outraged.

Unfortunately, my sister also abused alcohol. I could not cope that way anymore. I had made a covenant to not drink again. But she had not. Drinking worked for her as it had for me not too long ago. She had no other outlet. But still, as a younger sister, I was disappointed. I was disappointed with her weakness–I always had been. She was the older sister and never defended me. She was always off in another world. I guess we all were. She would have to go through what I did to quit substance abuse, and that was not easy. Alcohol not only loosened me up to feel more comfortable socially, it kept me from dealing with my past's reality. It was a fog, a mist to keep me from knowing who I really was and seeing the reality of my life.

It had been over a year since I had alcohol. I was stronger and better able to handle the truth, but I did not like it. I did not want it, but with the Holy Spirit around, there was no other way. I could not lie to myself or anyone anymore. I could not get on my knees and tell the Lord it was not true, that there must have been a mistake. I prayed morning and night to the Lord. I believed He was real and could not lie to Him. I had to deal with the truth.
My sister had to tell my father that I quit working for him. He called me, raging on the phone. He could not believe it. I could not tell him why. I just said I needed to make more money. He was screaming so loudly that Joey could hear him from the other room. I had to hang up on him several times. Joey could not believe how crazy he was acting. I told him

that if he did not stop calling I would call the police. That ended the conversation. He did not call back.

The next person I needed to talk to was my mother. I thought it would go much better. I actually had the thought that maybe she knew, but did not know how to protect us. I would accept any explanation. But then, she *could not* have known he was sexually abusing me or she would have protected me. She would have left him. What mother would not have?

Many months passed before my confrontation with my mother. I had been to therapy. At this point, many memories were coming back to me. I could remember things right up to the point of being raped by my father. I remembered him coming into my room and yelling at him to leave. I remember being so afraid to take a shower. I felt someone was going to attack me every time I took one. I would constantly look past the shower curtain to make sure no one was in the bathroom. I had many memories like these, but had never verbalized them before. I was so young. I was too young to be afraid of being attacked. It was not until I started dealing with these issues that I realized it was not normal for a young girl to feel these feelings or think these thoughts unless something was going on. My memories were still a little foggy, but as I verbalized all the things I did remember, I was starting to get a timeline. I was starting to see my father's inappropriate behavior when I was very young.

At this time, I had just undergone foot surgery and could not walk, but I could not wait to talk to my mother any longer. Being true to her character, she wouldn't even help me recover from surgery by helping me with dinner or going to the store for me. Being unable to walk, I felt vulnerable. Nevertheless, I could not wait any longer to talk to her about the family. I invited her over.

Up to this point my mother had a strange hold on me. I had never really stuck up for myself with her. Although we had our share of disagreements, arguing with her meant having to deal with my father. She knew he would always defend her even if she were wrong. He would rage at me if I disagreed with her. The problem was that she would let him. I was starting to see that she did have a role in the abuse but I could not put all the pieces together.

The night she came over Joey was home, but had to leave soon thereafter. I was nervous. My sister's response had been disappointing and a surprise. I was hoping and longing for a response of comfort. Perhaps my mother would hold me and console me and handle what I said like I imagined a mother should.

As the conversation went on I told her I called her for a specific reason. I was so nervous but finally said, "Dad, sexually abused me when I was a child. I knew it had gone on for many, many years." I expected her to embrace me and say how sorry she was. How I needed her to love me and support me at that moment. But she remained in her seat. The first thing she said to me was that she did not know and that she must have married a "monster." Her response was emotionless. I was confused. It was almost as if she had practiced her response. I agreed that she did marry a monster.

I shared with my mother how he would pretend to leave for work, then come back to drive me to school. He would come back just before I was leaving and do things to me in the car. I remember crying and being upset and running to class because he made me late. He would not even write a letter to the teacher, he would just kick me out of the car. After he made me do things to him, if I did not stop crying he would smack me. I would always be so embarrassed going to school on these days. I would be embarrassed thinking that

116

the other kids could see a red smack mark on my face. But once I got to class, I would quickly forget.

I explained that not too long ago, even I did not understand why I could not remember for so long. I continued that trauma can make us forget or we could go into denial. I explained that I thought I did both. I always hid behind playing with dolls, or drugs and alcohol. I could not technically explain why I did not remember all this time. But I knew now, and that is all that mattered. I told her the whole family had been living a lie. For a moment she acted like she understood, but for only a moment. Then she started to defend him. She started to defend the man she had not loved for so long, if ever. She treated him horribly and yet she was defending him. I was angered by her response.

I had been raped as a child and young adult and my mother's response was pathetic. What kind of mother does not defend her children? I told her this is not about whether it is true or not. *It is true*, and I had some questions for her. I grew so much from this confrontation. I was so tired of the lies. I wanted to know why, when my father was at his worst with his rages, she asked her place of employment if she could work the night shift. It was her request. We all had to fend for ourselves for dinner and had to defend ourselves from my father. Her face got gloomy and her whole demeanor changed. I had put her on the spot. I was questioning her role in all of this. It was as if a part of me knew she had known all a long, I just could not believe it. I could not admit it. Not yet. She *could not* have known. She made light of her choice as if she had to do what she had to do for her.

I asked her why she slept on the couch for most of their marriage. She told me that was none of my business. I continued, "Why did you not make him leave those Saturdays when I was lying out in the sun in the backyard?"

He would come into the backyard and water the yard while I was lying out. Sometimes, when he felt mean, he would squirt me and make me run into the house in my bikini. He always had a satisfied look on his face. As if he had done his mean action for part of the day. When I was lying out, he would just stare at me. I would beg my mother to take him shopping but she would not. He would be right next to me and I would be yelling at my mother to get him away from me, but she would not. It was as if she wanted to give him something she herself could not or would not. She would say, "In a little bit." He would not budge. He would not go in that house until he felt he was finished staring at my body.

He would comment on my bikini, but my mother would not do anything. After I finished lying out, which I would cut short because of his stares, they would leave together. Remembering this now is so uncomfortable. It would be just him and me in the backyard. I would be screaming at my mom to leave, and for him to stop staring at me. The reality that I had to ask my mother year after year to have him stop staring at my body hit hard. Why should a daughter have to ask her mother this, and why would a father do this? It was as if she let him leer at me blatantly because she did not want anything to do with him. Why did it not occur to my mother as odd and inappropriate for me to tell my father, her husband, to stop staring at me as if he were lusting after me?

I reminded her of all the times I would have to tell him to stop staring at my chest area. I confronted him by saying, "Stop staring at my chest!" I wanted to know why she let this behavior occur. She had no response. What kind of mother does not question this behavior? I told her I had lived with this horrible behavior, not understanding what it was. The next thing I knew, I yelled, "He was blatantly violating me and you let him!" The words just blurted out. She was stunned. I was stunned. I was blaming her for not protecting me. I had been a young girl pleading with my mother to make her husband stop doing inappropriate things to me and she never protected me from him. I would tell her what he was doing and she would not stop it. What was the matter with her? She would not act upon my pleadings. She was stunned and trying to regroup to come up with more excuses.

During the pause, I reminded her of a memory I had shared with her before I joined The Church of Jesus Christ of Latter-day Saints. I had a memory of my father coming into my room in only his underwear. My mother was in the corner watching as he approached my bed. He was going to rape me. She was going to watch. When I awoke in the morning I went downstairs and told my mother about this experience. I said, "I think Dad's been doing something to me at night. I often have to yell at him to get out of my room in the middle of the night." This memory seeped out. I was literally crying and she just stood there not looking up. Her only response was, "Wendy, don't talk about it." I sat on the kitchen counter crying. Within seconds my father walked around the corner in his underwear. He was a short, very overweight man. When he walked into the room in his underwear, I got the chills. I felt violated and wondered if something had really happened. I then yelled at him to get some clothes on. It was disgusting to see him walking around like that. I wanted to know why she did not want me to talk about it at that time. That was years ago.

I had forgotten about that talk until this confrontation. I did not realize it would be a confrontation, but that is what it ended up being. I knew the answers to all these questions. She just stared at me with her cold, dark brown eyes and said she did not know a thing had happened and that it had never happened to her. She had said that twice by now. I asked her, "Why do you keep saying it did not happen to you? We're not talking about your childhood." At that moment I questioned in my heart what *had* happened to her. She was so cold. She had no friends. No one was allowed to come over. She did not trust anyone.

I was flooded with tears and disgusted with my mother. Then I started to ask her about the other abuse. Why did she let him hit us and bully us almost every day of our lives? Why was this okay with her? She agreed he was so cruel but had no answers as to why she would let this happen. I asked if she was used to this type of behavior and did not think twice about it. She said she could not stop him. I asked her why she told me she was going to leave him time and time again, only to give me false hope. She had promised, year after year, that she was going to leave him because she did not love him. She told me a part of her hated him. Living with him was like walking on "egg shells." She would tell me that if they ever had a boy, my father would have "killed him or he would have killed my father." These were strong words. She apparently, however, thought this atmosphere was okay for girls to live in. I did not understand.

How can one really explain why she let abuse go on in her home? Perhaps it is all she knew. She did not discuss her childhood, just a few things. I told her, "The abuse stops here with Joey and me and there will be no more! Not in my family line." She got defensive and told me that my new life had changed me. She said I was putting down the life she had given me. But there was nothing she could deny. All the things I was confronting had actually happened before my life changed. There was no dispute over that. I was not confronting her way of life now, but then, when she was my mother in that home.

I saw things as they really were once again. This was her moment of truth. This was her opportunity to embrace it. She knew this had all happened, but to admit that he had sexually

120

abused me would mean she would have to admit that she did not stop it. She knew she turned the other way, with my drugs and with my father's abuse. There were too many covert, inappropriate actions from him. I felt that, if she really did not know, she would have defended me like any normal mother would. But she obviously felt guilty and that she needed to hide something. She was obviously a part of the family dynamics. A big part.

I finally said, "Mom, you did not love him, you hated him, just like all of us. Even up to this very moment, you hated him. Why are you defending him so strongly? What are you afraid of? You cannot deny all this covert sexual abuse. You know this is true!" She seemed to lighten up a bit. She shook her head, looked down and said, "Wendy, I don't know what to do!" We immediately got off my tragedy and became concerned with where she would live if she left him. I told her she could pack her bags and live with us until she found an apartment. I told her I would help her with everything. I told her she had never defended her daughters and had an opportunity to take a stand and defend us now. She just looked at me and said, "Are you sure?" I nodded my head firmly. For a short moment, I felt I had tapped into a part of my mother that wanted to defend me. A part that wanted to be what she never was. It seemed that a door was opening to her heart and that for a slight moment, truth and reality had hit her.

I remember how traumatic this was to me at first. For a short moment I believed she was going to be there for me. I reminded her how he would come up to our rooms and take our magazines and put them down into his bathroom. He would actually come into our rooms and raid our magazines and add them to his collection of pornography, which she allowed. Even though our magazines were fashion magazines.

121

Then another memory hit me. All of a sudden it occurred to me that he had a box of protection in his drawer. I just remembered it at that very moment. Sometimes the box was full, sometimes it was half full, other times it was empty. I knew about it because, when I put his laundry away, I saw it in his drawer just sitting there out in the open. I then blurted out "Mom, who was Dad using the boxes of protection on?" It was not her–we all knew that. But when I asked this question, her whole demeanor changed again. I questioned, "He was not having an affair, was he?" Her lips tightened with anger. I asked, "Mom, who do you think he was using them on?" I was sickened with the thought that he had used them on me. She got angry. I was insistent that she explain this one. She could not. She just looked at me with hatred in her eyes. What did I do? I was the one abused! It was an intimate question to ask, but we were talking about my father's sexual problem. A problem he took out on me.

Then I remembered that he knew all the spots around town where the "ladies" would be after hours on the street. If we were driving by as a family at night, he would tell the whole family where the "ladies" were at night. He would remind us that you had to pay for their services. This was always uncomfortable and an odd thing for a father to point out to his family. But he would leave at nights, at least three to four times a week, and go "driving" until two or three o'clock in the morning. Then he would come and visit my room. It all hit me.

My mother felt she could dismiss his inappropriate comments and looks, but she could not deny the reality of the box of protection he had in his drawer. I knew she knew. She knew I did also, and she hated me for it. She tried to cover up her actions. She looked cold and mean. As if she hated me for finally confronting this horrible issue. An issue to which I was new, but one she had worked so hard to hide. It was her moment of truth and mine as well. I had thought mine was just admitting what my father had done to me, but instead I had to admit that my very own mother knew about the sexual abuse. She looked at me and repeated that she could not believe she could have picked such a monster to marry. She was not consumed with my pain, she was just figuring out a way to hide the truth again and make it go away. I was disgusted with her and remember crying, "How could you? How could you not protect me?" She just sat there with no expression.

Then, with a smirk on her face, she shared that my sister had already told her about my conversation with her. I felt betrayed. She continued, "And, I already told your father." Serious fear set in. I'm sure that was her plan. My mother knew why I had invited her to come over. She already knew. I saw her as such a sly and devious person. Her smirk was cruel, as if she had one up on me. She abruptly got up and said she would call me soon to talk about this. She left as I sat there alone and cried.

Having to bear this trial was overwhelming. Admitting what my father had done was enough. But having to admit my mother knew was too much. She got mad at me for questioning her actions. I was questioning things she could not deny. I was afraid of what my father was going to do. He might have been short and overweight, but he was mean. At that point, I felt vulnerable. I did not know what the future had in store.

My father and I did not discuss the abuse. I was too afraid he would try to attack me. He did not just do these things to me while I was a little child. He was strong and would force himself on me. I was not about to be in the same room with him. He was so violent. I did not need him to admit it to everyone. I did not need him to apologize for a life of abuse and rape. No apology could be given for something that was done repeatedly, night after night, year after year. He consciously chose to abuse me. I knew, he knew and my mother knew. My whole family knew. I did not need him to admit he was a horrible father and a child molester. We all knew. I just happened to be dealing with it. What was a shock for me was something my parents knew all along. They hoped that none of their children would ever address it. I find this so confusing. My parents took no thought that, as an adult, I would find their actions inappropriate. My father felt he had no control over his impulsive behavior. He did not think about the consequences of his actions.

After the day I confronted my mother, we hardly spoke. Our relationship became strained and seemed to end in an argument. She had decided to defend a man she hated and did not love with little thought of how much that would hurt or destroy me.

During this hard time, I wanted to start an adult relationship with my grandmother, a woman I had only met a few times in my life. My mother was now concerned that I would tell her mother everything. She had to continue to cover up and that is exactly what she would do from then on. She would lie about me. She betrayed me as a mother and would tell my extended family members I was lying. She could not deny the physical abuse, mental abuse and verbal abuse, or even the covert sexual abuse. She knew he was perverted. She knew about all the nights out and all of her friends with whom he had cheated. She even knew he had me sleep with him in their bed at night! She was in the same bed. I was a teenager. He would wrap his body around me as if I were his wife and she would let him! She was two inches away, but she would not mention it to our relatives. She would say he loved his children.

124

What she would not tell my extended family, and what they did not know and could not know, was that, for the next eight years, I would spend my life trying to turn things around. I was left alone to deal with the family's truths. I was betrayed as a daughter by both of my parents. I was left alone to search for answers and an understanding as to why a mother who knows that her husband is molesting her children, would defend his actions.

What kind of a person can justify sexual abuse and stay with a man who does it to her children? If someone outside of the family had raped me, would not my parents have put him in jail? If so, why would my mother not want to put my father in jail? What was the difference? A crime is a crime, regardless of who commits it. I felt it was *worse* that a father did this because he did not do it just once. He did it night after night, year after year.

I do not think people understand when a father molests his own children, he is not "making love" to them. He is not doing the same things he does to his own wife. Rather, he is performing and acting out his most perverse acts and fantasies on his own children. These times are not loving, but usually violent. He is coercing, manipulating and physically abusing his own children–forcing them to perform acts that a child so young could not even imagine or understand. As a victim of abuse, I saw how I was exposed to such heinous acts at such a young age. I was exposed to sexual relations so young. I was a victim to my own father. I had so many questions that needed answers. But before I could go forward, I had to go back to my childhood and deal with those issues first. I had to get serious about therapy.

CHAPTER NINE

God Hath Not Given Us the Sr

"For God hath not given us the spiri
and of love, and of a sound m

I learned quickly that the Lord had placed Joey
help me heal. He had qualities that made me feel sa.
believed that each of us has to pave a new path in ou.
lineage, whether we come from a healthy family or not. At
this time, I felt the Lord was teaching me that my real family
was with Him and Joey. I would find solace in having a
relationship with the Lord. This next year would be a hard
year in regards to my family. I would come to understand the
pain of betrayal and loneliness. At the same time I would
find refuge in having a prayerful relationship with Heavenly
Father who would bring me peace where there was none.
Although my earthly father wanted me to keep quiet and
keep these things hidden inside, my Father in Heaven wanted
to help me. I believed the traditions of my father needed to
be changed. I just did not know how hard it would be.

When I started therapy, I went to a therapist of my same
faith. I was not comfortable with him. Not because of who he
was, but because he was a man. I had been terrorized by a
man my whole life. I trusted Joey, but no one else. As I
explained my memories and how I felt, I just did not feel
comfortable with him. I felt uncomfortable being alone in a
room with another man behind closed doors. When I told
him I had to see a woman, he understood. He encouraged me
to see someone with whom I was comfortable and who could
help me get through this ordeal. He did warn me, though,
that it would take a long time. He told me my journey had
only begun. He also explained that many women who were
victims of rape by incest or even a stranger often felt

rtable talking through their problems with a
ist of the same gender as their perpetrator. He
rstood that I felt uncomfortable verbalizing such
imate details with another man, even if he were a
professional. I felt like an open wound. Sharing my past out
loud was hard. I felt unclean and damaged, and sharing this
with another man did not make the situation any better.

I searched and found a therapist who was a woman. I started
from the beginning. I had just started working at a new law
office after I had quit working at my father's business. It was
very demanding of my time. I was a newlywed and
overwhelmed with the trial in my life. My new therapist did
not specialize in sexual abuse, nor did she share my same
beliefs and standards. I did not agree with all the things she
told me but I did have the Holy Spirit to guide me. I felt the
Holy Spirit helped me filter out what was correct from that
which was not. She was a strong woman and I felt I needed
her at the time. I had a dominating and controlling
personality and she knew how to get through to me. I wanted
to work very hard and she kept up with my pace. I remember
feeling overwhelmed with so many feelings, thoughts and
memories. Memories I only recently knew existed or
verbalized.

I did not quite understand why I could not remember all of
my memories. Not just of abuse but of holidays and certain
events. I took this time to get educated on trauma and how
the mind reacts to it. I shared with my therapist I had a
memory of me looking down from the ceiling of my
bedroom while someone was attacking me. There was a
sheet pulled over us. I knew deep down inside it was my
father. But I denied it over and over. Although this was my
only memory and experience like this that I could remember,
I did not understand why this memory would seep out every
once in a while. I just knew I would quickly tuck it back far

away, deep inside of me. I was just a little girl and it was at our old house in my old bedroom. I had not verbalized it. I did not understand it. It had always been with me in the back of my mind. My therapist informed me that as I experienced the trauma of sexual abuse I must have disassociated. Meaning the trauma was so great for me that it was the only way I could cope with the sexual abuse from my father. It was as if my mind would protect me against the pain I felt inside because as a little girl I did not know how to deal with so much trauma.

I remember fearing my father so much that once he was done raging, hitting or sexually abusing me I would quickly find something else to think about. I would count over and over in my mind to block out what had occurred. I did not dare ponder too much what he had done for fear of what even the mere thought would do. It is not that I was told what my father was doing was wrong when I was a child, but rather, as a child I just knew it was wrong. I was not supposed to share it with anyone. It is as if I knew this was wrong not by experience, but because of a higher power. My pure and sacred spirit! Because of his heinous acts against me, I felt damaged to the core.

I informed my therapist of my father's sexual comments to me. He would call me "sexy," even as a teenager. He would comment on my clothing and how my body had grown up. She confirmed that this is called covert sexual abuse. "Covert" meaning that a person was never touched, but the innuendos were there. A person whose father never physically molested her could have the same symptoms as one who was physically molested because the father is lusting after his child in either case. This was definitely going on in my home.

129

She explained that sexual abuse is not just having full intercourse with the child. If the perpetrator made the child touch him or do things to him, or he did things to the child, this also constituted sexual abuse. Anything that made the perpetrator sexually aroused by a child constituted sexual abuse. The child is too young to understand or consent to this type of behavior. Besides, the adult doing this knows he is violating the *sacred innocence* of a child. It is a conscious choice made by the perpetrator.

At that time, society did not seem ready to hear from all of us who had been sexually abused. So the "false memory syndrome" was developed. Followers of this syndrome believe that memories can be planted in people's heads. I was an adult now, not an impressionable child. I was disgusted by this mentality and the whole movement. I understand denial. I understand not wanting to deal with the abuse because I did not want to as a child or youth, but to say it never happened would be to lie.

I told my therapist I wanted to file criminal charges against my father. At that time, the laws were very much against the victim and more favorable towards the perpetrator. I also wanted to bring criminal charges against my mother, but that would never make it into the courts back then.

I had many questions but was consumed with the betrayal aspect of it all. I could not get over my family's actions. The longer I was away from them, the more blatant the sexual abuse seemed. The more violent everyday life was in that home. I could not believe I had lived through it all.

I wanted to confront my whole family and ask why they were defending my father's behavior. My sister and mother knew he abused me and all of us, yet they were defending his actions. I had not confronted my father as of yet. I just stopped talking to him. My mother told him why I stopped talking to him and, of course, he denied it.

I found out that many survivors of abuse felt they needed to know why the abuser repeatedly raped them. They questioned why the abuser hated them so much and why they were singled out. As if any answer might somehow make the problem go away. Perhaps they were hoping there really could be a legitimate excuse that would make the whole ordeal "go away." The only answer to this question is that a man or woman who sexually violates children does so secretly. They are consciously aware that what they are doing is not socially acceptable and is against the law. A parent who violates their own children is relentless in giving in to their secret passions. They have to take time to plot out when a good time to make their "visits" will be. They have to make sure they will not get caught.

Sexual abusers lead double lives. Many go to church each week. As a child it is hard to distinguish between the acts of parents to that of the truthfulness of the gospel.

Many who have been abused need an apology. Thinking like a small child, an apology usually makes the situation "all better and go away." But if you were to put the abuser right back in the same situation again, chances are he would do the same thing. I did not need an apology from my father and an apology would not keep my own children safe around him or any others for that matter. If he had verbally admitted it, my mother and sister would have had no choice but to deal with it. If I wanted him to verbally admit it that would be the only reason why. Nevertheless, I did not need to know why he did this to me. He did not care about anyone's feelings but his own.

His own sexual problems became my whole family's problems. He did not care about life. He only cared about what he could get out of it or get away with. He picked the perfect passive spouse to allow him to torment his own children. My mother was passive to him and emotionally absent to me.

I told my therapist I did not need to know why he did this. I knew. He was a man who had no self-control and no conscience. He preyed on his own children. He was a coward and a violent abuser. I knew he would say my mother denied him of the affection he needed. Although this was true, it did not make his actions right or excusable. It would not make my body memories or panic attacks go away. I believed the threats. And still, most importantly, I felt like a puzzle scattered all over and that the old pieces did not fit anymore. I did not know what to replace the old pieces with, and well, I just did not know where to start. I was betrayed by the only family I knew. What was I to do now? The pain was seeping from every part of my body. I did not know how to get past the initial shock.

I could not believe how many things I did remember. As I started verbalizing all that I could, more and more would come up. I did not care about explaining my father's actions and trying to figure him out. He wouldn't change because he did not want to, but my mother's story was different. She hated this man for as long as I could remember and yet she was ready to defend him. I wanted us to discuss as a family how all of this abuse happened under one roof. I wanted us all to discuss the family problems. How could it really have been that bad? But they would never come to a therapy session with me. Not one. What kind of family refuses to work on its issues once a serious issue of this nature surfaces? What kind of mother does not want to help her child or see what could have happened in a professional setting? My mother could see I was in so much pain and would not come to my aid. That was the sad reality of my life. She rarely came to my aid.

As a little girl I needed my mother to protect me from my father. His abuse became a way of life. I just thought that was how life was, and yet, I was always hoping that maybe it could be better. As an adult, I was confronting my mother on her actions and my father's. She did not like that. As a little girl, I obviously needed her protection, but as an adult I really needed her to help me through this trial. The thought of doing it on my own was unbearable at the time. This was my time of need. I needed her to kick into being the mother she never was. I guess my mother feared she would be accountable to the therapist for her role in it all. After many requests and pleadings for her to help me, she refused.

As if being a victim of sexual abuse were not enough to endure, my family abandoned me. We ceased talking. They refused to be a part of my healing process and because of their lack of support and help, my healing was delayed many years. They made it clear that it was better to get rid of me than to deal with the horrible truths in our home and their actions. I had to deal with that issue for so long. As an adult, the reality of their abandonment devastated me and broke my heart.

To them, my seed of worth was smaller than a mustard seed. It was hard for them to treat me any better than abusively. I would find that I valued my own seed of worth based on how other people treated me. Because of how my family treated me, I felt worthless and flawed. Therefore I was drawn to people who validated my self-definition.

When I started growing and stood up to my parents, they did not want me around. They did not like the fact that I was growing stronger and healthier. My role in the family was changing. If they could not abuse me, they did not want me around. I could not understand their mentality.

Still, amidst all of this, Joey and I felt our lives should not be put on hold. We wanted a baby. We wanted to start our own little family. Joey had a distant relationship with his family and I had lost mine. I decided I wanted to get reacquainted with my grandmother, my mothers' mother. She was quite old and I had only seen her a few times in my life. I planned a trip to see her. Amidst all of this chaos, I also felt a prompting to do more genealogy work.

I had also quit my job at the law office to have a baby. Immediately thereafter, I got pregnant. The day I found out was a wonderful day. I decided I would surprise Joey when he came home. I bought balloons and a banner and decorated our condo. I bought a hand drawn picture of a family with many children and proudly displayed it. When Joey came home he was surprised. We had planned it but just did not know when it would happen. I remember it being a peaceful night. We talked about our future and how wonderful it was to finally start our own family. I did not call my family to share the good news. Joey did not call his family for a few days. It was just for the two of us.

A few months later, just before my trip to see my grandmother, Joey and I ran into my mother outside a store. She looked upset to see us. It had been some time. I told her I was pregnant, although it was physically undeniable. It is hard to forget her coldness. As Joey and I held hands together, she just stood there stone faced. Her response was, "Oh." Joey just sighed and shook his head and all I could do was see things as they really were. Her coldness was an outrage. She was going to be a grandmother and did not care. She did not even want to know her own grandchild. Her cruelty at the most frail moments of my life added more devastation to my trial.

I still visited my grandmother, and that visit is dear to my heart to this very day. I felt I had missed out my whole life by not knowing my extended family. I did not understand why I did not see my grandmother more. As an adult with a baby on the way, I often wondered why I did not know my cousins. Why was I so isolated? Within the church, families were bigger, at times in the same wards. It was not uncommon for cousins to be playing with each other. Why did my mother not want me to know my extended family?

This was my first visit to my grandmother as an adult. It was summer, a hot summer. We visited a state that was known for its heat and humidity. I was not used to it. Being pregnant did not help but I was excited to see my grandmother. She would send me a birthday card with a dollar in it. If I were lucky, she would send two. She would send this even when I was a teenager. The dollar sure had changed its worth throughout the years, but always held its sentimental value. Whenever I would receive a letter from her, I would cherish her words and have kept the cards to this very day. Whenever I would talk with her on the phone, I could feel her love. Although I never really knew her, I never blamed her. My parents always kept me from anything good. I still never understood why she was not a bigger part of my life.

I remembered visiting her home at least three times when I was younger. Playing with my cousins seemed so natural and being with her seemed natural. I missed her hugs. It had been quite some time since I had last seen her. I hoped she hadn't changed much. As Joey and I drove into town, I remembered how to get to her home. The houses were small, as was the town. I do not know how long she had lived there, but it was the only home I ever knew her to live in. At one time when my mother was young, they lived on an Indian reservation. I never really thought about that until this visit. I wondered if my mother was ashamed of that. She did seem ashamed of her past.

My grandmother's home was modest with white, chipping paint on the exterior. The back had a chain link fence around the perimeter with a big German Shepard barking to greet all those passing by. She lived there alone. My grandfather had passed away when I was younger. I only remember meeting him twice. My uncle visited her weekly, if not daily. I was a bit nervous as we got out of the car and walked up her walkway. I knew my mother had said many things to her, my uncle and aunt about me. I did not know what to expect from them. They only knew what my mother had said about us. I could only imagine the deception she had created. I did not know what my mother had said about Joey. She had blamed him and the church for my "change." She did not like that I stood up to her now and confronted her on the abuse. Nevertheless, I knew Joey and I had to be true to ourselves.

As we knocked on the door, I hoped I would still feel the love I had always felt from her. I hoped whatever my mother had said would not lessen my grandmother's love for me. As she opened the door and our eyes met, she was just as I had remembered when I had last seen her. Her almond shaped eyes beamed with love. Her long gray hair was loosely pulled back in a bun and her skin was wrinkled with age. She was a Cherokee woman with light olive skin. She was a round woman who always seemed to be wearing an apron and dress. She greeted me with a hug and held me for what seemed a long time. We just rocked back and forth, talking in each other's ear and so happy to be together again. She then gave Joey a hug as she met him for the first time. It was better than I had ever hoped.

As we got settled, I noticed her home had been neglected. There were cobwebs in the corners and it looked as if it had not been dusted for quite sometime. Joey and I noticed her kitchen cabinets needed to be repainted. During our trip we decided to paint her cabinets and get her kitchen looking nice again. Upon painting the cabinets, we noticed a hole in her foundation where bugs were getting in and who knows what else. I had to call for help with her bug problem. Her home reminded me of my parent's home–neglected and unkempt.

One night, Joey and I wanted to take her out to dinner and get acquainted with her. She wanted to go to her small town diner. The menu was good, old fashioned, home cooked food. As Joey and I were about to eat, she started saying a blessing on the food. We quickly closed our eyes and bowed our heads until she was done. As I looked up, I was a little uncomfortable praying in public. But she was quick to say, "You should always thank the Lord for all you have." I just melted. She was so sweet and Christ-centered.

We did many things on this trip, but mostly I enjoyed just being with her. Being around family. I knew there would come a time when we would talk about my mother and father. I was not in a rush. I think we were both waiting for the best time to do this. On one of our last days there, we went to my uncle's home. The phone kept ringing and my uncle would talk quietly and hang up quickly. Then I realized something was going on. My mother was calling. She was so worried about what I would say that she could not control herself and called several times. It became quite clear that she had told them lies about Joey and me. I felt that if Joey and I were true to who we were, they would see past the lies.

I am sure my relatives felt uncomfortable with the whole situation. They did not know what to believe. They never really knew us. Out of respect for their feelings, I did not say much regarding the abuse. That was not the reason I went to visit them. I think they knew something was not right with my family. I did not need to tell them that. I could have easily told them all the things my mother had done since I came out with the truth but then I would be entangling them in something they were not even apart of. My father could not harm any of their children since they were older. Otherwise, I would have told them for their own safety. I think most people know that, when truths like mine come out in the open about a family, they are more than likely true. No one wants to go through what I did that first year of coming out with the truth. I knew my family was messed up and I also saw a side of my mother that was so desperate she would go to the lowest of levels to hurt me even more. Perhaps she thought her cruelty and continued emotional neglect would keep me quiet. She saw how my father's rage had kept me from other people. After so many years of being quiet, she had become abusive herself after I came forth.

The night before Joey and I left, we had a heart-to-heart talk with my grandmother. She wanted to know if it was true. She asked, "Wendy, were you abused?" I told her yes. She had tears in her eyes and took my hand and held me for so long. I told her what had happened to me by both my mother and father, though I did not go into great details. She did not need to know all the things her daughter had done. She would get the gist of it. I said I did not understand my mother's actions. Our home had been so violent. I guess I wanted to hear from my grandmother some excuse as to why my mother would allow the behavior to have gone on in my home. She did share that my mother had a hard life as a child. She lived on an Indian reservation. They never really had a lot of money. She felt my mother had a lot of shame at being an Indian when she was younger. She shared that perhaps my mother wanted to be something she was not. It's interesting, but I felt the same way. Although I do not remember my mother verbalizing her shame, I felt it. It was not until I was a young adult that my mother started accepting her heritage. My grandmother shared many things with me that night that would help me in my healing process. She responded to the truth of my childhood the way I hoped my mother would have. It seemed loving came so natural to my grandmother.

Unfortunately, my mother lied to her about my church. She told her it was because of the church that I said I was abused as well as many other untruths. My poor grandmother was confused. I bore her my testimony of Jesus Christ and told her I had only known of Him a short time. I shared that the abuse happened for years and years before I gave my life to the Lord. I told her Joey was a gentle man who served the Lord well and was supportive of my healing process.

I remember saying, "Grandma, I cannot have a relationship with my father. He is a sick man." I remember asking her a pointed question. I asked, "Grandma, you're a mom. Would you have turned your back on your own child?" She looked down, confused by her daughter's actions. She asked me if there was any hope for me having a relationship with my mother. I said I think there could be, but she needs to respond to the truth responsibly. I promised myself, for my own sanity, that I would not subject myself to their abuse. I shared I did not really think my mother was abusive, just neglectful, until I came out with the truth. I shared that I felt my mother hated me for it. She hated me even more for coming to visit my grandmother. My mother feared our relatives would question the perfect life she tried so hard to portray.

I remember the Holy Spirit was strong. My grandmother looked at Joey and said, "You have good eyes and a good spirit about you. I believe you are good for my grand-daughter and will treat her well." Then she opened up even more as she shared some insight into my mother and father. She also bore her own testimony and told me that I could only heal through Jesus Christ. She urged me to give my burdens over to Him so I could move on. She told me that someday forgiveness would set in and to leave room for it. She had a strong testimony. After being in the presence of my grandmother, I had a renewed sense of strength. I had family who loved me. I promised myself I would not entangle her in my family's mess unless she felt there were some things she needed to know. After that trip I would not bring it up. I just wanted a relationship with her. Not only did she give me hope, she gave me a lot of genealogy. I was able to see pictures of those in my line I had not seen before. We bought a book on my family's genealogy that was published with pictures and stories. I could finally learn some history regarding my distant relatives.

Apart from gaining a testimony of Jesus Christ and marrying Joey, I had not felt unconditional love like I did when I was with my grandmother that trip. She was family. Growing up, family to me meant everything was conditional. "Respect is earned," my mother would say. But my grandmother showed me a different perspective of family life. I wish she had had a stronger influence in my younger years. I was quickly learning that I could not change the past, but I could work on the future and our relationship. She was full of love and could love so many. My visit confused me even more about my own family. My mother's side of the family lived close together and interacted with one another on a regular basis. My mother was the only one who had moved away. I felt I had missed out on so much.

When we got home from the trip, my mother called the very next day. She wanted to know everything. I had not talked to her for some time. Her call seemed so invasive and inappropriate. She was afraid about what I had told her family. I was sure she would twist whatever she could. Trying to avoid another argument, I shared with her what a wonderful trip we had. But my approach to avoid an argument only turned into put-downs and ridicule from her. I told her that her sister had given our baby-to-be a beautiful quilt. It meant so much to me. My grandmother had given Joey and me wedding gifts as well as some of her own keepsakes. They are keepsakes that I cherish to this very day. Upon hearing of my happiness, my mother quickly told me her sister gave quilts to everyone and that I "was not so special." Her remarks were mean and cutting and all I could do was to get off the phone. She could never know the special times we had with my grandmother, nor could she ever take them away.

After the trip, my mother started calling again. I think because my grandmother and I started calling each other and writing letters. This was such a confusing time. I knew I had been abused but still engaged in conversations with my mother. I guess I continued my conversations to break out of the mold in which I had been with her. Most of our conversations turned into confrontations. Even though she was often cruel, I felt I needed to keep confronting her. There was also a part of me that wanted her to be the person she should have been. Another part of me wanted to help her. After visiting my grandmother, I had a little more compassion for my mother. I realized we both shared something in common-shame. Only I would not work hard anymore to cover it up like she would. I wanted to work through it and rid myself of those feelings.

My mother wanted somehow to convince me that things were not so bad. I guess I wanted to believe that too. I decided to put my therapy on hold, vowing that, after our first child was born, I would resume. I was consumed with my pregnancy and slowly started to doubt myself. I began to ease up on my quest to heal. The pain was intense. My therapist had warned me about denial. She told me that many people, as they start to deal with the realities of their past, revert back to the way things were. It is easier to do things the old way then to break through and learn new, healthy ways. People experience their pain and want to minimize it. *It is in this minimizing that the victims often go back to the way things were.* Literally forgetting the issue or wanting to avoid it so badly they go to great lengths to not deal with reality. She told me taking a break from the realities of my life could delay my healing. If I were not careful, I could find reasons to never return to dealing with the issues.

My therapist told me it would take courage to pull through. She had seen many push forward, only to be pulled back down by their abusers because that type of behavior is what the victim is used to. That is also what the abusers were used to-controlling their victims. Victims of abuse are conditioned to believe they are deserving of abuse. The abusers remind them through words and actions that they are of little worth. If the victim feels weak and worthless the abuse continues. Most people who are sexually abused do not have to deal with only that type of abuse. The abusers control other aspects of their lives. There is so much more to sexual abuse than just the sexual aspect.

My therapist was right. I was not comfortable pushing forward. It seemed my mother's influence was getting to me. Reality was not so bad when I was in denial. Although it seeped out in different ways, denial was much more comfortable to handle than the reality of being sexually abused by my father. My mother wanted me to keep coming back to her point of view. She was manipulating me just as she had always done, and I guess I was letting her, even

142

though I did not know it at the time. I was slowly withdrawing from everyone and Heavenly Father.

I was starting to feel depressed. With her influence and the depression, I felt weak and vulnerable. I felt as I did when I lived in their home. I did not seem to have the courage I needed. I was slowly forgetting all the good things that had happened to me during the last two years, the best experiences of my life. It seemed I had come so far and was moving ahead only to slowly fall back. The light of Christ that seemed so bright in my life was dimming as darkness was setting in. I was used to this darkness. It was so familiar. Falling short and falling back were deeply embedded in my makeup. I was used to avoiding reality. I was used to not questioning my family. I had come so far in confronting them and working on the family issues, but depression was getting the best of me. It was pulling me down. It seemed I always found a way to avoid confronting my life and its problems.

Things got worse with my mother. I do not know why I hung onto her. She began bringing anti-Mormon literature that she got from her new church. She felt if I stopped going to my church that somehow I would not have been sexually abused by my father. Nevertheless, I could not believe other churches were publishing untruths about the Mormon Church. Her church actually spent serious money on publishing and printing material for persecution. I felt their money and time could be put towards more noble causes.

On my birthday my mother called and said she wanted to stop by. She came in the evening and did not want to come into our condo. She waited outside of the gates. She knew I would not accept anything from my father. She had not turned me completely away from keeping my distance from him. So, of course, she told me all the gifts were from him and her. This was a real personal defining point in my life. I had always taken presents, no matter what age. No matter how bad things had gotten, the presents had become a way to excuse the behavior with which we had to put up. Nevertheless, in my confusion and depression, I gave them back to her. She had bought me things I was really in need of. Things that Joey and I could not afford. I wanted her to know she could not buy me anymore. I felt two forces working on me at this time. I felt pulled in two different directions simultaneously. I felt I was losing my identity, but then I would make a right choice like this and feel a sense of hope. I felt that I was moving forward, even if just a little.

After I gave her back the presents, she raised her voice and screamed "When will things be as they used to be?" I remember feeling angry and sorry for her at the same time. What kind of person longs for life to be like the one in which I grew up? What kind of person did not want it to change? I remember looking at her and saying, "Mom, things will never be the same. Why would I want to be hit by him or raged on? Why would I want to be molested by my father anymore? Why would you want me to go back to that kind of life?" I told her that ever since I had started dealing with reality, as painful as it was, I wouldn't want it any other way, and when she was ready to deal with it, I would be here for her. She did not speak another word after that. She abruptly turned her back on me and got into her car. I stood alone in the street watching her drive away.

Then my mother did something unlike anything she had ever done before. She started being a volunteer at her church for women who were raped. Of all the things for which she could have volunteered, she picked this. How interesting. She would try to help other people she did not know, but she could not deal with the issues that went on in her own family. She told me she would talk with these women on the phone and tell them they needed to "just get over it," to be "tough." I thought she was the cruelest person I had ever known, or else she was a very sick woman. She would blatantly dismiss my abuse. I felt sorry for the other women to whom she was talking. I asked her how she could do this when she could not even deal with her own issues. She dismissed the question and explained how good she felt to help these women. Of course she was quick to defend anyone but me.

I had put going to therapy on hold. The only thing that kept me going was my calling in the church. It was the only time I got out. I struggled with my pregnancy on an emotional level. I did not have anyone to whom I could go to ask questions. My relationship with my mother was strained. It seemed each time we talked, we argued. I was getting tired of it. I was home alone all day with just my thoughts. Sometimes I would think about what I was doing. Similar to the night before my baptism, I had doubted all the truth I had been taught. Sometimes my quest to heal seemed clouded. Just as my quest to join the church. I had lost so much. I would question–was it worth it? Then other days I would be strong and sure of what I was doing, knowing without a doubt that I was better off without my family. I was going back and forth with my emotions. I could not think clearly. I guess deep inside I had a decision to make, a permanent one. I had to decide whether I would continue to accept my family's abuse or move on without them. Deep inside I knew having a relationship with them was pulling me down, but I was used to feeling down. I was not used to feeling the happiness the gospel gave me or the love I felt from Joey.

At this time we were hoping for a change to occur in our life. We were open to a move and would feel safer in another state. My father would often drive hours to another state at night and come back the same night. We all had a good idea of what he was doing. We all thought he was cheating on my mother. So I was open to something a bit further than a few hours.

Shortly thereafter, Joey was offered a job opportunity in another state. He was offered a position and asked to come out as soon as the baby was born. This was just another example of the Lord looking after us. He knew what would be best for us. We had hoped that something would have occurred sooner so we would not have to move after the baby was born. But we could not see the Lord's wisdom at that time. My fears and anxieties were hindering my growth, and I felt moving to a new place would help me feel safe.

Our very special day finally came. The day our son was born. I had been in the hospital off and on for five days to have him. He was two weeks late and I had a c-section. I remember looking at him from a distance after he was born. He was so beautiful to my eyes. He looked like Joey. When I held him in my arms I felt a surge of love I had not felt before. I was not worried about how much I could love him, but he did touch a part of me that had not been tapped into. He touched a part of me that only a mother can feel for her child. I did not know I could feel so much love. As I held him, my family came to mind and I felt a sense of compassion for my mother again. I had not spoken to my sister for quite some time and longed for her to be with me. At the same time, I wondered if my mother had experienced the same feelings I did with my son for my sister and me when we were born. Perhaps, life's trials had made my mother forget what it was like to really love.

I wanted to call my mother, but was hesitant. I did not want to ruin the moment. Nevertheless, I felt so much compassion for her I made the phone call anyway. She asked if she could come down to the hospital. I had her promise that she would

146

not bring my father. She came down immediately. I was going to share with her my feelings and tell her that I would give her more time to work through our families issues. I wanted her to know that I would help her. I was tired of fighting. I still had to inform her that Joey and I were moving to another state in two weeks.

Joey was not happy about her visit. He thought I would just get hurt again or she would say something selfish and inappropriate. He was upset that we had been through a hard two years because of them. Nevertheless, he agreed. He did keep his distance though. He did not know with whom to be more disgusted–my mother for defending and protecting my father, or my father for molesting me. Joey was the one who held me when I cried or had a memory. He was the one who saw my pain day in and day out. He was mad that he would have to be around her at this beautiful time.

I was not prepared for what was about to happen. Upon entering my hospital room, the first words my mother spoke were, "You are so fat!" This shocked me as I had never been told I was fat. It was as if she had planned to say it before she even arrived. She did not say congratulations or ask to see her grandson. She only had cruel comments. I had just delivered my son and the I.V. liquid had swelled my face and hands. All the things I wanted to say to her were quickly forgotten and replaced with strong words. I was overwhelmed. Who did this woman think she was? It was at that very vulnerable moment, as Joey waited outside the door, that I gave her a piece of my mind. I let everything out. I could not get out of bed after the c-section and felt vulnerable. She did not know that I wanted to tell her that I loved her. I wanted a new relationship with her. But her inability to love quickly removed the feelings I had nurtured earlier that day.

I spoke clear and plain truth to her. I was confronting her with the games she played and the lies she told. I confronted her with her jealousies of me. I confronted her with what she had told her mother. She was shocked. She had done terrible things to me, but now she was confronted with lies she had told to people outside our immediate family. She did not know what to say. Her whole demeanor changed and she suddenly became nice. I saw it for what it was, though, a game. She changed to adapt to whomever she was talking. Once again I saw a very devious side of my mother.

After we fought for what seemed so long, she apologized for her comment. Then she asked if my sister could see my son. After hesitating, I said yes. She then asked if my father could come. I was tired and mentally exhausted. I was lonely that having her in the room with me at this very special time meant so much to me, even if we fought. It is hard to explain. I just could not let go of her because the fact was, after all her cruelties, I still loved her. I still believed she could be a better mother, even though I had not seen her character different. I still held onto the hope that the Lord would somehow bring us together. I was moving away from the only life I knew. Maybe the Lord would bring us together because of the birth of my son. But it seemed my yearning for family was stronger than dealing with the reality of her comments and the fact that she was manipulating me.

Since I was leaving in two weeks, she convinced me I should try to talk with my father. She said, as a family, perhaps we could all "regroup." These were the words I had wanted to hear since I came forth with the truth! I could not believe it. She actually wanted to work on our family issues. I guess I was willing to throw out all of the pain I had experienced in hopes that I could have my family back. Maybe she had hurt just as long and as much as I had. Maybe my father would go to therapy and get serious help. I had not really pictured him in the healing process, but I was willing to do whatever it would take to have my family back–or at least my mother and sister *if* they were willing to work on the issues, as she had just suggested. I do not understand why I agreed. It took me a long time to understand why I did it. I think I knew what would happen, but I went quickly into denial. Perhaps at the birth of my son I wanted to feel like I had some type of family relationship, no matter how painful the past had been. And mostly, I wanted to see my sister. We hadn't talked in so long.

Joey was upset. He did not know what I was doing but he counseled me after my mother left. He said I had never confronted my father face-to-face. Perhaps this would be the last time I would ever see my family. He thought it was an opportunity to say good-bye to them. For those reasons, he would allow the visits.

The next day, when my father entered the room, I got chills. I was in my pajamas and felt vulnerable. My uneasy feelings I had around him came back. I did not know what my mother had told him, but he thought everything would be fine after this visit. It was as if we all were in denial regarding what had happened the last two years. Nevertheless, I was happy to see my sister. I remember she looked so different, so beautiful. She was happy to meet her nephew. Joey just hung around in the background. He called this situation the best example of temporary denial that he had ever seen.

As if that visit were not enough, I invited them to our son's blessing. My mother had refused to come to any church meetings in the past, but she came to my son's blessing. She seemed so happy that we were a "family" again. She thought things would be as they were. Joey and I were giving a farewell talk. I was not going to say certain things I had written because my family was there. Instead, I bore my testimony, not leaving out a thing. I spoke of my family and some of my trials and temple work. Some of the people who knew about my trials could not believe I was around my family. But, denial has a way of making us do foolish things.

On our drive out of town, we stopped by to say a final good-bye to my family. My father let me borrow his childhood photo album. I told him I would send it to him as soon as I made copies. That book just happened to contain names, dates and places from his side of the family. His childhood was so elusive. His brother had passed away. He only had a sister he never knew and a mother to whom he had never liked to talk about. I could not have gotten this information any other way. So within my temporary denial, some positives had happened from an eternal perspective. A part of me knew this would be the last time I would see them. As we drove off to greet our new life, I was not sad. I was glad to be leaving. I was glad to start over, and mostly, I just wanted to get settled. I had been on a roller coaster for so long–now I needed a change.

CHAPTER TEN

Be Safe

"Whoso putteth his trust in the Lord shall be safe."
(Prov. 29:25)

I was excited for a new beginning. Moving to another state helped me feel safe. I quickly came out of denial on the trip to our new home. It was as if I had been in a fog for two weeks. My sister and I continued to barely talk and my mother went back to trying to keep up her deception to other people.

My mother refused to deal with her own issues and continued to belittle me and put down the church. Her plea that convinced me to see my father was a lie. She had no intention to go to therapy. None of them did. I had been manipulated again at my time of vulnerability and weakness. Of course, I wanted to be around family when my son was born. She knew that. She knew what my desires were and manipulated me. What woman does not want to have family around when she has a baby? I felt my mother had worn me down at the end of my pregnancy that I was weary. I wanted to believe her when she said she loved me. I wanted to believe her when she said she wanted me in her life. I did believe her for that brief time, perhaps trying to re-fill the void she herself had put in my life. After the move, reality hit hard again. I could not figure out why she would play her cruel games. What did she gain by coming to the hospital or blessing? Was it just to confirm that I was still under her control? I was confused about her actions and would spend a lot of time grieving over it.

Once Joey and I got settled, I was ready to get to work on my issues. I had contacted a lady who was an advocate for children and adults who had been sexually abused. She was frequently on television making the public more aware. At that time, it seemed no one else openly talked about sexual abuse. I admired her courage because I knew why victims would not come forth. I knew how hard it was because I felt re-victimized all over for finally dealing with the truth. She lived in our same area and I asked her for a referral to a therapist. I interviewed a few and found one that specialized in sexual abuse. This television personality told me it would be better for me if I found someone who specialized in my type of abuse. A general therapist could only take me so far. He or she might not know what direction to go and how to keep me on task. They might not really know how to support me in my time of need. She also informed me that therapists who do not specialize in my type of abuse may undermine some of my feelings and thoughts. There may be a lack of sensitivity.

She told me that, because that I was ready to work on my issues, it would be the hardest time of my life. I did not really know what was in store for me. She told me it would take a good few years of intense work. That seemed to be the average time to get over the tragedies of childhood. Unfortunately, many do not finish the journey. Many victims go through life as an open wound because they do not know how to heal or the pain is too intense to push through. I felt I had already worked effectively for two years, so maybe a few more years would not be too bad.

I had experienced a lot of pain those first two years, but I hadn't really jumped into my issues. I had just become aware that I was sexually abused and separated from my family. The therapist I had seen for a while was a family therapist. Some of the things the television personality would share with me were true. I would tell my first therapist things and she would undermine their significance. Not that she meant to. I thought she was a great therapist at the time, but she did not know how to support me. I second-guessed myself. It had become my nature. I did not need someone else making sure I continued doing it. I needed someone to validate my feelings so I could move forward.

Before Joey and I moved out of state, I had challenged my parents to attend a session of therapy with my old therapist. I had read in books how the whole family would be in the same room and the therapist would direct the meeting. I finally wanted to confront my father. Being in the same room with him was the scariest thought. I did not know what he would do. I could only imagine him hitting me like he always did, or raging and scaring the therapist. He could be so violent. I wanted my mother and sister back. We may not have had the ideal relationship, but that was because of my father. I felt we could start over. I was willing to confront my biggest fear which was him, and do whatever it took to save my mother and sister from his abusive ways. He had a hold on them and I wanted them to be free of the violence. I was free of it physically. Mentally I could still hear his words, and when I thought about him hitting me, I literally felt the fear as if it were really happening. Unfortunately, my family refused to come.

After interviewing several therapists, I finally met someone with whom I could relate. The ones I interviewed all specialized in sexual abuse. One had me sit on the floor surrounded by pillows with low neon lights. She insisted it made her clients feel safe. But I was too uncomfortable. Another told me what I was feeling rather than letting me tell her. Then I finally met a woman with whom I would meet eight times a month for a full year. I would visit her four times a month one-on-one and four times a month in a group.

The setting was an office in her home. It was comfortable. She was professional and seemed to have a direction for me. It had been two years since I started dealing with the abuse and I found that I had not really scratched the surface. My previous therapy had helped me understand family dynamics and everyday life. But starting up again, I felt like I had wasted time. I wish I had seen someone who really specialized in my form of abuse.

I had great motivation at this time in my life. I had a beautiful baby to love and nurture. He was my first and foremost drive. I took my responsibility of parenting seriously, even though I did not know how to parent. I did love him. He was so happy. I could not believe he would wake up every morning eagerly waiting for a new day. He could not wait to do things. He was so curious. I longed to have that kind of energy. When I awoke, I dreaded the day before me. I dreaded the reality of my past. But his curiosity gave me hope that someday I could have an outlook like him.

When I started attending my new therapy sessions, my therapist was wonderful. I was able to take my son with me at first because he was a newborn. She told me all that I had done with the drugs and alcohol was quite normal for what I had been through. I had not heard I was normal my whole life. Promiscuity was another form of acting out at such a young age. Many teenagers who have been sexually abused are in search of love to fill the void abuse brings them. Unfortunately, they mimic the only form of love they know—physical. My therapist informed me that my decisions to join a church and marry Joey were not normal. Many abused women marry someone just like their abuser and create the same environment they knew growing up. Some of these victims' own children would be abused by their husband. The thought of that scared me.

I was so grateful to have married my husband! He did not rage or hit, and was centered in Christ. I was so grateful that Heavenly Father had intervened in my life. I felt He had literally taken my hand and guided me. On my own, I would have made many different decisions. I could have ended up a tragic statistic. I could have ended up being an alcoholic or drug addict, or marrying an abusive husband. Thank goodness for the Word of Wisdom and the guidelines of the church! I was able to give up my addictions and strive to live higher standards. As a matter of fact, if the church had lower standards, I am sure I would have found a way to justify continuing my addictions.

My new therapist gave me the support I needed. I told her my whole story. With her I could let my guard down. Not only did I feel safe at our new home, I felt safe with her and our new surroundings. I did not fear that my father would unexpectedly visit us. It was because of this environment that I was able to grow and talk about my deeper issues.

She informed me that many mothers know the abuse is happening. There are many stories like mine where the child begs the mother to not be alone with the abusive father or relative. In many cases, the mother leaves the child alone, no matter how much pleading she endures. She said a *healthy* mother would find this behavior odd and question what is going on. She confirmed one of my worst fears.

I could not get over how cruel my mother had been after I came forth. My new therapist taught me that people's actions often tell of their innocence or guilt. She asked me some pointed questions. She asked that my son, as an adult, admitted he was abused when he was young, and I honestly did not know about it, how would I respond? I answered that I would believe him and confront the abuser. I would take

155

legal action. I would do everything possible to help my son to heal. She told me this is how most parents who do not know of the abuse would respond.

We talked about my mother's actions in great detail. Her guilt was so blatant. The compassion associated with an unknowing healthy parent was replaced with cruelty in a guilty parent. My father's conversations would often center on some sexual content. He leered at women as they walked by. It seemed life stopped for a moment as he strained his neck to stare at a lady passing by. I could finally verbalize how I felt when he did this. I was so ashamed and embarrassed that my father would do that. I would be standing next to him and it was as if nothing else were in the room but the other woman.

We discussed why my mother would let my father have me sleep with them in the same bed when I was a teenager. My mother obviously did not want anything to do with my father physically, so she let him use me as a surrogate replacement to satisfy his physical needs. My father would wrap his legs around my body. My mother would be next to him. Sometimes, I would catch her awake in the mornings, lying in the same bed as my father firmly held me. Although this was normal life in our home, discussing it in therapy literally made me sick to my stomach. How could things have been so blatant?

I shared that, at times during my teenage years, I would sleep on my mother's side of the bed on the ground because I feared I would be attacked by someone–not realizing that person was my own father. Being attacked at night was very real to me. It was hard for me to fall asleep at night. I just stared at my bedroom door, waiting for my fears to be confirmed. There was a time when my sister came screaming out of her room in the middle of the night, saying a man was in her room looking down at her in the darkness. Recalling this memory was hard because I now had a good idea of who it was. She was really shaken up by this experience. I was too. In therapy, this memory brought me to tears. That was the reality of being sexually abused. One just wants to scream, living a real nightmare night after night. Unfortunately, when sexual abuse is in the home, there is no safe place to run. The fear never goes away.

My mother's constant belittling after I confronted her with the abuse convinced me even more she knew. She had never been so abusive. She knew I was in therapy and hurting, yet she continued to get worse with her abusive ways towards me. I had grown up with an abusive father. I had known her to be the silent partner, letting him violently prey on us. But her new demeanor showed and explained why she thought his actions were okay. She had an abusive nature herself! Perhaps because he raged so much, so often, she felt she did not need to get mad. But now that he was out of the picture, she could not hide behind his rage anymore.

I was finding that she was just as capable of abusing me as him. Her abuse tactics were cruel mind games and manipulation. I was seeing that her actions were conscious choices as well as seeing a devious side of her. It was almost scarier than dealing with my father's issues. It meant I would have to admit that my mother was not a woman of integrity, but a woman who would go to great lengths to cover up something horrible of which she was a part. She did not hit me like he did; she just let him do it. She did not rage or scream like he did; she just allowed him to do it. She did not sexually abuse me, but she let him do it. I remember her as quiet and depressed and always sitting on the couch, watching television and overeating. She would even wear headphones to bed.

I was sinking more and more into depression. I could not keep up with day-to-day tasks. I could get to church and to my therapy sessions, but that was about it. The apartment was in disarray. Much like the environment I had grown up in. I could not even keep it clean. I could barely take a shower each day. Some days I did not. For most of my days I was alone with my son and on the couch with the television on. I would not even open the blinds to let the sun in.

I had lost my identity. My whole demeanor changed. I had been, on the surface, very social just before I joined the church. But the last two years, I could not help but turn inward and completely shut everyone out. It was a dark period in my life. I felt so ugly and dirty. I changed my hair color every other week, hoping that, if I looked good, maybe I would feel good. That is what the world would have a person believe. But it did not matter what my hair color was, I still felt ugly and dirty. I stopped working out and let my body go. I did not gain a lot of weight, but I did get out of shape.

So much had happened in a short amount of time. Now I had a sweet baby depending on me to give him the best life I could and the life he deserved. I was confused at this time, but still determined to heal and work through the life I had given up.

Reflecting on my first two years of therapy, I had even gone to an LDS women's group. It was down the street from my parents' house. Every week I would drive by, hoping to never run into them. In this group, I would hear stories from other woman who had been sexually abused. Some had clear memories of their whole life. They knew day-to-day what was happening and could not stop it. Most all said their mother knew. Their stories were much like mine, mothers knowing and refusing to leave their husbands. It seemed the mother's actions were just as devastating as the abuse itself. A mother's choice to stay with a man who molested his own children, her children, was just as devastating as the abuse itself. The group was not professionally monitored, but we had a lady who led the group and shared with us papers she had received from a group she was in previously. It did have order to it. It was helpful. I could talk with them about my feelings. Depression seemed to loom over the group though. Sexual abuse can be a depressing topic. I went for quite a while. I was grateful for the experience. I realized I was not alone, and had other women of my faith with which to talk about these issues.

After I started sharing my life with other people, they admitted to me that they knew my family was "weird" or "messed up." Our neighbors heard the yelling. People on the phone heard the yelling. My old friends admitted there was a cold feeling coming from my home. None of my girl friends trusted my father–they had weird feelings around him. They would comment on how dirty our home always was. Not just untidy, but dirty, unclean. They did not like to come over. I was ashamed of this.

To my new therapist, I described when I felt my life had really started. It was when I accepted Jesus Christ. I felt that was the beginning of my life. Then I went backwards to the time and life before I was baptized. Although talking about my mother's actions was a big part of therapy, I also discussed my body memories. I did not really understand them. She explained that, when a person has been violated, often those areas that were violated hold onto the rage. That is why I would relive the same feelings I had during the abuse. I would have uncomfortable feelings in those same areas.

I wanted to know if they would ever go away. She asked when they first started. I told her it was when I moved out of my parents' house for the first time. That was when both the panic attacks and body memories started. She explained that a part of me felt safe. It was safe for me to start feeling, even though I did not understand what was going on.

As I described my father to her, he was a textbook child molester. The things he did were all too familiar to those who have been abused. Rage, control, pornography, verbal abuse, physical abuse and sexual abuse all go together. She told me his actions were manic. He should have been on medication. He obviously could not control his emotions, nor would he even try. I would tell her that I could see when he was going to lose it. I became quite good at reading him. It was survival. I could be upstairs, hear his footsteps, and depending on how fast or loud they were, I would know if it was going to be a bad day in our home. He would often yell at me to come downstairs. If I did not respond in a time he felt I should, he would bang on the wall. If he was in a good mood, he would not bang very hard. But if he was in a mean mood, he would bang hard and fast, yelling at me to get downstairs. He was under the impression that I would not come on purpose. He thought I was playing games. I honestly would not hear him and tried to explain myself as he yelled at me. He usually only had a simple question, like asking where my sister was, but it turned into a huge, traumatic ordeal. In fact, the faster I responded to him, the less likely he was to yell at me. So I often found myself running to the edge of the staircase randomly just in case I did not hear him. I found myself doing this even when he was not home. I lived with so much fear.

There were many times when I was in my bathroom at the top of the stairs and I would hear my father whispering my name. I did not understand why he would do this. Then he would yell at the top of his lungs for me to get down those stairs and talk with him! I would tell him I heard him whispering for me, and then all of a sudden yell. He would blatantly lie to me and tell me he had been calling me for some time, and that I had upset him. He was an unstable man.

I told my therapist about my father's comments to me and how he just stared at my body and referred to me as "sexy" so often. I told her I still wish it were not so. I shared with her that I did not understand how, after all my therapy from before, even though sporadic, why I would still go into denial. I did not understand why I had invited my father and mother to meet my firstborn. I was so mad at being manipulated. I did not understand why I kept going back and forth regarding the abuse, and why I would let my father meet my son. What was the matter with me? I knew what he had done. I saw the true colors of my mother, and yet I still invited them to the hospital.

She explained that I was not out of full denial yet. I was still just trying to confirm my memories. I had forgotten and had not dealt with my abuse ever. She explained that, had I just been physically or verbally abused, it would have been easier to deal with. Having to admit that my father molested me from the time I was a little girl all the way until adulthood brought me so much shame. It was this shame that fueled the denial.

She said having to admit that my father abused me sexually would be hard to deal with. Not that sexual abuse by someone else was not as cruel. This is not to minimize abuse from a person other than a father. Abuse in any form by any person leaves the victim feeling shame. She was right. I was feeling the heaviness of the shame and disgust.

I believed my father's actions were quite barbaric-the indecency in treating me, an innocent young child, that way. I had to admit that my father was in the same class as those people I would hear about on the news. At that time, it was rare to hear of a father molesting a child, at least on the news. It seemed the public was against the victim. The victim would have to explain himself/herself in great detail to be believed. The victim was told it was serious to accuse someone of this heinous crime. Of course the victim knew all too well just how heinous the crime was. But every once in a while I would hear about a child molester and I had to admit that my father was no better than that person. Back then, when I first started my journey to healing, the public was outraged when they finally believed a molester was guilty. Sexual abuse was not commonly talked or thought about. Perhaps that is why it is labeled the "unthinkable" crime. No one wants to think about it. No one wants to admit it may have occurred in their own family, and the victim certainly does not want to admit it.

After I finally came forth and told people I had been abused, so many shared that they had been also. As a matter of fact, many of them shared that it had occurred in their home and was still going on with their siblings. I demanded with outrage why they had not told anyone. They responded they did not want to "break up the family." They chose to live the lie-consciously, knowing that their siblings were being molested by their father or grandfather. I understood their fear. But I found that many people who had been sexually abused were willing to sacrifice the truth and their own conscience to keep the lie going. After several had shared their family lie, I found it hard to be around them. Sometimes, they would praise their father or minimize the trauma that had occurred. They did not want to cause any waves in the family and used that as an excuse why they should not work on their issues.

I understood denial. I did not want these things to happen, but if I had known it was happening to my sister when she was still young, I like to think I would have told someone. My abuse was not known to me until I finally faced it as an adult. But to some of my friends, it had become a way of life. It is sad to think of fathers partaking of the sacrament, entering the temple, and then going home to commit those serious offenses against their own child. I could not understand it. Pornography is a big part of sexual abuse. Many assume that a man who looks at pornography has only that problem. But in almost 100 percent of cases of child molestation, pornography is apparent. People may admit they have a problem with pornography but fail to mention on whom they are acting out their fantasies.

One friend shared that, when she finally confronted her abusive father, he said he had mistaken her for her mother, from whom he had been divorced for years. It appears he had done this with all his girls with the same excuse. She thought he gave a valid answer and said she forgave him, never working on the issues or even questioning him. Although she publicly defended him, she acted out her denial in other ways. She was heavily overweight. I saw people undermining abuse all the time. I felt sorry for her and other friends who knew their siblings were being abused. They were sacrificing their own health and spiritual progression.

Seeing life through the eyes of a victim is hard to do and explain. Their actions are often unexplainable to someone who has not been abused. But I understood them. I also felt sorry for them. The abuse would continue until they stood up to it. They might lose their family as I did. It seems an overwhelming loss until we are given strength and a healthy outlook on life. I wanted to lie to myself about the abuse, but I could not. I would try really hard to minimize the severity of it. But deep inside I knew it was not going away. I had to work through it, and that was not easy.

I often wondered what their accountability would be in all of this. They were adults now. At the same time, I understood all too well the fear of breaking up the family. I understood the fear of having to face the reality of sexual abuse. It is the most shaming and ugly experience to confront. Nevertheless, it needs to be confronted. No one wants to go through what I did. Although I went in and out of denial, I could not defend my father's actions.

My therapist shared that it is all too common for someone to participate in the family cover-up. Especially those affiliated with a church. It seems the shame was put on the victim rather than the perpetrator. The victim was the one to carry the family shame. The perpetrator, devious in nature, would undermine the victim–just as my father had always done. The life of a victim is not easy. There are so many barriers to overcome. It is an uphill battle, but one worth fighting for.

CHAPTER ELEVEN

The Marvelous Light of God

"I was in the darkest abyss; but now I behold the marvelous light of God." (Mosiah 27:29)

When I attended therapy, I brought notes of thoughts that had come to mind throughout the week. I did my homework, which generally consisted of keeping a journal and putting down my thoughts on paper. Writing it down helped me come out of denial. I could not deny what I wrote. There were many times I would ask myself, "Could this really have happened?" Then I would reread my life's story and reconfirm that it *did* happen. It was hard to accept, but undeniable.

I loved going to my new therapy group. Although I was the youngest by many years, just hearing other people share their story reminded me I was not alone. None of them were members of the church. Some of their word choices and philosophies were different from mine. But only having the gospel in my life for a short while, I felt I could relate to them and accept them. At least they were working on their issues.

Every mother of the women in my group, when learning about the abuse in her home, chose to side with her husband rather than her child. I was surprised once again at how many mothers stayed with their husbands after learning of the abuse. They practically disowned their daughters. Just like what had happened to me. I was not alone. I was ready to deal with this issue. It was a sore topic with me. I was a mother now. I did not understand that mentality. This knowledge gave me more determination to heal.

As my son grew older and wanted to crawl around, I found myself faced with having to leave him with someone. I had to go to therapy during the day for my personal sessions. I did not have anyone I trusted with whom to leave my son. I knew the statistics of those who were abused. The number was high. I was afraid to leave my son with just anyone. Then the Lord blessed me with a new friend who immediately accepted me. She had two children of her own. One was the same age as my son. My stories did not scare her away as they had others in my previous ward. Although I enjoyed that ward, I really had no one I could just call and talk to besides Joey. My new friend, along with therapy and church meetings, became my only link to the outside world. Depression was still with me.

Joey was at work a lot during this time with his new job. But at night, he was always there to listen. We would spend hours talking every night about his life and mine. I would be emotionally drained by the time he got home from work. My days were long and lonely while Joey's were filled with talking to people. He would often complain there just were not enough hours in the day to get the things done he needed to do. Nevertheless, after working hard to support our family, he would stay up with me, listen and help guide me to healing.

I remember my therapist asking me about my mornings. I told her I would lie on the couch until noon each day. I could not get up. I felt physically exhausted and sleepy. On the mornings when I had my personal sessions, it was hard to even get there. She told me I was clinically depressed. My emotions were up and down. Or *really* up and *really* down. I did not know what was going on. I had never felt so out of control in my whole life. I would take naps with my son and found myself sleeping whenever I got the chance.

I did not want to interact with anyone else at this time. I could barely make it to church. I felt I was in a dark haze that surrounded me. I found myself not being able to relate to people. I was slowly drawing away from any social life. Joey was outgoing and wanted to do things with other people, but my depression kept us both homebound. I was starting to believe that I was ugly. I was sure others were disappointed in the way I looked. In Joey's line of work, he was constantly around a lot of women. Often times they told me they felt sorry for the long hours Joey worked and hoped I treated him well.

I had not lost all the weight I had gained during my pregnancy, but was starting to not care. I felt I did not measure up to others. I believed that once they got to know me, they would be disappointed. I felt dirty and damaged, and could not look people in the eyes when I spoke to them. I felt so worthless. Getting through each day was hard for me. Although I was finally away from my abusers, I was uncomfortable living life because of the many years I had been abused. I continued to do what I was comfortable with-I tormented myself with thoughts of doubts and self-hatred.

During therapy I would unleash a recurring dream. My image was shadowed. I was alone in a room, hiding behind a winged-back chair. I was in torn clothing bent over behind the chair, shaking and scared to death of what my abusers would do to me. I was a young girl old enough to know that I should be scared at what was about to happen to me. There was no light in the room and fear was the dominant feeling. When I would awake from this dream I would still feel afraid. As an adult I did not know how to protect myself. I still felt like a helpless little girl.

I shared with my therapist, before we had moved to our new home there was a night when I contemplated suicide. I had just read Mosiah 27, which explains how Alma was tormented for days because of his sins. I was also tormented because of my sins, and because I was abused. The shock was overwhelming. I realized that I had done nothing good in this life. I had committed a crime against life with my abortions and was still overwhelmed by my decisions. The feelings I had at my baptism were gone. I felt guilt, sorrow and remorse. On top of it all, I was convinced I was damaged to the core, violated by my own father. How shaming! Joey deserved better than me. My prayers that I could improve and be as good as he seemed not to have been answered. I felt dark inside without a glimmer of hope. Maybe it was better that I did not exist anymore. People had treated me like I did not matter my whole life, anyway.

My family had treated me like I was not worth anything. I laid on my bed contemplating the worth of my life. I was not thinking of how I would commit the suicide, only making a case for why I should. Just what was I worth and what did I have to offer anyone? I felt so bad inside I could not think of any self-value. Being with Joey was a blessing straight from a loving Heavenly Father. I knew that. But he deserved someone better than me. After joining the church, I questioned my purpose. I could see no value in my life. There was not one memory I could draw upon to change my view. Bad things had always happened to me. If I were a child of God, perhaps I was one He had forgotten about. As I was consumed with these thoughts, I remember being racked with torment like Alma described because of my past. Not just because of the things I had done, but also because of what my family had done to me. I was embarrassed to share my past life with people.

Very soon thereafter, I remember feeling the weight of my own sins and the sins of my lineage. My own sins were enough to bear, but the weight of my forebears' almost broke

168

me. This was a defining moment for me-realizing how sin can be passed from generation to generation. Like Alma, I felt I was in the darkest abyss, and amidst this darkness, I felt the Lord opening my mind to a state of feeling the full weight of the consequences of carrying on this destructive behavior. My thoughts abruptly switched from my own worthlessness to the consequences of not changing. All of a sudden I remembered feeling that I had a very special calling! A very special purpose in this life! My life was not just about the abuse I had endured, but what I could do to change it.

The dark depression I had felt was being lifted. Just as the Lord wanted Alma to stop rejecting Him and denying His teachings, I felt the Lord wanted me to do the same. I was rejecting the fact that I was a daughter of God-of divine heritage. My parents' treatment had blocked the thought that maybe I was loved by my Heavenly Father. My parents wanted me to believe I was worth only their abusive treatment. But at that moment, the Lord wanted me to know just who and what I was. *I was more than just an abused person who had made many mistakes in life.* His light shown through my darkness and confirmed that I was born of God and had done something right. Through my decision to get baptized, I had given my life over to Him.

As Alma's eyes were opened to preach the word of God to redeem others' souls, I felt I had an obligation to stop the abuse in my line and redeem the souls of my forebears through vicarious temple work. The thoughts of not being worth enough to live in this life were lifted from me. I did not like what was before me, but it was this experience that kept me going. I could reflect upon it any time I doubted or forgot my special purpose in life. I did not have an angel appear to me, but I *did* have an experience that took me from the darkest, loneliest place hiding within me to being rescued by the light and love of Christ. His love saved me once again and gave me the conviction to move forward. I did not feel like giving up on my life after that experience, although I did feel like giving up on healing many times. That experience planted something of great importance within me-an inner strength I never knew I had. Just when I thought I was on empty and alone, I was rescued by an undeniable feeling of love from my Lord and Savior, Jesus Christ.

Although my depression kept growing my therapist assured me this was normal and part of the process. Many people are under the impression that if you suffer from depression you have a chemical imbalance. But stress and trials can bring this state about as well. She informed me that I would be restored, without a doubt, to a fulfilling life. The depression I was feeling was only a phase during the healing process. Strength would prevail as I grew. She had a lot of confidence in what she did. I did also.

I did not know which night I would be tormented with a memory. I did not know which night I would awake crying, afraid to go back to sleep because of what my unconscious mind had leaked out. I was also having a lot of nightmares. I would be sleeping and suddenly feel my body start shaking. I never knew if it was really shaking or not, but a memory would start to come through. I knew something horrible was about to appear, so a voice in my mind would say "No!" It was a little girl's voice. I finally understood how I had survived all those years in that home-I literally blocked out the horrible truths and developed a way to not let them come back into my mind. The thing that made me cry most during these experiences was the voice-I was just a little girl.

I cried a lot during my therapy sessions-mourning my life as a little girl. I felt I had been ripped off. As I reflected on the few memories I had, I could not help but realize just how much fear I lived with day to day. I made sure none of those memories came out while I lived in my parents' home. I always found it amazing what great lengths I went to, to survive.

My therapist informed me that, when I blocked the horrible memories out, it was my mind's way of protecting me. But I felt it was a burden. I wanted to see everything, but could not. I was still so afraid. She worked with me on trying to break through the barriers that were holding me back from remembering more. When sporadic memories started coming unannounced, she informed me I was ready to work on my issues. The memories were coming, just not at the pace I wanted. She also informed me that I would not get all of my memories back. Some would be lost forever. I had worked really hard to hide them, so it would be really hard to recover them.

The first two issues with which I had to deal were coming out of denial and handling the betrayal of my family. I started looking carefully at my family dynamics. I did not understand my sister's reaction to this whole situation. She was not a mean person–she just could not deal with it. After watching her work for my father, I saw some odd dynamics between them. My sister would have formal outings and she would bring him. Many people thought they were married. Many of my friends thought she was my mother. My father and sister would drive to a certain hotel and have drinks together, then hang out for the evening. My mother would stay at home on the couch. When we were all together, my father would only talk to my sister about the day's business. The two of them would dominate the conversation. My mother did not discuss the business with him. She had no interest in it.

There were so many things I would recall in therapy. I recalled how my parents let my sister drive the family cars. They would not let me. My mother had a car she loved. It only sat two people. She would not let me drive it-only my sister. When I would ask her why, she would just tell me to stop asking. She told me I would not drive her favorite car. My parents knew my sister had a drinking problem and that she would drive while under the influence. After working on sister issues, I could only come to one conclusion-she could not deal with reality. I knew deep inside, my parents favored her. Although as a child I was aware of this, my response as an adult may be surprising-I was grateful I was not favored! Without my parents' strings attached, I was able to deal with my issues. I was able to see things as they really were. But as a child, it upset me that there was favoritism in my home. My needs were met last, if at all.

My parents had my sister bound financially and emotionally. Just before my move, she was like a puppet in their hands. I do not know what the material payoff was, but I know what the spiritual payoff was-she was bound. They had to keep her on "their side." If she ever revealed the truth of their marriage or the abuse, there would be no turning back. Our family, based on lies, would fall apart. There would be two people admitting this, but she could not break off.

My sister finally decided to marry a man she had dated off and on for years. She told him it was time to get married or their on-again, off-again relationship was permanently off. She invited me to be a part of the wedding. Being away from them for many months had changed my view of things. I had to admit that I had a very sick family. Going to the wedding after being in therapy and dealing with the truth for so long was a hard decision to make. It meant I would have to see my father and mother again. I did not want to make that mistake again.

My mother and I were hardly talking. She still blamed the church and Joey. I told her and my sister to blame the church for helping me gain the courage to face and deal with the abuse. They did not want to be accountable and did not understand what that meant. Although I faced the abuse, I still feared my father.

After much prayer, I called my sister and told her I could not come to the wedding. I confronted her by that the only reason she wanted me to be a part of her wedding was to show people that our family was fine. She did not care about me. I told her if she would deal with the family issues and would not let our father attend, I would come. I would not feel safe any other way. I confronted her with the blatant lies my mother was telling people and wanted to know why she was a part of what our parents were doing. She wanted her husband-to-be to think she came from a decent home. I also had been afraid to tell Joey my family was abusive when I first realized it. She did not want her fiancé to know that the grandfather of the children they would have was a child molester. No, then she would have to deal with the pseudo marriage relationship she and my father had. Too much was at stake. She informed me that our father would "give her away" the day of her marriage, with or without me. She told me she was hurt and thought I was so selfish. While she was preparing for her wedding, I was going through the most intense part of my therapy. Although I felt weak inside, I was so grateful to be able to draw upon the strength of the Lord to stand my ground. If I went, I could be sucked into the family dynamics again. I could not do that. I had come too far.

I was the scapegoat. I was used to that. But she was my sister and I felt a deep loss when I lost her relationship. That conversation would be the last conversation we would have.

I think, at the time we stopped talking, I realized just how powerful abuse is. I realized just how far people will go to hide abuse, even if it means losing the one coming forth with the truth. I still have a hard time with this way of thinking.

I just did not understand why my sister would defend my father. I had to finally realize that my mother and sister were willing to go to great lengths to keep the lies going. Dealing with the abuse was hard and having to deal with the betrayal of my own mother and sister added a weight I could hardly bare.

It is hard to explain the deep sadness I felt when I lost my sister. We were not that close, but now I knew why. It was the environment we grew up in. We did not have much interaction between us, but sisters still share a bond that is different from any other relationship and the fact is I loved her. I grieved at the thought that our special bond that sisters have would diminish and I thought because I was dealing with the abuse, our relationship may never recover from it. It was as if I went into mourning for the death of a loved one on top of dealing with the abuse. Nevertheless, I still had compassion for her and understood she did not know how to change her role within our family. I could not imagine going through my trial without the gospel.

CHAPTER TWELVE

He Is A Shield

"Every word of God is pure: he is a shield unto them that put their trust in him." (Proverbs. 30:5)

After mourning the effectual loss of my sister, I was once again determined to push forward. Although I was battling deep depression, the Lord was working mighty miracles within me. Just giving me the energy to go to therapy was a miracle. The sessions were inspiring as well as overwhelming. I was in a personal crisis. Had the Lord not been in my life, I probably would not have gone to therapy. I would have stopped. Each week I was either faced with a new memory that set me back or lacked the coping skills for day-to-day life. I felt pulverized each week. But I was given an inner strength that led me to those meetings.

I worked hard to lay a strong foundation of the gospel and set healthy boundaries in my life. I had some serious questions and did not know where they would lead me. I only knew I needed the answers. At this time, as I was prayerful and had rededicated myself, I felt close to the Lord. It was as if He were sitting with me in every session, guiding me to ask the right questions, to ponder the right thoughts and to have the courage to move forward.

Even when I was flat on my back with depression, He was protecting me and my son. When therapy got really tough, I would run. When I ran from my problems, money was always spent, although I had nothing to show for what I bought. Money was tight, but I would find a way to buy things. I was irresponsible. I was spending the money we were saving for a new house. Although I could be very frugal, I racked up debt with the credit cards. We would still have enough money to buy a home, but then we would have so much debt. Nevertheless, I felt the Lord by my side. He knew what I was going through. I felt that He stood patiently by me. Since He knows all things, I knew He knew the outcome already. It was my hope that I would prevail and remain faithful. It was my hope that, one day, this whole ordeal would be over and I could move on.

I was also for friends, but I could not reach out. I had nothing to give. I was often asked at church outings about my family. I did not know how to respond. My answers led to more questions about why there was no communication between us and I would often get emotional. When I would say I did not have a relationship with my family, they were quick to say, "Oh, one day you'll forgive and they will be in your life again." They would insinuate that I was the one with the problem, not even knowing the level of abuse I had experienced. Their shallow comments brought me no solace, only regret for opening up. It seems like such a simple and normal question to ask-"How often do you see your family?" But it put me in an uncomfortable situation. That was a very personal and weighted question for me. People assumed I was raised in the church and had a long history of Mormonism in my family line.

They would comment on things about which they did not even know. Some of them could not imagine not having family around. I could see the disappointment in their faces. I was not raised in the church. Even before my family and I had stopped talking, I did not have a big family. What seemed such a normal lifestyle to a typical church member was not normal for me. I was not allowed to get to know my distant relatives. Their comments hurt me and I eventually stopped going to places where such conversations would come up. I stopped any type of social interaction with people.

I was on a quest to find out why families betray the one who comes forth. Why would the lies continue? Why did I not know my extended family? I did not know my father's brother or sister or mother. I hardly knew my mother's parents or brother or sister. I did not know my cousins. Why? As I searched this out, truths of my parents' past surfaced. As I did their genealogy, I saw similar patterns of abuse in my family lines.

I always knew that my father had been married before marrying my mother due to an unexpected pregnancy. He had a daughter that his mother raised. He was divorced shortly after getting married. My father shared that he was put into a Catholic orphanage when he was young because his mother was abusive and neglectful. The state had taken her children away. He also shared that he had hardly any memories of being in the orphanage. He only knew that he was severely abused. My father's mother had divorced my father's father because of an illness that institutionalized him.

When my grandmother remarried, her daughter, my father's sister, was adopted by other relatives when my father and his brother came home with her. The abuse continued, but this time with her new husband. It was confirmed to me that sexual abuse was evident in my grandmother's home. Even the rage was there. My grandmother was a rager. I found out that rage and sexual abuse where clearly in our family line. I realized that this behavior could be passed down from one generation to the next. I was starting to feel the weight of my forebears again, and what a heavy weight it was! They had passed on some serious abuse. I was unable to trace how many generations back it had started, but I imagined many. During a genealogy search, I found one story in particular that was similar to mine. A few generations back, one daughter had run away from home and refused contact with any family members. No one ever heard from her again. I had a good idea why.

At that time, many people in the psychology world were claiming that certain behaviors were genetic. Anxiety, rage, depression and abuse were being discovered many generations before–therefore, it must be genetic. But if these behaviors were genetic, would the actions of a child molester be genetic? I believe abuse is an act and a behavior. I never believed it could be genetic. Nor did I believe my mother's depression was genetic, although I had grown up living with depression as a way of life. When I joined the church and changed my lifestyle, it was as if that dark cloud lifted. My depression was gone. When I started dealing with my trial, I started experiencing extreme depression. Only this time, I knew the causes. I felt that blaming one's actions on genetics did not hold a person accountable for their actions. It was not genetics that made my father hit me when he walked by. I am sure it happened to him, so he mimicked the behavior. It was not genetics that made my father quietly sneak up the stairs and visit my room at night. Rage did run in my family, but it was just a way to cope with things. It was a bad way. It was a behavior I felt I could overcome. I had been sexually abused and vowed to not become an abuser myself.

My mother had been depressed her whole life or at least as a mother. Why should I be burdened with depression just because she was? I did feel serious depression because of these issues, but I had to hold onto the hope that it could all be overcome, and that I would find peace and have a positive countenance. I did not want to pass on the rage to my children, nor the depression. I believed that my countenance would play an important role, and clung to the gospel to find answers.

178

On my quest to find out about my mother, I was told she left the only home she knew to start a better life in another state. One could say she had to prove something. That life was better some place else, any place else but home. Kind of like what I was doing. Life and family life had to be better than what I had experienced. Her plans were soon stifled when she got pregnant with my sister and was forced to marry a man she did not love. This was a secret I would not uncover until two years after I started dealing with my issues. That explained why my parents never discussed their meeting, their wedding or my sister's birth. It also explained why the atmosphere got so tense when these subjects were brought up. I looked up their marriage license and confirmed it to be true. My parent's marriage started out as a dark secret. My sister was born six months after their marriage, and she was full-term.

I started to see my mother in a new light. She had lied for so long about her life, at least from the beginning of our family. She had married a man who stopped her from fulfilling her dreams of a better life by getting her pregnant, and she always resented him for that. She did not want to get pregnant and have a baby at that time. But her resentment was based on blaming my father without taking responsibility for her own part in having the baby. This proved to be detrimental to her children. She resented us.

She was forced to marry and would do anything to save face with her family back home. She had to have that better life. I could imagine her journey. I was on my own journey in search of a better life, although mine started out a bit better. I felt sorry for her and had compassion for her. I could imagine being so young and on my own and making a mistake like that. I compared it to my own mistakes. I was so young when I had my abortions. I had no one to whom I could turn.

179

I think she really wanted her family to believe she was happy. But after spending time with her mother, I do not know why she felt she could not go to her. Perhaps it was her own father she feared. He was mean. She told me stories of him. I imagined my mother had a hard life too. She still had to prove that things were better where she was, at least on the outside. I did the same. But we were different. I did not want to live the facade-somehow living with the reality of my shame was better than lying. I could only explain our differences in dealing with the realities of our lives by having the gospel in mine. It was what gave me the strength to deal with my past.

After my visit with my grandmother when I was pregnant with my firstborn, I found out many other things about my mother. Although I do not know the extent of her situation like I did my father's, I did know that, whatever happened, she did not want to be a part of it. I know there was a lot of shame because of her heritage and where they were raised. She described her own father as a rager and her mother as passive. I found this to be most interesting since I was raised by the same type of parents. My father raged and my mother let it all happen. That was all my father knew and all my mother knew. So why did I feel I needed to give my child a better life when they did not? Why did I feel the need to change the behaviors I was taught?

When I understood their backgrounds, I was better able to understand why they stayed together. My father had gotten two women pregnant out of wedlock and was not about to divorce my mother. He too had to present a facade. He would do whatever he wanted to whomever he wanted and my mother would slip more and more into depression and overeating.

Still, I had compassion on her. I saw what an abuser's influence could have on a person's life. If she had a hard childhood and then married my father, she had only known hardship throughout her entire life. I did not like what her life had turned her into. I had mixed feelings. A part of me still loved her. She was my mother. I felt sorry for what life had done to her. As a daughter, I still wish she could experience the love of the Lord as I have. The other part of me understood that, once I realized what abuse was, I had to change. I confronted her and exposed the abuse. Her response made my healing process harder and, at times, very lonely. But no matter what a person has been through, all changes are possible through the Lord.

As I discussed these things in therapy, my therapist believed it was good to know as much about the family dynamics as possible. I still did not feel any better. It did not make my pain go away. It angered me. Hate was settling in my heart. The only life I knew was abusive, but I still knew it was important to become a better person. Why did my parents not feel the same way?

During this time, I was called by the television personality who had referred me to my therapist. She was putting together a victims' convention and wanted me to speak at it. I had never spoken at a convention or even been to one. My speech was to be only two minutes long. I could say whatever I wanted regarding my journey to healing. I accepted the invitation, but was overwhelmed. I could not believe she asked me.

I was excited to share this with my therapist. Then, something strange and unexpected happened. The therapist, whom I thought was so supportive, looked me straight in the eye and asked who was I to be invited to speak at a convention. I was shocked and disappointed! She had built me up and helped me to face the unthinkable. Her question crushed me. Who was I? I told her I had also been invited to work with some other ladies to get a non-profit project moving forward. My therapist did not understand what I had to offer. She noted I had no experience and was still in therapy. Our relationship changed from that appointment on. I did not trust her like I used to. I still felt she could help me a lot, but I felt she had crossed a line with me. I was tired of trying to figure out who I was, and I certainly did not think I should have to explain it to my therapist then pay for her time!

Nevertheless, I went forward and gave my talk. There were about five hundred survivors of abuse waiting to hear many of us share parts of our stories. I decided to talk about never being accepted and feeling worthless. I cried during my talk, but something was liberating about this experience. I was admitting to a lot of people that I was abused. I was being taped and would have a copy for myself. I thought journaling my thoughts and memories were helping me come out of denial, but this experience took me permanently out of denial. It was liberating. I would not go back into denial after this experience. I would not have to waste my time worrying about that issue anymore. It was a defining moment in my therapy and healing. My therapist's comments were also. Instead of being crushed by her comments, after my talk at the conference, I realized I was just mad at her and it was okay to feel as I did. I was not going to attempt to prove my worth to her. For the remaining sessions, I would go forth with the specific purpose of learning coping techniques for day-to-day life. I realized there was a time when I was emotionally fragile that I felt I needed her. At one point I did. But just like all of my past relationships with people who were significant in my life, I was let down. I made a conscious choice to not be emotionally tied to her. This experience needed me grow and realize that, although she was an amazing therapist, I could not depend on anyone but the Lord. He would never let me down!

Soon thereafter, my paternal grandmother died. This was yet another turning point in my life. I was told that my father was raging at my mother. He was upset that I had his scrapbook. He thought it stated that his father was mentally ill, and that it could potentially mean he could be locked up or provide proof so I could put him in jail if I sued. He believed whatever was in his family scrapbook would be held against him. I had recently sent confrontational letters to both him and my mother regarding their abuse towards me. I confronted them on everything. I did not expect a response. Nor did I ever get one.

I sent the first letter to my mother. I confronted her with all the lies. They were on paper. She could not deny any of it. I then sent a letter to my father. I confronted him on his sexual relationship with me. He did not respond. I had threatened to sue him if my sister had children and he was around them. I had to pray and ask the Lord if this would be the wisest decision for my new little family. Did I have the strength to go through with suing him?

Then I received a phone call informing me that my father was telling my relatives that my first therapist had told him she would not stand by me in a court of law because she did not believe me. He told my relatives that she had shared details of our sessions together, and that I was lying. I quickly called my first therapist and told her what I had heard and asked if any of it were true. She assured me she had never spoken to my father and that she would not violate our patient confidentiality agreement. She was so upset that she wanted to contact him herself. He was blatantly lying and doing it publicly. I finally had proof he was lying. I had a witness. I can only explain that I felt a sense of inner victory.

When my father blatantly lied about my therapist, I accepted it as his admission. I did not feel I needed him to admit what he had done because I already knew the truth. But, catching him and my mother and sister lying together was so sad and liberating.

His actions gave me even more courage to move on. He was lying publicly now. And I had proof he was lying. I felt a sense of relief. I could finally prove he was lying to many people. It was no longer my word against his. Now, my therapist knew also.

Deep inside I wanted to call all my relatives and tell them everything. I even wanted to call my father's long time friends. But I could not. What would it accomplish? No one really knew his true character in our home. His friends were not around when the abuse was occurring, nor were my relatives. My father was scared. The thought of going to jail scared him, but gave me a sense of relief.

During this time I received an unexpected phone call from my mother. It had been so long. She told me she needed my father's scrapbook. I confronted her. I told her I knew they were afraid I was going to sue them and that my father was caught in a lie. I had my therapist to defend me. During this conversation she lied so much that my stomach started hurting. I told her I knew why she wanted the scrapbook. My father was lying and so was my mother to cover up their abuse. But this time it was so blatant. So much time had passed and they were strategically trying to cover themselves. They were in it together. I did not feel alone though. All the ladies in my group therapy sessions had gone through the same thing.

During this conversation my mother shared with me that my sister had a little girl. My mother was personally taking care of her everyday while my sister worked for my father.

It reminded me, just before I married Joey, of my mother talking with me and told me to never ask her for money. I was leaving the family as an adult and should not expect that they would help me financially. She also told me she would not take care of our children. She said her "years of dealing with kids were over." She was not going to be our "babysitter." She had things she wanted to do, and taking care of her grandchildren was not one of them. She was so cruel as she gloated that she took care of my sister's daughter. I remember a sinking feeling settling in my stomach. She always knew what to say to hurt me.

Then I thought more about this little girl I would probably never know. She was being raised by an abusive grandmother. How irresponsible of my sister! I was disgusted with my sister and her role in all of this. I realized just how far my mother would go to cover up their abuse. She did not like to be around children. I know this because she barely raised me. She would do anything to cover-up. My mother said the final thing that would end our relationship. She told me she wanted to come out to see me and her grandson because she missed us. She was lying. She just wanted the scrapbook. She was going to great lengths to cover up and now she was so blatant about it. I told her I would send it to her and hung up the phone.

Immediately I felt prompted to call her back. She was already on the phone. When I finally got her again, I asked to whom she had been talking. She said her mother. Then I knew she was lying even to her own mother. I knew she was scheming and hoping that I would not call her mother to tell her everything I had confronted her with. I was betrayed once again and lied to once more. I made a promise to myself she would never hurt me again or lie to me. This would be our last conversation.

The next day I contacted a person in their state about the state laws of abuse and suing. He specialized in such court cases and was very honest with me. He said they are hard cases to try, and with all my family against me, the odds were also against me. He told me it would take a toll on my life and therapy. It could set me back. I had to imagine losing, and if I were okay with that, then go ahead–if I were emotionally able to. I had a decision to make. Do I sue my family to protect my niece and prove that my father was a child molester, or do I go on with my life? And how could I go on with my life knowing that a little girl was prey for my mother and father?

This was a hard decision. I had to ask myself why I would really be suing. Of course, my father should live the rest of his life in jail away from children, but I also felt my mother should go to jail for allowing him to abuse their children. I was at a fragile state at this time. I prayed to Heavenly Father for an answer. What was the best thing for me to do regarding my family? As I pondered and prayed for days, taking into consideration my conversation with the legal person from their state, I had come to a decision that was very hard to make.

As I pondered my sister's actions, I felt both compassion and disappointment towards her. I had compassion because I loved her. She was my sister, after all. I knew the life she had and I felt sorry for her. I was also disappointed with her as an adult. She lacked character and courage. She became an active part in the cover-up. She knew my parents were lying and she was lying with them. I thought of her as passive and weak. After defending my father, I wondered what she was capable of. I would have described my mother as passive and weak up until I confronted her. She then turned cruel and abusive herself. What was my sister capable of?

My sister knew what my father did-about all the lies. She also knew deep inside that she was part of all the lies since I came forward. She was responsible for her child along with her husband. I could sue and lose, and my niece would still be around my parents. Did I have the strength? I still feared my father. I also realized that it is the parents' responsibility, no matter what they have been through, to overcome bad traditions and behaviors.

I had my own new family to take care of. I had to change the paradigm of abuse in my own family. Having been in therapy for almost a whole year, eight times a month, I realized I still had a long way to go. I was learning to cope with everyday life and this issue, but I had so much to change. I trusted no one. I did not want my children to feel this way. Being non-trusting was so lonely–I would not rob my children of this essential ingredient to life. If I trusted no one, it was hard to trust God. And God was my salvation at this time. I could only lean on Him for things good and positive. I had so much to work through.

Being a member of His church brought great responsibilities to Joey and me. We were pioneers. It was hard, but I realized that I would rather be a pioneer to grow and stretch my soul. In my family line, abuse had to stop with me. My sister had to stop it in hers. I could sue and win and still not change them. Although this was a very logical answer, I acted on a prompting to not pursue the suit any further. The prompting was strong. I still do not know exactly why, but at times I feel guilty for not trying to help my niece. Nevertheless, I cannot deny what I felt. I also realized I wanted my parents to stop being abusive and my sister to stop being an active victim. I wanted the lies to stop. I wanted to see miracles in their lives as I had seen in mine. But I could not make it happen. I also had to access my emotional state. I was fragile. I was broken and afraid of them. I did not have the strength within me.

I'm sure Heavenly Father tried to touch their hearts and heal their pain, but sometimes, when we are so far from God, it is hard for Him to touch our souls. When we feel His spirit, we have to act. I do not believe I was the only one He tried to help in my family. I know He wanted to help all of them. I know He is still trying. But sometimes, when a person has lied so much, he loses his identity, his true identity, and it is hard to get back to God. I know Heavenly Father tries to reach us. I also know He knows our hearts and intentions. He knows if we, on our own, will change or not. Most importantly, we can change through Him but often times our own weaknesses hold us back.

I was finally able to let go of my family. At that time, I had an active relationship with my grandmother. But I could not stand to hear about my family anymore. It was too painful. So, unfortunately, my relationship with my grandmother faded also. I could not keep up with the lies my mother was telling her. I felt sorry for my grandmother. I did love her so. She was accepting of me, but I would get off the phone emotionally drained after I spoke with her. Not because she was inappropriate, but because I could not help asking about my family. She knew my pain. She comforted me. I did not want to feel like I was in competition for her love. I did not want her to feel confused as to who was telling the truth. I did not want to hurt her. I loved her too much. I decided to not let my grandmother be in the middle anymore. This was so hard for me. There were many times I wanted to call to just hear her voice. But I did not. I had to cut all ties.

Although still quite emotionally fragile, I knew without a doubt I had made the best decision for my family. I still regretted never taking action. I still felt weak and like a coward. But my son needed me. I did not have the strength to carry it any further. And for some reason, I did not receive a confirmation from the Lord that suing was the right thing to do.

CHAPTER THIRTEEN

Run with Patience

"Run with patience the race that is set before us."
(Heb. 12:1)

Throughout that year of therapy I experienced much anguish as I recollected many memories that had haunted me. Verbalizing them was still difficult. I shared many stories with the group.

I remember being a little girl, no older than eight. There were many times my father would wake up the whole family in the middle of the night and drive us on what I would term "night terrors." He would be mad at my sister for reasons I never knew. He would pull us all out of bed in the middle of the night and drive to the worst areas in town. He would drive through the alleys and take us to what he considered to be the "slums." He would scream at the top of his lungs for what seemed like hours, driving around in the middle of the night showing my sister what kind of life she would have if she did not straighten up! I remember being scared to death. I feared he was going to drop my sister off in a slum as he threatened he would. My "sissy," as I called her then, would be crying with fear and terror the whole time. My mother would just sit there in the front passenger seat, never saying a thing. Just letting him rage on my sister. I do not think I ever experienced more conscious fear my whole life. I remember them giving me a pillow and blanket as if they thought I would go back to sleep. I remember wanting to hold my sister because I was so afraid and I knew she was also. But we could not. We just sat in the back of the car, scared of what my father might do. Scared of what my mother would let him do.

It was not too long after these episodes that my sister ran away–twice. I remember my father looking for her and coming home saying he knew where she was. I did not understand why he would not bring my "sissy" home. Deep inside, I wondered if she was at one of the places my father would take us on a "night terror." We had no family meeting regarding this. I just remember him screaming and raging and leaving at night to look for her. My parents did not understand just how scared I was for my sister. I would often wonder if she were going to die or never come home. If she really were at a slum, I feared all the horrible things that would happen to her. I wanted to go to my mother to tell her how I felt. I never did. After some time passed and she came home, the circumstances under which my sister returned remained unknown to me. I just remember being so happy she was safe and alive! I also remember not trusting my father. He knew where she had been, as I heard him tell my mother so. I always wondered why he did not bring her home sooner.

The second time she ran away, my father hired a private detective. Again, nothing was said to me until she was brought home. I remember sitting at the kitchen table at nighttime. My whole family was sitting at the table with the detective. It was odd that we were all together like that. The detective was lecturing my sister on how selfish she was to put our family through what she had. He lectured her on being a better daughter and respecting the family rules. I did not even realize we had family rules. His words seemed like good advice, if my sister were selfish and disrespectful. But, she was not. She lived in fear just like I did. Of course, my parents failed to mention the abuse that was going on and the "night terrors" that transpired just before she ran away. As I look back, how I wish that detective had a clue that children did not run away when life was great in the home! Young children run away for serious reasons, usually from great offenses against them. My sister was not the selfish one. Rather, my father was. He would not admit the fact that his actions were the very cause of her leaving. Life was confusing in our home. My father was the cause of the fear, yet he blamed my sister for the bad decision she made in running away.

I, too, ran away in my teenage years. I could not handle the pressure anymore. I was gone for days. I did not want to go home, but I had no money and no other place to go. My parents went to my friends' houses looking for me. I hung out with my friends all night. I remember them feeling sorry for me. I never talked about my family, even then. But they knew it must have been bad for me to leave home as a teenager.

Upon returning home, my father had the whole family stand by the staircase. He raged on me. He did not care that he scared me. I thought he would tell me he was worried about me, or at least that my mother would. Instead, I was berated. He also threatened that I may end up dead the next time I ran away. I never knew if he meant by him or someone else. What a sad thought for a teenager!

Other memories were also painful to verbalize especially ones regarding our pets. We had dogs that were abused by my father. They were big dogs, too. They were not allowed to leave the backyard or garage. They did not have beds. They had to sleep on the cold garage floor every night. I do not ever recall my family cleaning out the garage. It was dirty and unsanitary. Our dogs were only fed when someone remembered to feed them. I remember they would be so hungry. They were not fed regularly. At times, I would go out and give them scraps of food because I felt sorry for them. We did not play with them or hug them because they were so dirty. If they ever put a paw into our home, they got hit by my father. I, too, learned to treat them badly.

I am saddened at having so much rage as a little girl and taking it out on the dogs. I would not let them touch me. They only wanted attention and love. I was haunted by their eyes. They did not just want food. They were trying to read my father. They wanted to see what his reaction would be to them. I did not know why we even had dogs. I wanted dogs I could hug, but they were so dirty and untrained–not even partially trained. I did not know how to treat them. I remember them living in fear also. Whenever my father would come around, they would always cower in fear. They would walk with their heads low. They did not know what my father would do to them.

Their abuse and neglect stayed with me for years and years. I actually had nightmares of their treatment during therapy. I felt so bad for the life we had given them! I had dreams of loving them, only to awake feeling guilty, as the reality was not so.

Our washer and dryer were in the garage. I would go out to do my laundry and my shoes would stick to the floor. My parents' living conditions were shameful. I remember one of our dogs sleeping in the dryer because he was so cold at night. When we gave them baths with freezing cold hose water, they whined. These baths, which they got probably once every two years, were violent.

As I shared this with my group, every woman there was crying. They could see my pain and how much I was tormented by these memories. I was also informed that abuse to animals is quite common in families where sexual abuse exists. It is a sort of sign that the abuser wants to be in control and can harm or kill if necessary. Abuse to my dogs when I was a young girl made me fear my father even more. As an adult looking back, my father's treatment of those animals reminded me he was capable of committing serious harm to anyone, especially to me. But it did not stop there.

There was another time, a morning in the garage when there were sounds of baby kittens. We were so excited to see them and were trying to stay quiet so we would not disturb them. My mother, sister and I were standing at the garage door looking for them. Unexpectedly, my father came raging into the garage with a bottle of ammonia. We started screaming knowing what he was going to do to them. He was raging and yelling at us to "shut up" and "get back!" He found the newborn kittens and poured the ammonia all over them. He poured the whole bottle. We were all screaming as we huddled behind him. I remember crying and yelling, "Stop, Daddy, stop!" I had never witnessed such cruelty. My sister and I were crying.

The mother cat did everything she could to save her kittens but could not because my father ran to the front of the house, got the hose and squirted it full blast on the baby kittens. We had to watch them roll out of the garage into the street. They were all separated. We were all screaming for him to stop but he would not. He was raging and in a crazy, unreachable mood. He did not care what he was doing or if he killed them. Although my mother was visibly upset, she did not tell him to stop. She just let it happen.

This was a very hard memory to verbalize. It was so traumatic. I did not know how many kittens died that day. I just remember the mother cat looking for days in the windows of our home and the backyard for her lost kittens. Then one day I heard a noise in the front yard in the bushes. One kitten had survived. I begged to keep him. After much pleading, my father said I could. Once he came down from his emotional highs, we were lucky if guilt set in. It was because he felt guilty that he let me keep the kitten. The kitten's eyes were not open yet. Apparently it had been born the night before he tried to kill it. I had to feed the kitten with a bottle until he could eat on his own.

I did not know how to take care of animals, so the kitten, too, suffered from not eating regularly. I did love him, though, and did the best I could, for a child my age without any direction from parents. I let him sleep with me every single night. The mother cat continued to look for her lost kitten for what seemed so long. My mother told me I could not give it back because she may harm the kitten. I did not know. I just know I loved him, but felt guilty we had him.

As I think of the pain and abuse these animals went through, it breaks my heart. After verbalizing these memories of animal mistreatment, my nightmares lingered for a long while.

My most shameful memories were not just the sexual abuse; they included the living conditions of our home. I remember discussing our living conditions. Our house was always dirty. Very dirty. Unsanitary dirty. It was also all I knew. Our new kitten found a place to go to the bathroom on the stair landing. He had a litter box that was not regularly changed, so that area of the house smelled accordingly. My parents did not seem to mind. I remember one Christmas Eve my sister and I decided to wait up for Santa. My parents told us to sleep on the stair landing where the cat would go to the bathroom. I did not want to sleep there but I was told it was the only place I could be outside of my bedroom on Christmas Eve. I was used to things being dirty and did not imagine they could be different. Also, I knew sleeping on that stair landing was not good. I was just a young girl who would do whatever I could to see Santa Claus. The thought of unsanitary conditions, I recollected as an adult, were so shameful to admit to my group.

As I told of my day-to-day life, I shared that my mother was never one to teach me how to do anything. Chores weren't taught, but done from what I remembered seeing, or from fear of being raged on. I was not taught how to fold clothes, make beds or clean the kitchen and bathrooms. We were used to filth. Clothes were rolled instead of folded and plopped on top of each other. There was no organization to anything.

I had to clean the bathrooms when they got unbearable. Of course I would be bullied and raged on to do it while my mother sat on the couch. She would not give me cleaning supplies or guidance. I would find whatever I could to scrape the mess off the toilets because it had crusted on there. Often times I would use a razor blade. I remember being so young and not knowing how to clean the toilets. I was too young to be using a razor blade, but I had to clean the toilet well or I would get into so much trouble. Algae were literally growing on the toilet sides in my father's bathroom. My father would force me to clean his own personal bathroom and leave his inappropriate, pornographic magazines lying about. I had to put them back under the sink cabinet. Why would he leave them out? I remember being as young as seven years old and being exposed to those magazines.

The showers took hours to clean. Things were growing on the walls and they were grimy. My parents would not clean their own bathrooms. Even to me it was disgusting. My mother's bathroom was just as bad. I could never see the counters because they were filled with trash that she did not feel like throwing in the garbage. Her toilet was the same. I would often use shampoo to clean up the bathrooms. Her bathroom was the one that people would use if they were ever invited over. I never remember any of my mother's friends coming into our house from the age of nine on. As I shared my family's living conditions, my own therapist was disgusted. What was once so normal for me had become a most shameful memory to verbalize.

One of the most painful and shaming memories I have about how cruel my father could be was when he came home and decided he did not like how messy the house was. He immediately started raging. Then he paused, looked at my sister and me and screamed at the top of his lungs to start oinking like pigs because that is what we were. He told us to get on our hands and knees and to walk around like pigs. I stood there in the living room, stunned and scared he was going to start hitting us. Though he repeated himself several times, I refused. I remember I started crying as I looked across the room, not because of his screaming, but because of what I saw. My sister was on her hands and knees oinking like a pig. I was screaming for him to stop. He had taken all dignity from her that day. She was different after that. I was too. I never forgot just how cruel and degrading he could be.

The neglect was atrocious. I did not realize how bad it was until I was journaling and reading back the notes of my life. It amazed me how blatant the neglect and abuse were. I'm sure that if social workers had come over, my sister and I would not have lived in that home for so long. We would have been sent to foster homes.

Another feeling I will always remember is hunger. I was always hungry especially at lunch and dinner. Often my mother was gone or she would not cook dinner. I remember my father having to order pizza two to three times a week. We would eat the leftovers the next day. I remember in the third grade I would go to school hungry and did not have lunch. My mother did not make snacks or lunches for me. I would literally go the whole day without eating. My mother was not home in the mornings to help get breakfast or lunches ready, nor did she show me what to do. I felt that, if she were going to work all day and not be there for me, she could have at least shown me how to take care of myself. She could have shown me how to pack my snacks and lunches. She did not discuss with me what to do. I would eat other people's food when they would share.

Going to school and coming home were hard. I remember being so young and my mother and father leaving my sister and me at home by ourselves, hoping we would get up in time for school. I do not know how we did it. I remember one incident, which happened frequently, when I was in the second grade. My sister and I were home alone. We did not have time to eat breakfast and I did not have any clothes set out, so I went to the hamper to find something. I dressed myself in mismatched clothes. I remember running down the street with a brush in my hand, yelling at my sister to please brush my hair. We were going to be late for school. My sister usually did my hair the best she could, but she was just a child herself. We had to walk so far to school. I do not know why we did not take the bus. We had to cross busy intersections to get there. Today, I would not let my children walk that route. It was dangerous.

The same thing happened when we moved to our second home. I was in Fourth Grade. I was consistently left on my own with no snacks or lunch and went to school hungry. I would come home alone. If I left home after school, I would get into severe trouble. I was not allowed to use the phone or go out front. I was alone for hours because my sister was in high school. After work when my mother came home, she would hurry to get her walking clothes on and leave again. There were times she would not even say hello to me. Sometimes, on rare occasions, she would let me come with her. That did not mean she wanted to talk to me about my day or anything, it just meant I could come along for the ride. But most of the time, I would not see her until dinner. That did not mean she would be cooking it either.

Analyzing the actions of my mother was perplexing. She did things that were hard for me as a child to understand. I remembered a time when my mother asked to be transferred to the night shift. It happened in my early teen years. Home life was getting harder and confusing. She was gone from early afternoon until after midnight. I did not see her for a long time. It was as if she did not live there anymore. We were left as prey for my father. She knew how he was. During this time, my father was the only one raising us. He decided that I should sleep with him at night. It was as if I were his wife during that time. Sometimes I would go to sleep in my own room, only to awaken in his. When my mother finally changed her schedule back a year or two later, he would still have me sleep with him on his side of the bed. My mother never said anything. No one ever told me a teenage girl sleeping with her father was wrong. If anyone should have told me, it should have been my mother.

During my teenage years, my father's abuse worsened. It seemed like he raged on me every day. If he missed a day, he would find a way to make it up. These truths in my life were hard to overcome, let alone verbalize. Because I had numbed myself for so long, my reflections of my home life seemed to hurt more as an adult. As a child, I always found an escape to cope with life. Those escape techniques no longer worked as an adult. I was left to verbalize all the truths in my life and feel the effects they had on me. Their effects were painful. It took a while to get through reliving the conditions of my home life.

I saw wisdom in reflecting and confronting the past. By verbalizing it and writing it down, I now had the power to make a choice. I could see life as it was and change. Although this was a painful process, I never regretted it. I not only had to deal with the abuse, I had to make conscious changes in my day-to-day living conditions as well. I, too, had to work on my rage and overcome my fear of having pets in the home.

It had definitely been a year of intense therapy. I had an inner determination and a knowledge that it would not last forever, even though it was hard to believe at times. I had to believe that confronting my abuse was necessary so a new life could emerge. By this time, I was getting tired of therapy. I was going eight times a month and was starting to know what my therapist would say. I was learning my coping skills and living them. They were becoming second nature. It was a good thing. But I started asking myself, "How much longer? When do I stop?"

Joey and I had decided that, amidst all the chaos, we would have another baby. I decided during this pregnancy that I would stop therapy. It was a hard decision. At that time, when a memory came, sometimes I would get depressed, but not every time. Sometimes, if it were really bad, I would physically get sick to my stomach. But I was not as depressed as I had been in the past when I was literally bedridden. I felt I needed to be in the present for a while to deal with my new, growing family. Our marriage had been centered on my issues. I needed to be focused on the present situation.

As I explained this to my therapist, she thought I was running from my problems because I had just had my worst memory of some things my father had done to me. The bad feelings that resulted lasted for days. My memories had come at night. It was usually hard for me to have memories at night. I would awaken just before they came. Much like when a person awakens from a nightmare–abruptly and scared. To my therapist, it was a sign that I was getting stronger. I believed her. A part of me wanted to stay in therapy. But I was starting to feel depressed when I left the sessions, not hopeful as I did at the beginning. I felt I needed a therapist at the beginning. I did need help. But after this huge and devastating memory, I really did not want to have anymore. My father was having sexual relations with me. Although I knew he had me do things to him, with this memory I saw just how young I was. I could physically feel his whole weight on me. He did not care that I was suffocating and gasping for air. It was this memory that helped me understand why I had forgotten my abuse and why I did not need to remember all of them.

My therapist thought I had been making remarkable progress and felt I was stopping because I could not take any more pain. There was a time I had asked her before I had my second child if I should start taking medication. The rest of the group was on something to cope with life. At times they would get lost in discussion regarding someone's medication. Either they were trying stop taking it or it was the wrong dose. But my therapist advised me that I had an inner strength to deal with the truth and the medicine would only hinder my progress and make me numb.

She was right. Deep inside I did not want medication because of what I had been through. I did not want to have to take medicine because of the environment I grew up in. Chemical imbalances seemed to be on the rise back then. Everyone seemed to be diagnosed with it. If you had any type of anxiety, it seemed something was wrong with you and you needed to be medicated. But I was actually *feeling* for the first time in my life, even though it was painful. I did not agree that so many people should be medicated. Even children were starting to be medicated. It seemed if a child could not sit still, something was wrong with him. Having confronted what I have, I strongly believe that children act out all the indifferences and problems in the home. Each handles the stress differently.

Behavioral change is not easy. It is even harder when a whole family is trying to work on change. I had an inner prompting and belief that this time would pass. My emotional problems and distorted beliefs would all dissipate in the future. Unfortunately, it seems with each passing year there is new medication prescribed for even the smallest of problems. I believed anxiety was not a chemical imbalance, but a natural emotion. After overcoming my addictions I did not want to be numb again. This was important to me. I did not want to be medicated. I needed to feel in control of my life even if feeling bad was a part of it. I personally believe medication should be taken with caution. The problems will not go away because of the medication. I also believe if medication is taken in conjunction with therapy it may be easier for someone to look at their issues and deal with them. If a person does not deal with their issues, once off the medication, the problems, issues and/and feelings can return if they are issues of abuse. There is no quick fix for healing from abuse. It requires hard work.

Although my emotions were becoming sporadic, I felt it was because I was in therapy. I noticed them being more magnified as I worked on my issues. My own husband thought I should go on medication. But I told him he would have to be patient. I would not be in the middle of this storm forever. My abuse was bad, that was certain, but I did not believe it would affect me my whole life. I had the hope that, someday, this trial would end. And, if I worked really hard to overcome it, I would be whole. I believed my depression would leave and I would be healed. So taking medication would never fix the problem. It was a temporary solution. Medication would not take the reality of my past away, but it could prolong my dealing with it.

As I kept talking about when to stop, my therapist was disappointed. At my last group visit after saying my good-byes, everyone said, "You'll be back." They were sure I would see them again. What they did not understand was that I was not coming back. I did not want to stay in group therapy for years and years. I did not want it to be my only social life, which it had been that whole year. It had helped me grow, stay on track and get out of denial. I could not minimize the great impact it had on my life at that time. It educated me and saved me. I was in a crisis. I was able to verbalize things I never knew I could before in a safe environment. But, at that point in my life, I needed to focus on the present. I did not understand God's role in all of this yet. I just knew that, amidst all this chaos, I could find rest with Him.

Besides, I was about to be the mother of two precious children and was determined to not be in therapy for years to come. I had a lot of work to do. Time was not a luxury. It was a reminder that I needed to work hard to move on. I needed to be a mother and be on my own for a while.

People said my second pregnancy was a mistake. I had heard this before with my firstborn. But it was because of his birth that I sought help. I worked even harder because of my responsibility to him as a mother. With my second pregnancy, I saw it as an opportunity to move on, yet again, with my life. I did not want to be such a victim in this trial that I had to halt my present life. I did not want my past dictating when it was time to have children, or whether or not I should go on medication. I had to believe that, somehow, the convenience of medication did not hold a candle to the hope of being healed of my childhood trauma through Jesus Christ.

CHAPTER FOURTEEN

Benevolence

"Let the husband render unto the wife due benevolence:
and likewise also the wife unto the husband" (1 Cor 7:3)

At this time in my life, my intimate relations with my
husband had suffered. Our intimacy had changed once I
started working on my issues, which was not too long after
we got married. In the beginning, I could not have asked for
a husband who was as tender as Joey. He respected me even
though I felt unworthy of his love. He helped me feel safe,
beautiful and pure. I had never felt that way before. It was
hard not to love a man who loved me for myself. Especially
when I felt so badly inside about who I was and what I had
done before I met him. I also felt guilty once I started
working on my issues and remembered the things my father
had done to me. They affected me greatly. They changed me
so much that I could no longer share those beautiful
intimacies I had with Joey.

Upon joining the church, I valued the counsel of waiting to
have intimate relations until I was married. This teaching
gave me boundaries that I respected. Before I joined the
church, I had no guidance. Intimate relations were not sacred
or beautiful. Intimacy to me was more a signal of whether
my date liked me or not. There was no loyalty, and many
thought it odd to be with one partner in this life. After the
conduct of my father, I had a lot of fears regarding loyalty
and marriage.

I learned that love between a man and a woman is to be
cherished. Going through the temple to be married for time
and all eternity was sacred. I remember feeling the Holy
Spirit when Joey and I were sealed and made sacred

promises to each other and the Lord. Any doubts I had about marriage were put to rest in the temple. My worldly views had no place there. I remember feeling very special to be married to Joey. It meant everything to me, that he also wanted to stay committed to our marriage.

That is what I loved most about him—his commitment to us and our future family. It was also this fact that helped me feel guilty when I could not enjoy being with him in an intimate setting. We enjoyed the love a man and a woman should experience for only a few short months. I treasured these experiences because he made me feel safe and pure. But for the next few years, our marriage was robbed of these experiences as I delved deeper into my issues.

When sexually abused, it is hard to not have intimacy problems. It does not matter if the spouse is gentle or not. The problem was there before the marriage. I viewed intimacy differently from other women who had not been abused. I discovered that, having been molested at a young age, I was plagued with guilt and low self-esteem. I felt re-victimized during our intimacy. These feelings were hard to escape and just as hard for my husband to understand.

Unfortunately, my body memories would get in the way and I would confuse Joey's touch with my perpetrators. I was grateful for our first experiences together because they gave me hope that I could be restored to the way I felt when we were first married. At first, Joey and I did not really know how to react to my predicament. As my memories kept coming, I did not want to be touched by anyone, even the one I loved.

At first, I felt guilty for taking away something special that Joey and I once had between us. This guilt lowered my self-esteem because I felt like "damaged goods."

At first, Joey was understanding. We talked a lot about my feelings and his. I often apologized and felt bad. After a while, Joey started taking the rejection personally and asked frequently when I would be over it. Intimate moments that were once so special had become something I dreaded.

I loved Joey, but I did not want physical contact anymore. I got so sensitive, if Joey touched me in a way my father had, I would pull back. Sometimes we got into arguments. I would try to explain. Sometimes he was very understanding, but other times he was just sick of my trial and how it affected our intimacy. I could not stand the pressure.

Every touch by my husband was a reminder of what my father had done to me–a reminder of what my father had violated.

I felt re-victimized. It was not Joey's fault. I know intimacy between a husband and wife is normal and desirable. But what I was going through was not normal. My therapist had informed me intimacy problems were normal. It would pass with time and healing. She said the abuse would not be as magnified as it currently was. She told me to be patient and give myself time. I informed her that I did not mind the time, but my husband did. I wondered if I would ever be in the present with him. I wondered if the past abuse would always be in the present. It seemed the more Joey and I dwelt on this issue, the worse it got.

Not many books were written for husbands to understand what survivors of abuse go through. But arguing and coercing only made the matter worse. Not that Joey coerced me, but I felt obligated. I felt he was being pacified for a moment and I was being re-victimized. He took it personally.

He would constantly say that he did not abuse me, but I could not feel my husband's touch anymore.

It seemed my father still had a hold on me. He would want that. He would want me suffering. I could not understand why my body could not just forget about what my father had done. I mentally knew about it and was mentally dealing with it. But it seemed, in the heat of the trial, everything was magnified. I had not felt this way before, regarding being touched. Even as a child, I would blank it out. It seemed that, for all the times I blanked out what my father had done as a child, they came back tenfold now. My heart was filled with hate towards my father. He had taken something from me and could never give it back–my innocence. Unfortunately, the bitter feelings I had for my father were taken out on Joey. I knew logically Joey hadn't abused me. But I argued with him about what my father had done to me and how the intimate pressures were too much.

I eventually had to examine why a father would abuse his own little girl. I would look at pictures of myself when I was so little and could not believe he was abusing me at such a young age. I had to find the answers to stop being re-victimized by him as an adult. He was not even part of my life anymore. His abuse would continue to have a hold on me if I did not fight to be free of it. I had to make a choice that I was not going to give him power to ruin my relations with my husband.

As I was getting stronger mentally in some areas, I started setting boundaries, even if it meant an argument. I told Joey we could not discuss our intimacy problems for a while. They were too magnified. I still had things to sort out and he was going to have to deal with it. His feelings of rejection would have to be put into the right light. I was not rejecting him, but with each intimate moment he had to understand that I felt re-traumatized. That had to mean something to. him. He would have to give me time. More time. This was not about him, it was about me. Each argument only made me resent being with him even more.

I told him if he loved me like he did the day we were sealed in the temple he would not want me re-traumatized. He would have to respect my space and understand just how important it was for me to be able to say no. I told him as a child I could not say no. But, as a woman, he was not going to take that right away from me. Joey would have to find peace with my boundaries. He responded that he knew this was my problem, but now it was hurting our relationship.

I shared with him that I would not want to do something to him that made him feel violated, or do anything that reminded him of being violated. I expected the same in return. I told him he had to be stronger and respect my fragile state. If being with him made me feel violated, then he was right–our relationship would suffer. We could not continue the way we were addressing our intimacy problems. I could not make these physical feelings go away, but he could have more respect and patience for how I felt physically and emotionally.

At that particular time, I needed space. If he loved me, he would give it to me. It would be difficult in the short term. But I promised to keep working on my issues. In the long run it would pay off.

I also told him how I liked to be touched during this time and what I felt comfortable with. I did not want anything to remind me of my father. This was a time when he would have to pray and be supportive of me.

Sometimes were better than others. But we both decided it would be good to not make it such a big deal anymore. We understood each other. Sometimes we still argued, but over time I noticed he was becoming sensitive again. He took to heart a commitment to try to not re-traumatize me. He did not want to be a part of that or the cause of it. Setting down firm boundaries during this time finally eased our marital tensions.

I was also pregnant for the second time. When I found out we were having a little girl, I was deeply concerned. It is not that I did not want a little girl; it is just that I wanted to protect her from ever being abused and all the hardships I had endured. My fears that I could not protect her were extreme and out of balance. My biggest fear was for her to grow up with all my fears and insecurities.

With this pregnancy, I was determined to not have a c-section. To eliminate all the reasons to have one, I hired a labor coach. She knew I had been abused and was sensitive to the subject. She believed I needed to have a birth with no epidural. She shared that it was symbolic for a person who had been sexually abused to take charge of her body again. I was ready to. I felt I needed to do this to regain my "womanhood." I worked hard at all the homework. I worked hard on trying to not worry so much that I could not protect my little girl.

Nevertheless, my fears of having a girl were overwhelming me. I called my therapist for a "tune-up" to understand my anxiety. This session was different from all the others. She helped me put things into perspective regarding having a little girl. Going back to her one more time was interesting. I could see that I had grown and had made the right decision to quit intense therapy. I also felt she was disappointed with my decision. At the time, it hurt. I wanted her to be happy for me. Looking back, I can now understand her feelings because many victims of abuse do not finish their journey to healing. She and I were making progress, but I needed to be in the present as much as possible. I was still determined to heal, just not at the pace she thought I should.

The morning our little girl was ready to come was amazing. I called my labor coach and told her to come over. Our plan was to stay at the apartment as long as we could. By the time she got there, I was in serious pain. Joey and I had taken a class specifically for having a natural birth, but nothing was working. We finally left for the hospital. I believed that the only way I could be a "real woman" and regain control of my body was to not have an epidural with this birth. However, my main goal was to not have a c-section.

When we got to the hospital, I informed the staff I wanted medicine. The doctors read a note I had previously written to them. They reminded me it said to not give me medication, even if I asked for it. As they were reading my own words, my perspective immediately changed. I had been working for months to overcome my worries about being a mother to a little girl. I thought the only way to regain my womanhood was to have a birth with no medicine. Maybe then I could have a healthy, intimate relationship with my husband. But the physical pain I was experiencing put everything in balance.

First, I vowed to never write another note putting my own comfort at risk. Second, I realized that taking pain medication did not signify my level of womanhood. I was a woman, medicine or not. My goal was to not have a c-section. I did not want any limitations on my body. I did not want to feel damaged anymore. And, well, even if I could not have a normal birth, I needed to make sure it was not because of my past. I was thankful to even be able to have children. And what if I could not? That did not signal my level of womanhood either.

After this quick revelation, I demanded an epidural immediately. I suppose it was my tone of voice that made the doctors set me up quickly. Joey and my labor coach looked worried. My labor coach felt she had failed me because I wanted medicine and the doctor said he felt I needed a c-section. I did not let her response affect me. This wasn't about her. When I informed the doctor I was not going to have one, he was upset with me. He was also about to get off work in less than half of an hour and a new doctor would take over. I knew he just wanted to have a baby on his watch and I told him he would not rush my body. I was dilating at a normal pace. What I really felt was that no man was going to have control over my body anymore. No man was going to intimidate me to do something I did not want to do regarding my body. I would let my body work through this on its own timetable.

After a while, my little girl was in distress. The cord was wrapped around her neck and with every contraction her heart beat faded. I still felt at peace though. I asked the labor coach if there were anything she could do because they were prepping me for a c-section. She started to move me side to side, and with each contraction, my little girl's heart beat did not fade as often.
Much to my surprise, a new doctor came in. The other one left without saying good-bye. That was okay. I could not help his reaction to the boundaries I needed to set. I cannot explain it, but as I looked into the new doctor's eyes, I felt at peace. He asked me why having a natural birth was so important to me. I told him I could not explain to him why, it was personal, but to please help me to have the birth I wanted. I did not want to tell him that having a normal birth was some sort of victory to me–a sense of gaining something

back. It is even hard to explain now. But being a victim of sexual abuse and having the birth I wanted were kind of tied together for me at that time. It meant I did have control over my body and it was not damaged.

The next thing I knew I was ready to push. The doctor told my husband he would only let me give three pushes, then if no success, would rush me for a c-section. I did not know this at the time. Since my first baby had been taken with a c-section and I had only dilated three centimeters, this was, in a sense, my first natural birth. They thought I would have to push for a while. The atmosphere in the room was tense.

Again, Heavenly Father was watching out for me. Although everyone else was tense, I felt at peace. Much to everyone's surprise, our little girl came out in two pushes with her fist and arm coming through first. I likened it to a victory stance–for her and for me. What a miracle! The doctor and nurses were amazed. They asked if I wanted to hold her. At my son's birth, I did not get to hold him right away. With a sigh of relief, I wanted desperately to hold my sweet, little girl. I held her for so long. I remember the nurses trying to rush me. But, I would not let anyone take her from me. I had gone through so much during my pregnancy and birth. I had finally met the little girl for whom I had worked so hard. I had finally met the little girl with whom the Lord had blessed me. This was our time together and I cherished every moment of it.

CHAPTER FIFTEEN

Looking Beyond The Mark

"Wherefore, because of their blindness, which blindness came by looking beyond the mark, they must needs fall; for God hath taken away his plainness from them, and delivered unto them many things which they cannot understand because they desired it. And because they desired it God hath done it, that they may stumble."
(Jacob 4:14)

Adjusting to two children in less than eighteen months, was a handful. I no longer had my therapist and group to support me. I did miss them. Not so much the therapy, but the relationships. I was now on my own. I wanted to adjust to everyday life. I felt I needed to be in the present for a while. My trial had been at the forefront of my married life. I needed to just be myself. I was hoping that I would find some sense of happiness and a different relationship with my Heavenly Father. It seemed my only relationship with Him had been one of absolute dependency. I wanted to be less dependant. I wanted to be strong and able to stand on my own. I believed that, by being less dependant, I would grow more. I thought I would mature as a woman and mother. With this as a conscious thought, I soon found that the Lord would indeed allow me to be on my own.

As I embarked on a new identity, I did a lot of self-introspection. I was able to see another part of my life–my role as a mother. I had two beautiful children and found much happiness in being with them. But my own actions would leave me frustrated with how to parent them. I realized that I had a tendency to be like my father. I found that I had the same lack of patience he would display. I did not know what I was doing as a parent, nor did I have anyone I felt I could ask for advice. I read books on parenting, but it was a lot harder to apply the principles than I realized. The way I was parented was haunting me as a parent myself. I was finding that the actions of my own parents had a great impact on my life. At the time of a frustrating situation, I did not know how to act, so I did what I was taught by their actions. I never hit my children or even had that tendency but I did lack patience.

In addition to parenting, I began to focus on other weaknesses that I had not addressed. I focused on trying to work out and take care of my body. My body image was poor. I wanted to be healthy, but I did not want to be attractive in any way. I did not want anyone looking at me like my father did. I was haunted by his lustful eyes. Just as I would start to feel good about my body image, I would find myself stopping the workouts. Feeling good about me was not something with which I was comfortable. If I looked good, I feared I would get hurt. I was taught in therapy it was not uncommon for victims of abuse to be overweight. The reason is simple. If they look unattractive, maybe the abuse will stop. This was a hard mentality to overcome, even when I was away from my abuser. My body image was already tainted.

A better job offer took our family to a new place of residence. We thought a change of scenery would do us good. We moved to a remote mountain area where the homes were used as vacation retreats. It was a beautiful, scenic place in which to live. It was also a place where I would have to step out of my comfort zone to make new friends, and I had to let some of my walls down. But I found almost immediately that my relationship with the sisters in our new branch would be a struggle.

I was realizing that it took a special person to have compassion on a sister like me who had experienced such hardships in life. It took a caring person to accept me for where I was in life. I had a friend who did that in my last ward–a dear friend who would just listen to me. She had grown up in the church and had a very different childhood from mine. She did not want to fix me or give me advice. She would just listen. She was always there for me. I desired that again. She looked past my faults and pains and accepted me for who I was and where I was in my healing process.

Unfortunately, at this time, I did not realize how uncomfortable other people felt about my story. The fact is I really could not contribute a lot in any relationship. I was in need and when a person is in need, it is hard to give. I knew of others who had similar backgrounds and felt much like I did. It was never my intention to make others uncomfortable. No one seemed to understand my journey. It is such a deep issue and if you have never experienced abuse, it really can be an uncomfortable thing to listen to. No one really understood how memories of my childhood could set me back a few days and that I needed to talk about it. I desired sisterhood but my issues became a barrier to receiving it. I realized it was hard for others to know how to act around me.

In the past, I had been so engrossed in my healing process that I was not really in search of friendships. But now I was. I was starting to feel alone in a crowd of people. The fact that I could not connect with them was heartbreaking. I did not know how to work on my social issue. I would keep trying, in the hope that maybe I would be accepted. But after my visit invitations were consistently rejected, I started turning inward.

I soon realized that no one else wanted to help carry my burdens. They were too deep and uncomfortable for others to deal with. I felt bad for making others feel uncomfortable, and at the same time I was hurt that no one reached out to me. I started falling back into depression. Being alone all day and not socializing sent me back to focusing on me.

I was finding that the superficial person I used to be had become a deeper person. The numbness I experienced regarding my feelings was gone. I became amazed at the depth of my feelings. Life had become incredibly serious. In my therapy group, we all talked about the deepest things within ourselves. Group therapy put me in touch with who I was. I was starting to miss that. They understood me. They accepted me. I was looking for an answer to make the hidden pain go away. My quest for finding out whom I was became very lonely.

Shortly thereafter, we found out we were having another girl. I was so happy. This time I was able to accept the news with peace. All the fears I had with my first girl were gone. I was growing a little. Instead of spending time with friends, I would spend more time with my children. Although I was mildly depressed I did get out more. It was not as debilitating as it had been. I would go hiking with my two little ones and started to bond with them. It was just the three of us until Joey would come home. During this time special family memories were created.

But, with depression lingering I started to slowly get mad at the Lord. I was slowing losing touch with the healing powers of the gospel as doubt crept in. My old beliefs seemed to still be a dominating force in my life and were always there for me to fall back on. It was hard to believe that the abuse made me feel so damaged. My therapist had told me that my parents' abuse had torn me down.

After only being in our new place for eight months, Joey had another job opportunity that would bring us to a more convenient community where people lived closer together. Our new move sparked some interest in growing again. I was a little nervous about meeting new people again. But as I reflect, I am sure in my own weakness, I would not have known how to have a relationship with someone like me. I wondered if my own insecurities had shut them out. I pondered if I was the sole reason I felt unaccepted. Could depression be that isolating and distort my views on relationships? Maybe I thought sisterhood could fill the void I felt. Nevertheless, I would be more aware of my social issues in our new ward.

The next few years I focused on getting settled in our new community. The Lord once again blessed me with a good friend. She set an example for me. She showed me pure charity. I will always be grateful. I would work really hard at this friendship. She kept showing me kindness. After a while, I accepted it and wanted to reciprocate. I did not know how to be a good friend and did not want to mess things up. She did not seem to mind my insecurities. I felt I could tell her anything. I was realizing it takes a rare person to do this. Her friendship made me want to be a better person.

The Lord also blessed me with other special friendships. Some are still friends. Although I tried to work hard at all of them, some would somehow lose touch or drift apart. I was starting to learn that friendships take a lot of effort. At least the good ones do. I was also starting to believe that I *could* connect with people. Not just rare ones filled with charity, but more typical ones.

My deep conversations still scared many away though. I remember a few telling me that my story made them uncomfortable. I was still very serious and always searching for answers to fill the void I felt inside. I found I would end up in deep conversations with people. I found that many women had a hard time expressing themselves, and that as they shared personal stories they later felt uncomfortable that they had verbalized them. Nevertheless, I still did not know how to lighten up my conversations. But I was getting okay with that. I was getting comfortable with the fact that I did have some issues I had to work through. Although I was still plagued with insecurity, I would still reach out. I was trying to break through my fear of rejection. I thought by having everyone like me, my fear of rejection would dissipate.

I tried to be myself, but did not know who exactly that was yet. So I tried to do whatever it would take to make people like me. I learned if the situation came up to keep my story short and to the point–that was all people could handle. I did not wear my issue on my sleeve because I did not want to come across as a victim, even though I still felt like one inside. I did not get offended anymore when someone asked about my family and made a condescending comment in an attempt to end the conversation. I just accepted the fact that they did not know my situation or how to accept my answer. I felt I could finally reach out to others and I was starting to relate to them. For the first time in my life, I was bonding with people in general.

My dear new friend taught me it was okay to just be me. She did not come from an abusive family, but had similar concerns and worries as a parent. She had the same parenting problems which helped me to feel somewhat normal. That was rare. I had always felt something was wrong with me. Now I was learning that I did have the same concerns and problems many families have. She definitely had a gift for friendship. I began to believe that, if she could accept me, maybe others could, as well.

After living there a while, I was called to serve again. But this time it was different. Because I felt so insecure about myself, my callings became my new identity. Instead of focusing on the past I decided to try and find out who I was. I associated my worth with my callings and those who liked me. I was also feeling uneducated and wished I had gotten my law degree. I was contemplating getting a job. Being a mother just was not good enough for me. I did not feel like I was an important person without a degree or a job. *Within insecurity lies the culprit of pride. Pride is bred from insecurity and confuses us as to what really matters and what is really important.* I wanted to be able to describe myself as something more than just a homemaker. Perhaps if I was an important person, maybe the void I felt inside would go away.

I quickly learned that there were other women who felt this same way. They did not verbalize it, but in serving with other sisters I found we were all starving for attention. Although my background was different, we all suffered from wanting to be more than we were. During this time I still had a lot of compassion for those who were seen like me or who were less desirable. As I heard sisters' points of views on these other sisters being "painful" to deal with, it hit me hard. I became defensive and upset that there was not more compassion. As I felt compassion for certain sisters who were struggling, my desire to reach out to them was seen as a nuisance and an act of overstepping my boundaries.

In our first family ward, I was given a calling that I thought was overwhelming for a new member. But I was told my ideas mattered and that we were a team trying to strengthen others' testimonies. I always carried this mentality with me and had good experiences with my callings and the sisters with whom I served. But this situation was different. I was hearing the points of view people had about people who had hard lives or who had sinned or did not live the basics of the church. At first, I just listened and wanted to fit in, but I just could not. I now knew that in some circles, women like me, struggling and lost, were seen as difficult and not worth other sisters' time. This hurt because I did not want to be a "pain" to anyone. I did not want to be a difficult person. My life was just hard and I was dealing with my trial the best I could. I may have been insecure, but their comments about other sisters hit home to me.

It was a time of confusion. I felt I had come so far regarding my trial. I knew I had put it on hold, but something within me changed because of my experiences with these women. For all the courage it took to make the decisions I had regarding my family and therapy, I started to feel shattered inside again. I would slowly start heading into a downward spiral. The treatment of these sisters seemed to open up a vulnerable side of me—my need for acceptance. I was so desperate for people to like me. I started to feel hopeless. My trial was not going away any time soon. Although I did have friends who loved and accepted me at this time, I would put my walls back up and shut almost everyone out. Even the good people in my life.

CHAPTER SIXTEEN

Ye Shall Have Tribulation

"In the world ye shall have tribulation, but be of good cheer; I have overcome the world." (John 16:33)

I found that my abuse issues seeped into all aspects of my life. Sexual abuse not only created my perception that I was flawed and damaged, and caused me to suffer intimacy problems, it affected every part of who I was as a person. It molded weak character and bred insecurity. As day-to-day childhood life was unpredictable because my father raged, I never developed self-discipline. Abuse did not groom me to be a confident woman who felt the love of the Lord; rather, it made me emotionally fragile and scarred by images of being hit, abused and neglected. I was afraid as a child, and realized I was still afraid of nearly everything as an adult. Although I worked hard in therapy, I found most of the time was spent dealing with betrayal, coming out of denial and haunting memories. I learned coping techniques and had passed through major depression. I realized that I never worked on my social anxieties and insecurities. What I found was that part of the old me was still there–it had never matured, never developed. I felt weighted down by all the things I needed to overcome. Everything I had not addressed or tapped into would hang over me.

For the first time since my conversion, I started to make excuses to not go to church. I felt guilty for not wanting to go. I found myself attending meetings only for my children and husband. I did not want to tell Joey my feelings. Being hurt at church and my need for acceptance were causing my testimony to become weaker.

I found my insecurity to be rooted in my past. I had not learned how to resolve conflict with people. The only resolution I knew was to hold a grudge and disparage them to others. Although my natural reaction was to blame myself for deserving bad treatment from others, a part of me was tired of this kind of treatment. My outrage sent me inward. Some people do not seem to care if they hurt others, nor are they capable of taking responsibility for their actions. They rationalize their bad behavior by insisting the other person needs to just "get over it." I know there are those who do not realize when they are hurting others, and would feel badly if they knew. It was the ones who knew they were being inappropriate that added another weight for me to bear. It reminded me of my mother's actions of purposefully trying to hurt me. My thoughts were my worst enemies. I was consumed with thoughts of those who had hurt me. I was trapped, mentally. My whole demeanor changed as depression was seeping back in. I would go through the next few years hurting and searching for an answer. It seemed easier to dwell on how the sisters had hurt me than to focus on how to heal from my past.

It was confusing, but as my father would act inappropriately by hitting, raging or doing something cruel, my mother would make me apologize to my father for making him act that way. I remember defending myself and being confused as my father would blatantly lie to my mother about his part in the argument. He knew I knew the truth, but it was somehow a game to him. He wanted me to know he could get away with anything. Confused by this happening time and time again, I learned to internalize his wrong actions as my fault. Over time, I started to believe I must have done something wrong.

When I was hurt in the church, I did the same thing. I would internalize it as *I* had done something to deserve their cruel words. It would take a long time to realize that no one deserves being treated badly just because another person or a group of people feel like acting that way.

I started to obsess over my behaviors more and more, and became critical of myself. I was once again afraid to even talk to people. I did not want to say the wrong thing, or be put in a situation where I might be noticed or belittled publicly.

I learned that a natural issue of abuse is anxiety. One of the most common manifestations of anxiety is "social phobia." I started to withdraw from day-to-day life and stopped inviting my children's friends over. I did not even know I had done this until years had passed and I was able to reflect back on the situation. But my insecurities were symptoms of a bigger problem—a void in my life.

I went to great lengths to convince my husband that my symptoms were a necessary part of my life. I started to blame him for my unhappiness instead of addressing the real issue—growing from my past.

Another symptom of anxiety is hypochondriacal behavior which I was starting to display. The slightest pain meant something very serious was wrong with me. I came up with the most distorted stories about my health, and even believed them. Everything was exaggerated. I had real physical symptoms for which doctors could not seem to find a cause. I went to chiropractors. Then my medical doctor told me she thought I suffered from stress and that it was related to my unresolved issues.

I later learned that many people who suffer from anxiety or unresolved issues somehow make them manifest in other ways. Medical doctors are unable to diagnose such a problem because it is more mental than physical. A person in pain, mentally, will find any escape from dealing with what he or she really needs to. Vitamins and herbal treatments did not help me either. I was hoping I would be cleansed inside because I never felt clean enough. Many victims are obsessive about washing their hands because they never feel clean. After being addicted to drugs for many years, I sought remedies I thought would help me feel cleansed of them. I believed if that happened, I would feel better at my core. But after many treatments, I still felt bad, and deep inside I still felt tainted and damaged.

People who suffer from depression, overeating, addictions, and health fanatics are all trying to fill a void in their lives. I was no different. I also believed going back to my past and finishing the job would hurt more. No medical doctor could satisfy my need to feel whole, nor could they heal me. I sought medical attention in an attempt to heal my problems anyway.

I went as far as looking into aroma therapy and seeking herbal remedies to heal my pain. I contemplated hypnotherapy and past life regression. As I studied this I realized that I did not need hypnotherapy to help me remember my past. I had enough bad memories. How many more did I need? I did not need to remember anymore in order to heal and it kept me stuck in the past. I realized my strength was not found in how many memories I had, but rather what I did with the ones I did have. In regards to past life regression, it opened doors to so many things contrary to what the gospel teaches. Reincarnation and seeing beyond what we need to see. As I talked with sisters of my same faith who believed in this, I saw sisters trying to find an answer in the wrong place. As I talked with people not of my faith regarding past life regression I felt it did not bring me closer to my Savior, but it took me further from Him and his doctrine. Although I did not have the answers, I knew this was not it. People will search anywhere and listen to anything to fill the void within them. I realized that I could not be healed with any herbal remedy or a doctor's prescription.

The medicine might work in conjunction with a conscious choice to work on my behavioral changes, so that when a crisis hit I would know how to act appropriately. Many take medicine just to numb them and often find they are not any better off at handling stressful situations once off the medication. I saw this time and time again.

If there is one thing I learned about the gospel, it is that people can change. That is what it is all about–taking personal responsibility for my actions and changing them for the better. Although taking personal responsibility was a conscious thought and my goal, it was a long journey to fulfill it.

As if all were not enough, my anxieties not only hurt me, they hurt everyone I loved. It is amazing how our anxieties can make us unknowingly selfish. Because of anxiety, I kept my husband and children from going places and doing things they enjoyed.

Finally, my growth stopped completely. My problems were magnified until they became the center of my family. We all lived around whatever mood I was in just like we did with my father. His selfish impulses and unpredictable moods were the center of my childhood just as my mother's depression was. I was disappointed with myself as a mother and wife. I became more depressed from my present actions than the pain of my past. I needed to change. I needed help. But I felt I was being held captive by my anxieties and pain.

I felt the Spirit withdraw. He could no longer guide me. Occasionally, I felt his presence, but only rarely and slightly. I was left on my own. I did not want to go back to the past and pick up the pieces and heal. I did not really believe I could. If I did not believe healing could occur, why even try? I knew I needed to change, but lacked the faith that I could.

After being plagued with so much anguish, I started to journal. As I wrote, I started to see similarities between my behavior and my parents' behavior. Thinking about it was different than reading about it. I started to get motivated again. I was getting scared that I would leave the same problems for my own children to overcome. They were going to have their share of problems in this life, so why give them my burdens from a life they never lived? Abuse was passed on in my family and I was determined that it would stop with me. Even though I had stopped the sexual abuse, I still had much to overcome as a result of being abused. *I needed to overcome these things, not my children.*

I finally came to a breaking point where I realized that I needed to finish my healing, but did not know where to turn. I bought more books on psychology. Books on how to control my moods, deal with anger, and change who I was. I bought workbooks on how to develop higher self-esteem. Joey told me I was wasting time and money on these books, and that I had a free book to which I could turn. He told me I had gone through the crisis. Now it was time for *spiritual healing*. I told him he did not understand what I was going through. I needed "real" help from people with doctorate degrees. They understood what I was going through. But as I completed their workbooks, I was not changing and was starting to get frustrated. In the end, I was still the same— unhappy, unable to talk with people or go to certain surroundings. I still felt like I was just going through the motions of attending church. At church meetings, the messages did not mean anything to me. I attended in person, but not in spirit.

I was trying to restart the healing process. I did not understand why the books were not working for me and why I had not changed. I had been unhappy for so many years. Enough was enough!

I prayed that Heavenly Father would take away my burdens and leave me alone for a while. I could not hear the still small voice that had powerfully changed my life years before. My anger was stifling the Holy Spirit from penetrating my soul and moving me forward. My actions and mishandling of situations kept me from God. I was mad that His presence was gone from my life.

My past lingered like a project you do not want to do, but know you must. The weight of my trial was always looming over me. I was longing for something wonderful and peaceful, but was unable to obtain it. I was stuck in a state less than desirable, unable to move forward because the future meant going back to the past one more time. I was not ready to face what I needed to do–be healed. It was like reaching for something out of my reach, something always there that was beyond my grasp. I wanted a solution but could never seem to find peace. I needed help, but no stone I turned over gave me the right answer.

Mercifully, Heavenly Father knew just what it would take to ease my burdens. I'm sure He looked down in frustration at my meager attempts to heal and was tired of me looking in all the wrong places. So, He finally decided to intervene and give me a wake up call. Just when I was starting to doubt there really could be an end to all of this, He wisely sent me another trial.

CHAPTER SEVENTEEN

Awakened

"Behold, he changed their hearts; yea, he awakened them out of a deep sleep, and they awoke unto God. Behold, they were in the midst of darkness; nevertheless, their souls were illuminated by the light of the everlasting word."
Alma 5:7

Joey got laid off. We just had our fourth child, another beautiful girl. She was only a few months old, and the fear of having no health insurance scared me. This layoff was the wake up call I needed. Joey had never been laid off before. Amidst this new trial and feeling nervous about the future, I remember holding my newborn at night promising her a better life. Between the anxiety and fear, I was filled with so much love for her. Holding her brought me peace when nothing else would.

Joey's layoff, to me, was a clear indication from Heavenly Father that I needed to heal. It is hard to explain why. I did not hear a voice telling me it was time to move forward. The Holy Spirit is not always audible, but more like a feeling. It was as if the Holy Spirit spoke to my mind. Amidst the layoff, I felt comforted that, if I would start the healing process again, I would finish it this time. I would be led down the right road and not feel alone. A part of me knew there was an answer. There had to be. When I was a new convert so many years before, I believed all answers came from a loving Heavenly Father and knew all pains were eased through Him. It was my conversion to the gospel that kept me close to the Lord once my trial hit. But I seemed so far from that new convert now, who leaned on the Lord those first few years.

I did not want to pick up where I had left off. I did not know how painful it would be this time around. I remembered that, with the Holy Spirit by my side, I was able to do courageous things before. I felt the Lord was saying to me, "Wendy, wake up and free yourself!" My thoughts and actions had bound me for too long. I could not let go of the past. It was as if life had suspended itself for the past few years and hardly any growth had occurred. My memories still hurt and I could remember the actual physical pain I felt when I was betrayed by my family for coming forth with the truth. Those memories were punishing me, and I was letting them. Even though my family and I had not spoken for many years, I was still a victim of their cruelty.

This wake up call put me in a new mindset and gave me some courage to start the process again. I felt a renewed energy to do whatever it would take to overcome and face my fears, no matter how painful it would be. Being unemployed with a big family causes one to have a thicker skin. I needed it. I felt a renewed spirit regarding my sacred duty as a parent. I had to get out of my mind and stop focusing on the things that brought me so much pain.

There were times during my break from therapy when the pain seemed to be eased and I thought I was healed. I felt I did not have to do any more work. I just needed to work on my social skills. But time proved my issues were still unresolved and still affecting my life in a bad way. I could not imagine what it would be like to be free of this trial. I did not really believe there would ever be an end–not really. I thought my pain would always be with me to some extent.

The very next Sunday after Joey was laid off, we went to our bishop. Both Joey and I had decided to repent, to start over and rededicate ourselves to the gospel. Joey took one minute with the bishop and I took a good hour.

I confided that I did not want to come to church because of how I had been treated. I had a testimony but my treatment from others distracted me. I discussed with the bishop my point of view. I did not want to be around those who had hurt me. Clearly, I was a sister insecure and in pain. I found myself defending others who suffered from low self-esteem and explained how we all desired one place we could look forward to coming to each week–church. I shared with the bishop that I was mad at the Lord. I was mad I had no place I could find refuge. He explained it is a shame when sisters do not feel connected with other sisters. He was sad to hear that maybe there were sisters who were not sensitive to how fragile I was at that time.

The general advice given is that if a person it more optimistic and had a positive outlook that person will get along better with people. For those of us who are wounded, we do desire charity and more understanding. It is hard to be optimistic, positive, and outgoing because of how we feel inside and because of what we have experienced. To other people it may seem as if a person suffering from personal pain is taking too long to "get over it." We seem to be judged that we are hanging on to our pain. When a person has had a hard life, freeing ourselves of pain is not an easy journey. There are so many things we need to overcome in order to be free of it. It is not as simple as people perceive. Nor did anyone understand I had already come a long way on my journey. The strides I made on my journey may not have been noticeable to others. My desire to feel more comfortable around people would be a long road to get to. Until then, I needed charity, not judgment.

I also learned that being a victim changed my view of reality. I could not see clearly what others could. I was so full of pain that my anxieties controlled my life. I was a prisoner to my past. I had heard time and time again lessons on pride and how it keeps us from the gospel, how it keeps us from having loving relationships with others. I had also heard how my own hurt could turn into pride if I did not let go and forgive. But I had a hard time forgiving because my hurt had tapped into a part of me that still needed work–my worth.

I was not holding onto grudges because I did not want to let them go. I *did* want to. I did not know how to. I did not know how to forgive. I had never really studied it. There were many times when I tried to go out of my way to be nice to the people who had hurt me to help them feel special. As I worked hard over and over again with certain people, I realized I was the only one who wanted things to change. They were comfortable with their behavior. But being the recipient of it, I was not.

As I met with the bishop, I did repent for not forgiving the sisters. I was so tired of being hurt and yet I still needed to forgive them. I started realizing a connection among others' behavior and my worth. It's hard to explain but after I had repented for still being mad at the sisters, I felt a barrier come down. Although I had not forgiven them yet, I wanted to. I also realized that forgiving them would not change them, but would change me.

This experience set me on a journey in search of my worth. My repentance helped break down the barrier that was holding me back.

I also knew I needed to forgive my family to be free of them. It was liberating to just talk about it to the bishop. It was not that my heart had been changed in an instant, but repentance opened a door that had been closed for a long time. I felt the Holy Spirit again. I told my bishop I wanted to go to therapy or meet with him to get me started back on the right track. I had grown leaps and bounds in the past with the help of others, and had also found that, when left on my own, I had no direction and seemed to get lost.

As I spoke with my husband, he told me I had suffered from being a victim for too long. He counseled me to dig deep and to find the answers that would heal me. He had not seen me do that for so long. He reminded me that I had dealt with my issues at one time. But now I had lost my courage. I had given into the pain instead of fighting it. He had not seen a fighter within me for so long. He reminded me that, when we first started dating, it was my confidence that he found so attractive. Now I had let my life experiences strip me of strength to move forward.

At one time, I had soared with truth and knowledge and a belief that the future could only get better. Now I was beaten down just like the abused little girl of my childhood. He told me it was time to soar again to even greater heights. He reminded me that, when I first started dealing with my issues, a very noble and courageous part of me came out. He bore his testimony that I could only find solace in the teachings of the gospel.

Joey was always so insightful and spiritually prepared as a leader in the home. He told me that overcoming my "victim mentality" would be hard since I attached my worth to it. I was like a leaf at the mercy of the wind, landing wherever the wind would take me. It was time to get grounded and stand firm. He shared that the shame I felt was the reason I felt flawed. Feeling flawed had nothing to do with people hurting me. Their actions would just bring me back to this state. Because my self-definition was poor, it would take me longer to get over things because a part of me felt worthy of being treated horribly. He told me that, as I worked on my shame and worth issues, my perception of who I was would change.

By this time, Joey had written a program called "Worthy to Win." It is a program designed for athletes to overcome their anxieties and to dig deep into that part of them that is holding them back from performing at their full potential. He recognized my shame and worth were holding me back from my full potential. Joey also reminded me that, not too long ago, I believed I could be healed. I just had to tap into that part of me again. We discussed at length having a victim mentality. But, not in the way most people think of it. Most people think a person who has this mentality, purposefully wants attention and wants others to feel sorry for her. Perhaps there are those who deviously have the "poor me" mentality and take advantage of others. Nevertheless, that was not my goal. I did not want to take advantage of others. Just as those grounded in the gospel have it to fall back on, those who have been abused have their abuse to fall back on. Abuse becomes so engrained in our thought process it is truly a hard state to change.

As for the sisters who consciously have a "poor me" mentality and take advantage of others, I learned to have compassion on them also. I understood what it was like to grow up a victim and did not know any other way to view life. I was not a victim on purpose and I believe they are not either. Abuse affects our character. Some are not raised in a home where they view character to be sacred.

I do feel strongly that people who are offensive need to be more careful about offending and walking over others. Their very actions can bring people in my situation to a fragile state and set us back for a time. Deliberate put downs are abusive and not reflective of the ones they are hurting, but rather reflective of the ones doing the hurting.

Joey helped me understand that I had to stop being a victim. Many people had treated me badly, but I could not let that stop my healing any longer. I had been conditioned to accept abuse from my family and it trickled down in all my relationships and interactions with other people. Although Joey admired my so-called confidence and determination when we were dating, it was all a facade then, an exterior shield to not get hurt. Now I would have to find *real* strength and courage to deal with my issues.

I decided to start my final healing journey. I was not going to give up, no matter how hard it was until I was free. Instead of describing myself as a victim of sexual abuse, I replaced the word "victim" with *survivor*. I had survived! My parents could not change that. *Changing from a victim to a survivor required conscious thought on my part.* The effects of my childhood abuse would not stop even if my parents decided to change. The effects would only stop when I decided to stop being a victim. I had to take responsibility for my own feelings and actions. Although I knew where I learned my behaviors, dwelling on that history would not change my behavior or enable me to hold myself accountable for my actions. I now realized that I had to take responsibility for my own actions, no matter where I was in life. I had to hold myself accountable for how I treated my own family and other people, regardless of my background.

I did not come into this world depressed and rageful. I was not born feeling like damaged goods. I was not born with body memories or an inability to connect with people. I came into this world with tremendous potential and worth. I came into this world a daughter of God. My parents had taught me I was worthless–only an object of abuse. Enduring all the abuse made me forget just who I was. So here was my new quest–I had to remember the time when I joined the church and gave my life over to Jesus Christ. I had to remember that the Holy Spirit can penetrate the most depraved souls and change them for the better. I had been one of those souls and He saved me. Even though I had a lot of pain, so many blessings had occurred in my life because of Him! My life could have been so much worse, but a loving Heavenly Father placed certain events in my life and the Holy Spirit pierced my lost soul and brought me unto the Savior. I had to try to remember this. I had to try to remember the courage into which I was capable of tapping.

I had to take responsibility as an adult for my life just as I was. Feelings of being flawed and all. No one was going to make me feel any different. Only *I* controlled that. I had to understand why I felt like damaged goods. The core of it was that my identity had been completely marred by the abuse I survived. We all have an eternal identity that defines us on an eternal scale. I am a daughter of God and I am a part of a divine heritage, which means I have the potential to become like Him. That is my eternal character and identity. My quest was to not only hear these words, but to believe them and gain a testimony of them.

I finally knew there was not a pill or a store-bought item that was going to heal me. My anger was not going to heal me. I had used anger as a tool to keep people out, even Heavenly Father. I needed to start a spiritual quest. I needed to believe I would be made whole and that no scars would be left behind.

I decided to start with my unresolved issues of the sexual abuse. I hoped that, if I started with the biggest thing, perhaps a lot of the other issues would dissipate or not be as intense. I decided to rededicate myself to the gospel. I fasted and prayed and studied the scriptures for answers. To my amazement, the answers to my pain were right in front of me the whole time! I was reading from it night after night, but not allowing its power to work in my life. I had been lost for so long. Although I had the gospel in my life, its power could not change my life until I let it.

My bishop decided he would meet with me first. Although I looked forward to meeting with him to tackle my issues, I feared he would not understand–not to the level I needed. He spoke mostly of gaining a testimony of the gospel again. Becoming reconverted. How wise he was! He set me up on a reading program and gave me books to read on forgiveness. He did not know a lot about sexual abuse, but he did know where I could go to be healed.

I started meeting with him until my issues started getting really deep. I was feeling vulnerable. Although I trusted him, my issues were getting complex. I was feeling insecure again, so uncomfortable with myself. I was starting to hurt and feel pain again, and I did not like it. I was afraid that I might get depressed like I had so many years before, that I would wind up flat on my back on the couch, unable to move or cope with life. I was afraid I would not be there for my children. I constantly prayed for courage, strength and energy. I prayed for the Holy Spirit to be my constant companion.

Many people I have known who had gone to their bishops for help found them to push forgiveness and counsel to just "get over it" and move on with their life. Those not trained professionally to help a person in a crisis often lack the compassion needed. Many bishops, and people in general for that matter, do not really understand how to help someone who has been molested by a family member, whether once or repeatedly. Sexual abuse is a wound so deep that, unless you have experienced it, you cannot understand the inner turmoil a victim goes through. It is hard for people to understand just what has been taken from us. And without understanding, an untrained leader can send a person further from the gospel.

If a person has been robbed of her innocence, it is hard for others to have the compassion needed to help her. On the other hand, if you have experienced something another person has, it is easy to understand what she is going through. When a bishop has not experienced extreme abuse, he needs to rely solely on the inspiration of the Holy Spirit. Spiritual advice should be given to victims of abuse so they know where to turn for spiritual solace. A leader telling a victim to "get over it" or that "it was your fault to some extent" is not being led by the Holy Spirit. He does not know how to deal with the situation appropriately. Most victims are not coming to such leaders to stop the pain, but rather want information they can read to ponder the answers for themselves. Advice on abuse itself should be left for those professionally trained.

How grateful I was for a bishop who did not pretend to know all about my issues. He did, however, know where I could find the answers, in the gospel. I gained a great respect for this man, a bishop who did not want all the glory of my healing. When he felt he had done all he could for me, he sent me to someone else to help me with my deeper issues. He wisely referred me to an LDS therapist.

I finally met with this LDS therapist–a man. Although I had felt I had not grown much over the last few years, meeting with him changed this perspective. Men did not intimidate me anymore. I did not realize this until my first session with him. I did not need to describe in detail the abuse like I needed to in my first round of therapy. Just talking about the abuse was a big deal to me at first. But this time, I was not nearly as afraid. It did not seem to hurt so badly. I felt good about seeing him and was comfortable with him. I told him a short version of my life, asked him where I should start and how I could heal.

I wanted to start where I had stopped years before. I wanted all my memories back, even though the books I had read said a person may not remember everything when serious trauma like sexual abuse has occurred; especially, if the person has had out of body experiences or shut her eyes during the whole ordeal, which I did. When I was young, there were times when I would just stare at a toy and fixate on it to drown out the abuse while it was occurring. I felt I could break through and remember everything. But my parents' abuse had stolen many of my memories–permanently. I did not even remember birthdays or holidays, even though I wanted to.

My new therapist told me that Heavenly Father was protecting me. Did not I understand that? Not remembering was a protection for me, not my family. Then he asked how many memories I needed, to go on with my life. He said he believed I was using this as an excuse to not heal. He told me I would never recover all of my memories and that I was avoiding the real issue. It was not about recapturing all my memories, it was about healing from the ones I did have. He said there comes a time to look into the past and a time to let go of the past. The reality was that I was afraid to look to the future.

I was afraid to deal with the issues that were holding me back. I had so many! My lack of faith kept me from opening that door for so long. Only the recognition of my personal responsibility to my family allowed me to open that door. I could not do it for myself at first, but I could do it for them!

I know many therapists do not believe in going back to the past to heal. They believe a victim of abuse should just pick up where she is and move on. They believe and teach that the past does not hold any value in the present. But I believe the past is a springboard to healing. It enables us to not repeat bad traditions. Looking at the past helped me break through so much. Had I ignored the past, I never would have traced the root cause of my anxieties and problems. If I had just "let the past be the past," I would still be tied to my abusive family. Going back and remembering my parents' actions made me want to break through and be a better person. Looking to the past helped me move towards a healthy future.

If I carried on a relationship with my parents, my children would either be abused or suffer from covert sexual abuse. I could never explain to them that, although my father had molested me as a child, I still had a relationship with him. It would put them at risk and confuse them to imply it was okay to have a relationship with a man who had molested an innocent child. Dealing with the past was key in my healing.

Now, it was time to move forward. I had visited the past and confronted a lot. Now I had to start moving towards the future. Remembering all I could at this point was enough to move forward.
At my next meeting, I told my therapist my decision. I wanted to move forward but I did not know how. The future was hard to see. I asked him boldly if he really believed I could truly heal from sexual abuse and all the other abuse I had survived. Could all the shame I still carried with me and the feelings of worthlessness really ever leave? I wanted to know if forgiveness could really occur because, if I were going to go down that road, I wanted to experience true forgiveness. I did not want to just "let go" or "get over it."

I had met many people who testified they had forgiven, only to hear anger and hurt in the tone of their voices. They would share how mad they still were, but testified that they were healed. I never believed them. Not because I struggled with my own answer to all of this, but because I could still see the hurt in their eyes. When I asked how they forgave, they would say they just gave it over to Jesus Christ. It seemed simple enough. But why did they still seem to suffer so? I did not want to hurt anymore. It was hard for me to believe that, if I really gave my pain over to Jesus Christ, I would still be hurting–even a little. I wanted to experience the miracle of real forgiveness. I wanted to be rid of this issue once and for all.

I had also seen people on television saying that abuse will always be a part of a victim. The pain never really goes away. Not really. Forgiveness is not really obtainable with severe abuse. I would get discouraged when I heard this message. Why should I work so hard towards healing if it really could not occur? I believed this message for so long, not understanding the power of the gospel. I did not know anyone personally who had overcome sexual abuse and lived a fulfilling life. I knew many who were hurting just like I was. Some told me they had moved on, but believed the scars would always be with them. I had read a few stories of some who had successfully healed and forgiven. How I wished there were more stories out there of women and sisters in the gospel who had overcome abuse! I wanted to hear of their stories, their struggles and their journey. I longed for a fulfilling life and knew that, in order for me to achieve it, I had to have faith that the gospel could make me whole.

At my third and final meeting, I asked my therapist if he had any books he could recommend to help me. He told me I did not need any more books because I knew what they said and, quite frankly, I already had many of them. He told me my answers did not lie in more psychology books. They could

245

only take me so far. I knew this to be true. I had not read a single book on psychology that had opened the doors to forgiveness.

During my last session, my therapist reached over towards his side table and picked up the scriptures. He held them in the air and testified to me that all of my answers to healing lay within these sacred writings. He said it was time I healed and forgave my family, and that my answers were contained within the scriptures. He explained that I had been through therapy to help me cope with life. Now I would be leaning on the gospel to find my answers to healing and forgiveness.

The presence of the Holy Spirit was strong. I remember having tears in my eyes. Finally, after all these years, there was that feeling I had so many years before. That feeling I was doing something right, as when I decided to join the church, get sealed to Joey for time and all eternity, have my children and break away from my family. The Holy Spirit was back in my life! I knew I was on the right path.

I felt I needed to continue with therapy. It was true I had done a lot of work, but always with the help of a therapist. I did not feel I could do it alone. But I was quickly reminded by Joey that I was not in a crisis like so many years before, when acknowledging my sexual abuse and my mother's lies devastated me. I needed professional help at that time and the Lord provided a way for me to find a person who specialized in women's issues and sexual abuse. I needed help and guidance then. But now my new therapist felt the void I was seeking to fill could only be satisfied through the gospel. He told me I could be whole again, but I would have to let God in. I would have to stop being angry at the Lord.

After much pondering, praying and talking with my husband, it was clear that I needed more help and guidance. But not like I had before. It was true I had been led to a great therapist years before, but I was in a different mindset then. I was also led to my bishop at this phase of my life. He testified that answers to healing were found in the gospel. The LDS therapist felt he could not help me because my journey would now be spiritual. After having a heart-to-heart talk with Joey, he told me no one could help me but Heavenly Father. At first, I was afraid and did not believe I could do it without additional help besides Heavenly Father. I had not given the Lord the credit I should have. He had, after all, led me to the right people before.

Now I was to go on a journey of healing with just Him. I did not trust myself to stay on the right track. I felt I needed serious spiritual intervention to really understand His gospel and His role in my life. But I knew I would have to apply His teachings and *get started* even though I felt inadequate. So I set off on a new journey, a soul searching journey, with just the Lord to accompany and comfort me.

There was so much work I needed to do. I needed to work on my anxieties and confront them. There were many. I needed to gain a stronger testimony of the gospel. I needed to learn to forgive and become whole as Heavenly Father would want me to.

I needed a new foundation in my life. Although I was a convert, at one time I had a very strong foundation–but hatred and bitterness slowly ate away at my strength, and I eventually found that I had no foundation on which to build. Now, only in the scriptures could I find that firm foundation. For too long, I hadn't had the Holy Spirit with me to make what I read, touch my heart. Now I would have to draw strength from within myself with the help of the Holy Spirit. I could not draw it from other people. I would have to learn to have faith in the healing powers of the Lord.

247

CHAPTER EIGHTEEN

Seek Him

"Blessed are they that keep his testimonies, and that seek him with the whole heart." (Psalms 119:2)

To pick up the pieces again and start my final journey would be difficult. I still remembered just how hard I had to work before. It was all consuming. I had to cling to the hope that Jesus Christ had the power to heal me. I was afraid of what the journey would entail. A part of me did not really believe I could ever feel whole.

I began to study the scriptures in earnest. Many stories brought me comfort. I became especially familiar with the story recorded in Mark 5:25-34 and in Matthew 9:20-22. It is the account of a woman who had suffered from a blood illness for 12 years. After seeing physicians and spending all the money she had to be healed, she was desperate. Instead of being healed, she "grew worse." I felt much like this woman. I had searched all over for answers to heal my pain. Because I could not find an answer, I felt I had "grown worse." Being aware of my issues but not healing from them put me in a state of suspension. I could not move forward. No amount of searching made me feel whole. I had become a victim to my issues and in doing so was lonely and bitter. I shut the world out because the world had only brought me pain.

The woman, realizing nothing of men or the world could heal her, turned to faith in a greater power. She did not give up hope that an answer would come. That is why she kept searching. She had so much faith that she vowed, "If I may touch but his clothes, I shall be whole." Jesus felt "virtue" leave Him. Looking for the one who touched him, He turned to the "certain woman" and said to her, "Daughter, thy faith hath made thee whole; go in peace, and be whole of thy plague." "And the woman was made whole from that hour." I find it interesting that she never verbally told Him what was the matter with her and she never told him it was she who had touched him. But He knew her and He knew from what she was suffering and He healed her because of His love and because of her faith.

How I longed to hear those words–"Daughter, thy faith hath made thee whole." *She never had to worry about her problem again.* She was free of her burden and trial. If He could heal her and make her whole from a physical ailment, surely He could heal my emotional wounds! I pondered how I could ever develop that type of faith. How could I ever really believe I could be made whole? And if I could believe, how much longer would it take? Through my experiences with the gospel, I knew that things spiritual in nature came gradually.

I had a new mission and a determination I had not felt since I first started dealing with my issues. As I pondered my history of this trial, I realized I was still hurt, but not devastated. I had already faced the worst. I was looking to heal this time. I might feel some pain, but could it really be as bad as it was before? I knew it would be impossible to go through the healing process without some sort of pain, and made a commitment to move forward regardless.

My first step was to gain a testimony of Jesus Christ in my life again. He was not gone completely, just enough to keep me from becoming the person I knew He wanted me to become. I used a study guide for the scriptures and read diligently every single night. I had read every night before, but only a verse that was quickly forgotten. Now I had repented and opened a door I had shut long ago. My testimony would be the only anchor I would have as I started on my journey again, as I began my journey of faith.

As I started to gain a stronger testimony, I needed to work on my prayers and decided to keep a new journal. I called it my healing journal. I would pray for something whole heartedly one night, only to forget it the next night. In my new journal, I wrote down what I knew I needed to change and work on.

As I prayed for a better understanding and testimony of the gospel, I also prayed that my deep-seated bitterness would leave and be replaced with peace, and that my anger would be replaced with charity. As I focused on forgiving my parents, the thought that I needed to forgive everyone who had ever hurt me kept coming to mind. I noticed that my prayers on forgiveness were hard, but I was willing to change my thinking at this point. I was also willing to be directed towards the answers He would want me to read. I saw myself being humbled right before my very eyes, all on paper in my journal.

Between my prayers and reading the scriptures, I had not spent more daily time on the gospel. I felt protected. I started to feel strong inside. I started to feel like a new convert again.

With the Holy Spirit guiding me, I was able to take an honest look at myself and do some serious reflection. I had some important questions for Heavenly Father and did everything I could to find the answers. Notions such as "I am flawed" and "I deserve bad things to happen to me" were common, everyday thoughts.
I started to verbally acknowledge my anger towards the Lord. During my reflections, I realized I had been mad at Heavenly Father for quite some time. Before I joined the church, I just thought life was hard and confusing. Then,

when I joined the church, so much happened in a small amount of time that clinging to the gospel seemed the only way I could hang on to life. But as time went on, I started wondering, "If there is a God, why does He allow for so much tragedy to happen in the world?" Sexual abuse has become so common place in the home! There are so many wounded in the world–too many from the time of their infancy and innocence. It seemed unfair to me to not give those who had been abused from infancy a better chance in life. Growing up scared, terrorized and beaten down is a hard thing to overcome. Many become so hardened because of their own hardships that they become abusers themselves.

I had to find a personal answer as to why the Lord allowed me to be abused. This question haunted me day in and day out. Why did I have to endure the childhood I did? I was so tired of it affecting my adult life! I had missed out on so much happiness and friendships because I was "messed up."

A few sisters had shared with me a common belief amongst those who have been abused–Heavenly Father appointed the trial to occur. In other words, the perpetrator was chosen and it was predetermined that the abuse would take place. These sisters made their quest in life finding out why they were chosen to be abused. They believed they could not have had a different life because it was their predestined lot to suffer abuse. This belief kept them from gaining a strong testimony of the gospel. If Heavenly Father had predestined them to experience the tragedy of sexual abuse, why should they trust in a religion that claimed to be able to heal them? It was hard for me to believe that Heavenly Father would instigate abusive behavior towards anyone. I was mad at Him for letting so many bad things happen in my life, yet it was hard for me to believe that He would appoint someone to abuse an innocent child. If we are made after His likeness, would not

He understand the effects of abuse on us? Would He not be as outraged by abusive behavior as I was?

I could not believe He was behind the actions of these perpetrators. I could not believe that Heavenly Father would appoint a parent to treat his children so shamefully. I could not believe that, when my father would rage uncontrollably or be physically violent with me, the Lord was the inspiration behind his actions. I also could not believe that the spirit of the Lord was with my mother for lying and betraying me.

I could only find one source who could be the instigator of my father's and mother's abusive actions towards me–Satan. I could imagine him leading my father into believing that no one would ever find out about what he did within the walls of his own home. I could imagine him encouraging my father to believe it was okay to let unbridled passions take over his life and to indulge in the indecency of violating his own children. Satan–the source of all evil. The evil one behind anguish, rage, worthlessness and abuse.

I could not believe that Heavenly Father predestined my father to abuse me. I had been taught that we are all sons and daughters of Heavenly Father with great potential here on earth. Not to do evil, but good. As I was studying and pondering for answers, it became hard to believe that, if I was a daughter of God, He would predestine me to a life of abuse and feelings of fear, worthlessness and insecurity. Since I did not believe my father was predestined to commit these acts against me, I would have to find out why he was allowed to do these things and why Heavenly Father did not intervene.

I looked for my answers in the scriptures and in words of modern church leaders. I fasted and prayed. It seemed each time I fasted my spirituality deepened a little. My heart also softened. With the Lord's help, I was preparing myself spiritually to accept the answers that would come. Then, as if it were a revelation, I remembered that, when I joined the church all those years before, a person shared with me that I would be accountable for my actions no matter what I had been through. I did not know why this thought came up then. I just know it would not leave. I knew we are all accountable for our actions towards others. Still, it did not explain why Heavenly Father would allow abuse to happen. But it led me on a quest to understand personal accountability.

As I read counsel by leaders of the church, I found them reprimanding those who abuse their family. They said abuse is not in accordance with the Lord's will. There were many talks on abuse that I studied. Never once did the leaders give way or leniency towards priesthood holders, or anyone for that matter, who abused their children or spouse.

I needed to understand my father's actions. My father grew up in a Catholic orphanage. The news is replete these days with examples of child abuse by Catholic clergy and leaders. My father had been abused as a child by his Catholic caretakers. I found it hard to understand how someone could be a representative of the Lord and abuse children. I now understood why my father was a professed atheist. He did not have anything good to say about the Catholic Church. Now, I was understanding why. But as an adult, he became just as hardened as the leaders who abused him. Just as those leaders felt they were accountable to no one, so my father followed in their footsteps. Yet my father is still a son of God, free to act according his own will. Free to choose good from evil.

I started to learn more about free agency. Understanding free agency is a cornerstone of the gospel. Without it, I would be doomed to a life of misery, predestined to feel unclean and worthless. Predestined to be a victim during my whole experience here on earth. How could I look to a Savior if I was already doomed to be a victim? Free agency was the key to breaking away from my father's evil actions. I had the free agency to find those answers that would make me whole. I could find the answers to healing in my Savior's teachings.

As I continued to study, I learned that my scars from the abuse "need only be temporary." If I made a choice to not be a victim, the Lord would rush to my aid and, in His timetable, heal me. Just as my father had a choice to be a man of integrity, I had a choice to draw on the powers of Heaven to be healed and made whole.

I began to realize that the Lord created the eternal law of free agency so I could choose to heal or not and my father could choose to abuse or not. Heavenly Father did not predestine my father to be an abuser. If we were all spirit children of Heavenly Father before we came to earth, then we are still His children now. Understanding the plan of salvation helped me to heal by leaps and bounds. I stopped putting my father in a different category than being a child of God. I had thought he was created to be evil. I had thought he was just born wrong, like I had been. I stopped blaming Heavenly Father for putting him in my life. I realized my father was a son of God, created by the Master Himself. As stated in Matthew 5:44, "For he maketh his sun rise on the evil and on the good, and sendeth rain on the just and on the unjust."

My father's innocence had been violated as a little boy, and he seemed to blame Heavenly Father because it happened by people who were leaders in a church. His abuse was continued by his own family after he was brought home from the orphanage. But, as an adult with children of his own, he still had a choice. I know he was never taught how to be a good father or a man of integrity. He was groomed to be an abuser. But an adult who was horribly abused when he was a child still knows that molesting a child is wrong.

The violation of a young, innocent child is a premeditated, *secret* act. It does not matter what the person has been through. The *secrecy* of the act is an admission of a conscious choice to violate. It takes conscious effort to plan a time to violate the innocent. It takes a conscious choice for the abuser to continue to violate when the innocent pleads for him to stop. It is usually because of these pleadings that great threats occur to the child. Scaring her to the point of believing that, if she does not do what the abuser demands, she will be removed from the home or the abuser will kill someone close to her, even her pet. It takes conscious effort to threaten the innocent so the abuse can continue.

My father's lack of faith in any church led him to believe that pornography was okay. His world had told him that the out of control actions he saw in his abusers were okay to mimic as an adult. *He learned that unrighteous coercion is acceptable if no one external finds out.* No wonder he believed that infidelity was expected in a marriage. But I could not accept his ways. Many men have been sexually abused themselves and have never harmed an innocent child. Why didn't my father become one of those men?

There were times when I could remember my father in deep regret for some of his actions. During those times, he was best conditioned to choose to stop his behavior. But instead of nurturing his remorse, he would quickly squelch his conscience. Because of those memories, I realized my father really did know what he was doing–always choosing to be weak and give way to unrighteous actions. Nevertheless, his unbridled, indecent passions for his own children are heinous sins for which he will be accountable to the Lord.

I realized that Heavenly Father's law of free agency gives all His sons and daughters the opportunity to choose right from wrong, to know the bitter from the sweet. I realized that we are to be tested in this life. *Adversity is meant to test us to see if we can find our way back to the Lord.* Although it seems unfair for a child to be molested by her father, that child can choose to break the chain of abuse and experience complete healing through Christ, and her eternal reward will be great for doing so!

As I studied free agency I learned that opposites exist in the great plan of salvation so that we may know the good from the bad. In the second chapter of 2 Nephi, I found many great understandings when I was spiritually prepared to comprehend them. In verse two, Lehi states, "He shall consecrate thy afflictions for thy gain." This sentence gave me hope that something good would come from my trial. I had been abused, but I could choose to be a victim my whole life or put the gospel to the test and heal. Healing would open a new door to a fulfilling life. Lehi goes on to say in verse 13, "And if ye shall say there is no law, ye shall also say there is no sin, if ye shall say there is no sin, ye shall also say there is no righteousness. And if there be no righteousness there be no happiness. And if there be no righteousness nor happiness there be no punishment nor misery. And if these things are not there is no God." This verse made me realize that there are eternal laws to which we are all accountable. They are eternal in nature.

I realized that the effects of my father could be overcome by living the commandments. This truth seemed to confirm why the only time I ever really felt happiness was when I was living as righteously as I could and trying hard to live the commandments and stay close to the Lord. I had suffered too long in misery blaming the Lord for my trial–distancing myself from Him. Not understanding that His laws go above the laws of the land. He not only is my creator, but the creator of eternal laws that helped me understand that my father would be held accountable to the Lord.

In verse 16, Lehi states, "Wherefore, the Lord God gave unto man that he should act for himself. Wherefore, man could not act for himself save it should be that he was enticed by the one or the other." Lehi shared that the devil was an angel of God who had fallen from heaven and sought the misery of all mankind. Men are free to act and choose for themselves, whether good or bad. This verse explained to me that Heavenly Father was not behind the actions of my father, nor was my father predestined to abuse me. Believing my father's abusive actions as predestined would put the blame on Heavenly Father, not my father. The truth is my father was free to choose just like anyone else was. He was not different from anyone else. Rather, eternal law states he is free to act in accordance to his own conscience and will. I could no longer ask why Heavenly Father let this happen because I understood the eternal law of free agency. Now I had to choose if I was going to continue to be a victim of the abuse and let it eat away at me, or cling to the gospel and put it to the test to help me to heal and forgive.

Of course my parents' behavior was an outrage, but holding on to the hate was destroying me. My hate was not holding them accountable, it was hurting me. I understood that being outraged was normal. Of course. But I had not been able to let go. It was time to make a conscious decision to let go. I had to trust where letting go would take me.

Before this crucial decision, my anger had turned into bitterness, binding me from growth, turning me inward, and making me associate pain with the gospel. My bitterness took me to the very gates of hell–believing there could be no end to my trial. This way of thinking took me further and further away from Heavenly Father.

It was time for me to let go of my past. Holding onto it did *more* damage to me. It was time to stop the hate. My parents' resentment towards me for telling the truth was something they were going to have to work through. My hatred towards them for the abuse was something I was going to have to work through.

My rededication to the gospel broke down barriers one after another. The shadow of doom that had become a part of me gradually vanished as hope and gratitude for wisdom in the Lord's plan emerged. I started believing that I could be healed. One day I would feel whole and free of this burden. My hope became a stabilizing compass to find healing. My determination seemed to come back with more vigor than when I first started. I had learned so much by now. Holding my father accountable for his actions freed up my anger towards Heavenly Father and opened a door in my heart that led to a belief He could heal me. I was realizing that Heavenly Father was going to help me. He was the only way to healing. I felt another journey coming my way. A journey to forgiveness.

CHAPTER NINETEEN

In the Strength of the Lord

*"I know, in the strength of the Lord thou canst
do all things." Alma 20:4*

In the past, my faith and hope seemed to dangle by a single
thread. As I grew stronger in the gospel, I realized that,
although I was experiencing a fragile hope, it was still hope.
A part of me knew without a doubt that I could accomplish
what I needed to. But it was just a still small voice. My anger
would easily overpower it. I was realizing my bitterness had
a lot to do with keeping me from my answers. It was a
dominating voice that had guided me to make wrong choices
in my life. How could I find peace with so much anger? The
reality was simple—I could not. I could not find peace with so
much hate inside of me. I needed to let the full impact of the
gospel into my life. I found that my inconsistencies were my
enemies, not my past. My lack of constancy in the gospel
brought me unneeded heart break. It prolonged my healing.

I truly wanted to forgive, but that did not mean that it was
going to happen overnight. I knew I was never going to get
rid of my memories. I could not erase what really happened
or what each member of my family had done to me.

As I thought and prayed about forgiving my family and all
those who had hurt me, I realized that I needed to focus on
my family first. There was my biggest wound. It was hard to
forget that, because of them, I had been stripped of all self-
esteem. I had carried a lot of shame with me day in and day
out. I had been plagued with negative self-talk. I had always
come back to that way of thinking. There was not a
psychology book anywhere that could help me overcome my

negative outlook on life. It would have to come from within. I would have to experience a change of heart towards my family.

It was hard to imagine telling my mother that I forgave her. It was hard to forgive her for knowing about the abuse and doing nothing. Her actions towards me after coming forth with the truth were deliberately cruel. Her behavior was even more confusing to understand as I became a mother myself. I felt great love and a strong desire to protect my children. I understood all too well that abuse could confuse my outlook on life, but it did not confuse the fact that, as a mother, I had a responsibility to my children.

Quite frankly, I love being a mother. It naturally puts me in a selfless role. I was not held as a child, but it seems so natural to hold my children and nurture them. My trial could not take this away from me. At times, it seemed harder to forgive my mother than my father because of her coldness and her deliberate attempts to cover up the family secret. I guess I had never really known just how much she lacked integrity. She just could not do the right thing.

I was concerned that forgiveness would make me vulnerable to her. I promised never to be hurt by her again. When I would dwell on the things she had done, anger would set in. My anger would tell me I had a right to be mad at her. I was also mad at her for joining a church and pretending she had a good life. It seemed there was no stopping her in how far she would go to cover up. It seemed impossible to forgive her. My journey to healing was hard enough, but I felt unnecessary heartache because of her lack of self-responsibility.

Envisioning forgiving my father was different altogether. I could not imagine being close to him again and having him look at me and violating me with just his look. I still felt vulnerable whenever I thought of him. I could still hear the noises he made when he was molesting me. How could I ever forgive a man who would rape his own child night after night? So cold and without feeling! His unrighteous passions were more important than my pleadings to stop. I was at the mercy of his strength and his cruel disregard for his own child. It was as if I was not even a person to him. He treated me like a thing with no feelings. He took advantage of the fact that, as a man, he was stronger than I and would do whatever he desired, whenever he desired. How could I ever forgive him? I knew I could not do it on my own.

I started to read everything I could on forgiveness. I read church magazines, talks by the leaders and books written on the subject. I watched church videos and would attend the temple. I prayed intently, sharing with the Lord that forgiving was even harder than dealing with my issues because it required of me something I did not think I could do. My healing so far had only been about me. When I went to therapy, we talked only about my issues and how to get my life back in order. We talked about what my parents did, of course, but we also talked about how to handle what they had done. The sting did not seem so bad until I had to forgive their actions. It meant that I would have to stop hating them.

To most people, I'm certain that hate seems a normal reaction to extreme cases of abuse. Most would think it perfectly acceptable to be angry. *And, there is a time and place for it. But hate has a way of not letting a person forget what happened.* My hate had kept me suspended in the past.

I continued to read, fast and pray. As I read the scriptures, I was touched, but never enough to fill the void. I was getting to the point that I would rather go back to therapy and uncover more memories than move forward with forgiveness. What I did not realize was that, with each article

I read on the subject of forgiveness, I was growing, even if it seemed slow. I was spiritually breaking down the barriers holding me back. Barriers that wanted to hold onto the hate and continue the bitterness. Each time I was touched by an article, a song or a talk, my heart was softened. It was hard, but I kept moving forward. I had to put the gospel to the test. I learned that, with forgiveness, I needed to be spiritually grounded and strong.

I started attending the temple more regularly. I came away with great insights, only to be disappointed that I still had hate in my heart. After all this time, I was finally ready to forgive, but it was so elusive! Although I *wanted* to forgive, I was not convinced that I should and that it was obtainable. How could I ever really be at peace with my trial?

I still believed I was damaged because of my parents' actions. If I still felt worthless, how could I forgive them? I was still affected by their abuse. To forgive, my whole outlook on dealing with them would have to change. I did not know if I were capable of that change. Hating them had become a way of life. I had always carried a big load and could not imagine life without it.

What would life be like free of this burden? I had always been the neglected, abused little girl. It was hard for me to imagine describing myself as healed and whole. It was hard to imagine describing myself as a survivor and a woman who actually had something to offer this world. Perhaps my journey to forgiveness was long because there were so many things I had to change about myself. Changing my thought process would take some more time.

There are many lessons to be learned on the journey to forgiveness, and they are not all about the ones who have trespassed against us. Often our own transgressions keep us from experiencing the sweetness of forgiveness. There are things we need to change about ourselves also.

When I decided to rededicate myself to the gospel and talked with the bishop, I admitted my own inability to forgive myself for past transgressions. After all these years, I had never forgiven myself for my two abortions. How could the Lord ever forgive me? I had carried that weight the whole time. I remember crying and feeling ashamed as I confessed to the bishop. I had not verbalized my own dark secrets to anyone but Joey and my first bishop. I was overwhelmed with guilt at this confession. I was ashamed that the bishop I would see every Sunday now knew my deepest, most shameful sins. How could he ever look at me in a good light?

He asked if I went through all the correct steps of repentance at baptism. I told him I had not gone through any except admitting them. I told him I was sorry when I first admitted it, and that my first bishop told me I was right before the Lord upon my baptism. But I did not believe him. How could I be right before the Lord for such terrible sins? My newest bishop told me he would check to see if there were anything more I needed to do regarding this issue. During that week, I prayed fervently to the Lord and asked Him to forgive me. It seemed the weight of all those years was heavier than ever. I remembered the spiritual experience I had with my first bishop, but the shame had returned.

When I met with the bishop the next week, he read to me that, since my former transgressions occurred before I was a member, there was no process which I had to go through because I had confessed them to my first bishop. Because of my baptism, all my former transgressions were forgiven. He said the Lord had forgiven me, but I had not forgiven myself.

He was right. I had not. I still suffered from self-hatred and shame after all these years. I did not love myself for who I was then, nor for who I was now. After all these years, I still carried the self-hate I experienced as a child. *Self-hate was Satan's best tool for keeping me from Heavenly Father.* I felt unworthy of His love and acceptance. I knew I was not the cause of the abuse, but the effects of it made me hate my very being. If I hated myself, how could I love those who were the cause of my self-hatred? How could I love those who had instilled shame as a natural feeling in me? I thought guilt was the tool Heavenly Father used to prick our conscience. But I felt guilty for my father's actions against me! I also felt shame for the abuse—as if I had something to do with it. I had become so afraid of stepping out of my comfort zone that I was afraid to open my heart to the hope that maybe I could really be rid of these feelings. I had experienced self-hate, shame and guilt my whole life.

It was hard to imagine what feelings would replace them. Self-love and self-acceptance were feelings I had experienced only for short times in my life. But something within me kept pushing me to go on. Although I wavered, my inner spirit kept pushing me forward. I felt a part of me hungry for the peace the gospel promised. This was the motivating force that kept me going. I finally understood that a change would have to occur within me, not others.

In the days of our strong and faithful church pioneers, physical anguish and loss of life were the main challenges. But in this day and age, people seem to suffer more from mental anguish and spiritual death. Sometimes I thought we are so weak, compared to the early saints. But depression and mental anguish are just as challenging to us as a physically challenged life was to them. While they experienced the physical loss of life of a loved one, I felt a loss of life from within because of a lack of self-love.

I imagined the pioneers trekking across the plains, pushing their loads and having to lighten them a little here and there depending on the weather or the strength of those remaining to push. I envisioned them adjusting the weight of their carts according to the extremities of the land. Possessions once held so close to the heart were abandoned for life itself. Family heirlooms and children's toys were thrown aside as survival and freedom became more important. These pioneers had a goal they believed in with all their hearts. They never loss sight of it. It was to obtain religious freedom and live in peace. Upon seeing their rescuers, many left their handcarts behind, seeing no value in them anymore. They left them on the side of the trail and kept going forth with a lighter load.

Many claimed angels gave them their strength. They never complained about the journey, for they got to know God in the wilderness and would not take that back for anything.

I compared this mental vision to my own trek of having to let go of some of my bitter feelings that were becoming too heavy to bear any longer. I needed to let go of those things that were preventing happiness in my life.

I saw myself trekking across my own wilderness, only I was not letting go of anything. My biggest dead weights were my own thoughts and my inability to just let go. I was not surviving my trek. I did not know how to adjust my load and how to let go of those things holding me back. I was in the middle of a storm and I did not know how to survive.
The pioneers had a goal from which they never wavered. They would do anything to obtain their goal, acknowledging God's presence to sustain them. He was the secret to their strength.

I had to believe, as they did, that the Lord would be my strength. I had to set my goal, which was to find peace within the gospel. I needed to keep an end in sight. But I also realized that no one was going to come to my rescue like the pioneers' rescuers. My journey was not about religious freedom; rather, it was about spiritual healing. My only rescuer would be Heavenly Father Himself.

In order to move forward, I had to forgive myself of my past transgressions. I could not do it on my own. Although I still had so much to overcome, I pleaded with the Lord that I could learn to accept and love myself. I needed to know that He really forgave me. I did not understand how I could ever know if He did. I just knew I could not move forward until I knew without a doubt that He had forgiven me.

Miraculously, within days, I was blessed with this confirmation. It seems a compassionate Lord knew I had suffered enough from guilt and finally eased my shameful feelings.

In a dream I was standing and was encompassed about by the most glorious white light I had ever seen before. It seemed to have feelings associated with it for I felt love beyond any I had ever experienced in this life. There was no talking, but thoughts, that I was a daughter of God, not only entered my mind, they pierced my very soul. For a brief moment I understood just what this meant. The eternal capabilities we each have overwhelmed me. I realized how much potential I could tap into, and that I had not tapped into hardly any of it. My inability to let go of the past was debilitating my eternal possibilities and all the good works that I could do in this life. I awoke with a clear understanding that there was more to life than just the pain I had experienced from my past. *I realized that the Lord required more of me.*

If He is all knowing and can see the future, then He *knew* that I would overcome my trial. That was why He required more of me. He saw an end to my pain, and with this very remarkable experience, I felt a new hope develop within me. I could not see the future, but I knew that I would be doing more in this life than battling with this trial. That was my end in sight! That was the hope I needed! I had to believe in this experience and focus on trying to feel that love again. This is a message He would want all those suffering from pain to know. Through Him personal pain can be lifted and a fulfilling life awaits.

My journey to forgiveness would lead me down a path to find my own worth and my divine heritage. It made sense to me. How could I forgive others if I could not forgive myself? How could I love others if I could not love myself?

CHAPTER TWENTY

Remember

"Remember the worth of souls is great in the sight of God."
(D&C 18:10)

As I searched to reclaim my worth, I realized I was going to have to start from scratch. I could not fall back on my past. My very identity was being tested. Anxiety, guilt, fear, depression and even self-hatred were natural day-to-day emotions for me. I saw life through a dark cloud. I could pick out the worst in a situation. I had lived with this mindset my whole life. How was I going to change it? I am sure many saw me as weak or complaining, but it was all I knew. There were many times I had tried to be positive, but my old mindset would come back. It was deeply engrained. It would be very hard to replace my old patterns. They were the only life I knew. I wanted a more positive outlook, but it would take a lot of hard work to change my ways.

I had to rebuild my self-esteem. I could not be a victim anymore to my past or how others treated me. It was the mistreatment from my family and others that had convinced me I was flawed. To many, low self-esteem means insecurity and weakness. But it goes to a much deeper level if the victim believes she is damaged goods or flawed. And, well, being a victim of abuse did something to me. Naturally, I am outgoing. But addressing my issues closed that part of me for years so I became fragile in my relations with others.

At this time during healing, I had no sisters to call upon. No one understood what I was going through. I was alone again and I could not stand feeling lonely. It seemed, during my path to healing, as often as I would have breakthroughs, I would also have set backs. But this loneliness would come to benefit me. It was an opportunity for me to rely solely on the Lord once again. I could not depend on anyone at this time except Joey. Even though I was hurting at this time, I was also learning. I was learning that I needed the Lord. As I would fast for breakthroughs and understandings, I could only find solace in His teachings and the comfort the Holy Spirit brings. If I slacked at this time spiritually, my pains hurt just as bad as if they had just happened. Being spiritually prepared was strengthening me from within.

As I tried to strengthen my low self-esteem, I came to many realizations. I had to stop associating my worth with how others treated me, whether they were family or just people. It was okay for me to avoid people and family who hurt me. It was okay to find the courage to start standing up for myself and separate my own self-worth from other's acceptance. I had a choice. Admitting and taking responsibility for our own actions is not easy.

In the past, I felt trying to be accepted by others would fill that void of worthlessness that I felt. But why would I want to have a relationship with someone who continued to verbally harm me? By trying to gain their acceptance, I was reaffirming that I was worthless. I had to disconnect emotionally from any abusive relationships to be able to grow. I had to separate myself from any type of degrading relationship to gain a new perspective on life and just who I was.

The words in D&C 50:41-44 had a great impact on me. In fact, I was touched by the Holy Spirit and read this scripture passage over and over. It helped me overcome feeling like damaged goods. "Fear not, little children, for you are mine, and I have overcome the world, and you are of them that my Father hath given me; And none of them that my Father hath given me shall be lost. And the Father and I are one. I am in the Father and the Father in me; and inasmuch as ye have received me, *ye are in me and I in you.* Wherefore, I am in your midst, and I am the good shepherd, and the stone of Israel. He that buildeth upon this rock shall never fall. And the day cometh that you shall hear my voice and see me, and know that I am. Watch, therefore, that ye may be ready. Even so, Amen."

This scripture helped me to imagine a loving older brother, Jesus Christ, holding his arms open, accepting, embracing and comforting me as he softly speaks, "Fear not, for you are mine." I imagined Him telling me that He will show me the way, and I will not be lost. And if I receive Him, He is in me. If He can dwell within me, then I cannot be the damaged person I thought I was, but whole. I was not damaged goods! That is a worldly term to describe how I felt inside. It was just a mindset. Mindsets can change. I was not damaged because of what my father did to me. I was still a daughter of God. My father's actions did not change that. I needed to make Jesus Christ my foundation. I had tried so many other ways, but fell short of peace each and every time. I had not really prepared myself to accept His powers of healing and love. I had not been ready. I realized the more I stayed repentant with a humble openness to look at myself, the more I understood the Savior. I began to understand what He meant when He called for a sacrifice of a broken heart and a contrite spirit.

A deep part of me still felt unworthy of His love. I felt I did not deserve happiness. I would enjoy spurts of it, but it would not last. To be happy all the time was an uncomfortable thought. Experiencing the power of the Holy Spirit was a miracle to me, and the way it penetrated through the negativity gave me hope. I realized in order to truly heal I had to make a conscious choice to do so. I could not ask for my trial to go away, but I had to remember that Christ could repair even the most severe damage to one's very soul. By doing this, a whole new door opened to me.

What was I worth? I had to dig deep inside to find the answer. I decided to draw on the powers of the priesthood. I had my husband give me a blessing. I needed an inner strength to grow within me. My old beliefs and doubts seemed so powerful and overbearing. I realized that I had to stay close to the Holy Spirit at this time. I knew I was going to make a breakthrough, but felt opposing forces doing all within their power to muddy the waters. After my blessing, I felt protected. It was time to get to work. For too long feelings of worthlessness had plagued my life and I had continuously fallen victim to the belief that I had nothing to offer.

I love the story in John Chapter 9. Jesus heals a man born blind. His disciples ask the Master, "Who sinned, his parents or him?" They questioned if the man was flawed–in a sinful state before he came to earth deserving of this curse–or were his parents sinful so he had to pay the price for their sins, carrying a heavy, lonely burden? That was what I had done my whole life. But none of these assumptions were correct, for the Lord replied, "Neither hath this man sinned, nor his parents; but that the works of God should be made manifest in him." When Jesus healed the man, He demonstrated His absolute power to the unbelieving. This story opened my eyes to an understanding that I did not come to earth in a sinful state, deserving of bad things. I also learned I need not pay the price for my parents' sins. Paying for their sins had become too high of a price in my life. I needed to prepare a way to make the Lord's power manifest itself in my life. As He stated to Paul, "My grace is sufficient for thee; for my strength is made perfect in weakness."

In D&C 93:29 it states, "Man was also in the beginning with God. Intelligence, or the light of truth, was not created or made, neither indeed can be." And in verse 33, it declares, "For man is spirit. The elements are eternal, and spirit and element, inseparably connected, receive a fullness of joy." Verse 38 tells us, "Every spirit of man was innocent in the beginning; and God having redeemed man from the fall, men became again, in their infant state, innocent before God." In Abraham 3:23, it states "And God saw these souls that they were good." I realized that these scriptures aptly describe my divine heritage. All intelligences, including mine, have been described in the scriptures as the light of truth, innocent in the beginning, and God saw that we were good. This is a very different picture than the life my parents showed me. These scriptures' description of all spirits before they came to earth made a great impact on me as I searched to discover and reclaim my worth. I had become so focused on my pain that I could not see beyond the abuse or my abusers. These scriptures opened a door to the truth of my self-worth.

I found that Heavenly Father was very patient with me. I realized the Holy Spirit was my guide when I was on the right course. I was the only one who seemed to give up and get discouraged at times during my healing journey. I finally realized that Heavenly Father never gave up on me and realized He does not give up on anyone. The information I was learning was wonderful. Had He just taken my burden away, I would never have gained such amazing insights. He knew my personal struggle and would gently lead me in the right direction. For each mistake I made and each wrong direction I followed, He was always there to pick me up and help me to start over again. My heart was touched by this insight.

The wisdom of the world would have me believe that my worth was connected to how others treated me and the things

I had. That is why I always went shopping to fill the void inside of me. I believed if others treated me badly, then I must be bad. I believed for too long that my worth was connected to all the bad things that had happened to me. I believed I was flawed because of the cruelty of others.

It was not until the scriptures came alive to me that I was able to understand my divine heritage. As I looked to my divine roots, I saw a broader picture than I had ever seen before. I had been seeing only what was just before my eyes. When I separated myself from all the bad things that had happened to me and the bad choices I had made, I was able to see my true self. I realized I was a daughter of God and a spirit of light with just as much potential as the next person. I realized the abuse was something that had happened to me, not something that made me flawed or damaged. That was only a distorted perception abuse leaves with the victim. *The correct perception is to understand that the abuse I endured did not hinder my eternal possibilities.* Only I could do that by not forgiving and trusting that the Lord could heal me.

The abuse was not who I was. Rather, it was the result of someone using his God-given free agency. Even though I had been robbed of my virtue, eternal law states that I would not be robbed of my eternal potential. As church leaders have counseled, a person may feel scarred because of abuse, but the scars do not need to be permanent. The scars on our body may stay with us throughout this lifetime, but spiritual wounds can be made right as we do our part.

I learned that Satan's influence on me was as powerful as I let it be. As I succumbed to his temptations of feeling constantly bad, he had power over me. I had to keep remembering what Heavenly Father would want me to feel and believe. He would want me to feel hope and exercise faith that He could heal me. As my testimony strengthened,

Satan's influence became weaker and weaker. I found I had more control over my feelings. I was realizing Satan really does not have power to take away any good feelings or deteriorate my testimony. Only I could do that by succumbing to his temptations.

I continued to search for answers as to how to get over feeling guilty and shameful because of the abuse. After all my studying, I realized I was carrying a burden I did not need to. All my prayers, readings and listening to talks were paying off. I was growing inside and gaining an inner strength I had not experienced before. Why should I feel guilty for being abused? I was the child. *The greatest turning point in the life of a victim of abuse is when the shame is lifted by the realization that it was not your fault–nor were you ever deserving of such crimes against your innocence!* My eyes were opened to understanding that this is the greatest lie a person can believe about herself. This is exactly what the adversary wants you to believe. He wants us to feel flawed, impure and unworthy–not only of the help of others, but of Heavenly Father Himself. He wants us to believe we are not worthy of acceptance and love offered by others and Him. I was an innocent victim, helpless from fear and overwhelmed with the authority and power of my father. The less I felt the Holy Sprit in my life, the easier it was to forget what love felt like, and the easier it was to feel Satan's influence more than Heavenly Father's.

The abuse could not keep me from Heavenly Father. He was not disappointed with me because of the abuse I had endured. The abuse did not signify my worthiness to be in His presence or the presence of others. But because I had endured abuse, His works could be made manifest in me by showing His absolute power in healing me just like the blind man.

CHAPTER TWENTY-ONE

The Light of Christ

*"He that ascended up on high, as also he descended below
all things, in that he comprehended all things, that he
might be in all and through all things, the light of truth;
Which truth shineth. This is the light of Christ."*
(D&C 88:6-7)

I had finally forgiven myself for my transgressions and felt
freedom from shame. I was not embarrassed that I was
abused. Before I was weak because of the abuse–now I felt
strong because of the journey I had completed thus far. I felt
of worth to a loving Heavenly Father. If I could forgive
myself, I could forgive my family and all those for whom I
held grudges.

I continued to study the life and atonement of Jesus Christ. I
wanted to get to know Him better. I kept asking myself,
"What would Heavenly Father want me to know?" The first
thing that came to mind was He wanted me to know that
healing would occur if I did my part. Without even
experiencing it fully, I knew He had a path of success laid
out for me. I had found answers to hard questions. I not only
found answers to my lack of self-esteem and worthlessness, I
felt whole inside. I literally felt that my worth was separated
from how others had treated me. For the first time in my life,
an inner love and strength were growing from within.

Miracles had happened. I did not think I could love or accept
myself. It was humbling, the feelings precious. I finally felt
at peace inside. I finally believed I was a woman of courage.
I had been through so much! I had lived a life with
uncertainty about my purpose. Now I realized it was my

uncertainty that kept me from moving towards the future with purpose. It was not until I understood my divine nature that I was able to move forward with strength and certainty.

The Lord had enlightened me as much as I could handle. Loving me, He gave me no more than I could bear. There were plenty of times I felt overly burdened, but that comes with such a trial. I was on a quest to finish my work, and this time the changes within me were lasting. The Lord never sent surface changes, only life-changing answers.

At times the journey seemed harder than the abuse itself, because now, as an adult, I was finally dealing with the emotions of it all. But if having to deal with abuse meant being blessed with the inner changes and feelings that had occurred, I would do it all over again. Nothing filled the void in my life like the gospel. Healing is a time to dig deep down and purposefully intensify the light of Christ in our lives. For that is the only hope we have of successfully completing this hard journey. He was my strength. When I felt no person's love reach out to me, I felt His. I was fully dependent on the Lord. I thought being independent and finding my own way were signs of strength. Rather, they brought confusion and no growth. I looked beyond the mark many times in search of the answers, only to be disappointed.

As I set out on my quest to forgive, I realized many things had to be in place. First, I had to stop asking myself why so many do not heal. It was the track record of those abused who did not heal that scared me. It was the thought that abuse will always stay with me that made me doubt. Now I knew the answer. To heal I had to confront things I did not want to. I lost my family and missed out on many friendships. The journey required hard work and courage. I knew that I had to have faith that I could be healed. It was my lack of faith that had kept me stuck. I had to believe I could actually be free of this burden.

I studied the miracles Jesus Christ performed while on the earth. The stories became real to me. To help strengthen my faith that I could forgive and be healed, many scriptures led my way. I read Luke 4:18: "He hath sent me to heal the broken hearted." And in Psalms 147:3, "He healeth the broken in heart, and bindeth up their wounds." I was finally starting to understand the magnitude of Jesus Christ's purpose. I did not have a testimony of it before. I had read about so many physical miracles, but wondered how He was going to heal my broken heart. These scriptures gave me hope. I finally believed His purpose was to not only heal every person, but *especially* a person who suffered from abuse–like me.

When I read the Sermon on the Mount, I felt His words speaking directly to me. "Blessed are they that mourn; for they shall be comforted. Blessed are the meek for they shall inherit the earth." I did not understand that meek in this context meant "the humble, those that had suffered." *I believed these words. I believed He would comfort and heal me. I could not deny the miracles that had taken place in my life.* It was because of my studying that I found out how to tap into the powers of Jesus Christ's promise that He would comfort me.

I drew great strength reading about Jesus Christ in the Garden of Gethsemane. "Father, if thou be willing, remove this cup from me: nevertheless not my will, but thine, be done. And there appeared an angel unto him from heaven, strengthening him. And being in an agony he prayed more earnestly." (Luke 22:42-44). Jesus prayed to his Father to, if He be willing, "remove this cup." Instead of removing the hard experience from Jesus Christ, Heavenly Father sent an

281

angel from Heaven, strengthening Him during that crucial time.

There were many times I had asked and pleaded with the Lord to take this trial from me. But this scripture taught me that the Lord will provide the strength needed to endure a little longer. He will stretch us. If there is one thing that I learned, it is that trials do not disappear. Rather, if we are faithful, they become less painful, and through our faith, we can see an end in sight.

The scripture goes on that, while He was in continued agony, "He prayed more earnestly." I found that when I let up spiritually, during my hardest times, my agony stayed longer than if I prayed for help more "earnestly." I prayed to endure what I needed and to learn what was required for me to move on.

Although there were many times I felt the Lord comfort me during my journey, there were times that I did not. I understood why I did not feel His presence when I lacked faith, but it was during the times I felt close to Him that I questioned why He seemed silent to my pleadings. I did not understand why until I was studying when Jesus was on the cross at Calvary. Jesus Christ asked His father, "My God, my God, why hast thou forsaken me?" Although in the garden of Gethsemane an angel was sent to help comfort and strengthen him, on the cross of Calvary no angel came. The Savior endured a private agony. As I studied His loneliness in suffering, I came to my own understanding that the Savior had to endure parts of His suffering on His own. I realized that the Lord may be silent at times to allow us to struggle on our own. Will we get angry at Him and lose faith? Will we continue to be strong believing in His own timetable that answers and comfort will come? It is during these times that our character is tested and the strength of our testimony is questioned. But if we move forward in faith, our soul is strengthened and we become closer to God.

I was starting to understand the love Heavenly Father had for me. He sent Jesus Christ to lead the way. I was touched when I read in Matthew, Chapter 18, about Jesus preaching, "If a man have an hundred sheep, and one of them be gone astray, doth he not leave the ninety and nine, and goeth into the mountains, and seeketh that which is gone astray? And if it so be that he find it, verily I say unto you, he rejoiceth more of that sheep, than of the ninety and nine which went not astray. Even so it is not the will of your Father which is in heaven, that one of these little ones should perish."

As I had been lost for so long, I imagined His sorrow for my experience. I imagined Him searching for me, wanting me to know that He would bring peace and freedom to my heart. He loved me and wanted to protect me just as I did my own children. This scripture had a great impact on me. The Holy Spirit bore witness to me that Heavenly Father knew my pains and *was seeking opportunities to reach me*. It made me feel that Heavenly Father loved me on a very personal level. I felt I was important enough for Heavenly Father to send real answers and comfort to me during my trial so that I would not be in a stuck state. I reflected on the many times He had tried to help me. He sent people into my life to bring me back to Him, helping me experience small miracles to strengthen my testimony of Him. I could see His works through people and insights. He had been searching for me and trying to help me.

In Mark, Chapter 9, a father goes to the Master and asks, "Have compassion on us and help us." His son was possessed with a "dumb spirit." Jesus replied, "If thou canst believe, all things are possible to him that believeth." The father said, "Lord, I believe; help thou mine unbelief." And

Jesus healed his son. This story touched my heart. It confirmed to me that healing was predicated by my faith. If I did not believe I could be healed, then I would not be healed. I would stay stuck in a state of confusion, just as I had been for years. I had to do something different. Ignoring my problem would not make healing come sooner; rather, it prolonged my happiness. I realized I would get from healing what I put into it. A strong testimony and faith in the Lord would lead me to the solutions I longed for. I could not move forward when I doubted.

Talks by church leaders state that peace, comfort and love await me as I exercise faith in the Lord when times of turmoil come. There is always a solution. There are some things that just will not change in this life, and they include Heavenly Father's unfailing love for His children. This is a constant, binding love that could not be changed, no matter what my circumstances. I had to tap into that support by finding strength in my faith in Him and in His willingness to bless me. He could help heal my unbelief and doubting. "If thou canst believe, all things are possible to him that believeth."

Jesus performed so many miracles–healing the sick and physically afflicted, raising the dead, cleansing the leper, giving sight to the blind and hearing to the deaf. The lame walked and He brought wholeness where there was none. He performed so many miracles within my own life. I may not have been physically challenged, but I was spiritually and mentally. I understood in a spiritual sense the cleansing of the leper as I experienced something similar upon baptism and when I would repent. I understood the returning of sight to the blind and hearing to the deaf as my testimony was strengthened through reading the scriptures and applying the truths to my life. I understood healing the physically afflicted as I had experienced the miracle of feeling whole even though I had been physically and sexually abused. Surely, I could forgive! He would want me to experience the miracle of it! It is hard enough to imagine and believe that a blind person could see. And yet, the Master gave him sight. There was physical proof of His power. It was equally as hard to believe He could heal me of my burden. The only proof I would have was a change of heart. But with my spiritual foundation laid, I was ready to understand forgiveness and what it required of me.

In the scriptures, many stories are told of the Lord forgiving those who sinned. But the forgiveness is always predicated on the person's repentance. He is a merciful God, but to us forgiveness is mandatory. As the Lord states in D&C 64:10, "I, the Lord, will forgive whom I will forgive, but of you it is required to forgive all men." This scripture bothered me for so long until I finally believed that this commandment from the Lord was possible to obey. He would not have given it otherwise. To forgive can only bring us closer to Him. I was experiencing the wisdom of this principle. As my journey was coming to a close, it brought me closer to the Lord and I never felt happier nor a greater peace in my life. If I were this happy now, I could only imagine the elation I would feel once I had experienced forgiveness.

My trial was an extreme experience. It is hard to find the right answers and the way. But, as Jesus states in John 14:6, "I am the way, the truth, and the life." I doubted and therefore suffered needlessly for too long because of my lack of understanding the gospel. He was there the whole time. I looked at my trial as a curse, not recognizing the potential within me until I strived to learn from it. Through my trial, my character was strengthened, my soul was stretched, my heart was softened and I received a testimony of Jesus Christ I could have not received were it not for this trial. "The trial of your faith, being much more precious than of gold that perisheth, though it be tried with fire, might be found unto praise and honor and glory at the appearing of Jesus Christ." My faith in Jesus Christ and His healing powers had become much more valuable than any item I could possess.

I realized that true healing cannot be obtained without an understanding and testimony of the atonement. The prophets and apostles of old and modern times have testified of this fact. I have heard time and time again that it is through the atonement that our sins are forgiven and our pains are healed. But I did not understand how the atonement could be a part of my everyday life. For too long, I could not answer this question.

A loving Heavenly Father has set a plan of happiness in place for *all* His children that is clear and understandable. My quest led me to this plan. It gave me hope towards my eternal destiny. With my worth strengthened, my divine heritage reclaimed and affirmed, an enlightened understanding of free agency, and an unshakable testimony of the Lord's plan, joy entered my life, daily. I had a foundation in place to understand and experience the healing powers of the atonement of Jesus Christ.

I had needed a higher power to open my spiritual eyes. Just as so many miracles in the scriptures could only occur with the assistance of the Master, I needed to become open to the miracles of Christ's atonement. The sting of abuse was softened as my testimony grew and my understanding of the atonement became clearer.

I could not understand how Jesus took upon Himself our sins and sorrows. But as my understanding grew, I came to know His purpose. "For this cause came I into the world" (John 18:37). Jesus Christ, the ultimate example, led the way for us. He trod a path that had not been laid before. He was the only one who could do it. Jesus was persecuted and afflicted physically and emotionally, but he never wavered in purpose because He knew *His* purpose. Before, my lack of testimony about my divine heritage made me uncertain regarding my purpose. Now, understanding my purpose here in life gave me something to work towards. I now believed overcoming this trial was just one of my purposes.

Though part God, He was still tempted with evil and could have sinned. But He did not. His example showed His dedication and commitment to His own standards. Just as Jesus drew on the powers of Heavenly Father to fulfill His purpose, I needed to draw on the powers of Heavenly Father to fulfill mine. I was a pioneer in my own line. The abuse had to stop with me. I had to heal from it.

On earth, we are separated from God's presence because of Adam's transgression. No unclean thing can dwell with Heavenly Father. But Jesus Christ broke the bands of death and extends His mercy to help us live once again with Heavenly Father. He did this alone in the Garden of Gethsemane and on the cross of Calvary. It can be hard to fully comprehend, but is understandable when you need to tap into its power to heal. The Savior took upon Himself the sins of the world. To help me better comprehend this, I imagined the Savior in the garden with a beam of light coming down from the Heavens that was filled with every emotion known to man at that time and in times to come. That beam infused Him with our griefs and sorrows so He could understand us "according to the flesh." (Alma 7:11-12) Not only did he take upon Himself the sins of the world, He makes intercession for those that transgress. Thank goodness for repentance! He became acquainted with our griefs. He knows us each individually.

The following thoughts deepened and humbled my heart with gratitude for the Savior: "And he shall go forth, suffering pains and afflictions and temptations of every kind; and this that the **word** might be fulfilled which saith he will take upon him the pains and the sicknesses of his people. And he will take upon him death that he may loose the bands of death which bind his people; and he will take upon him their infirmities, that his bowels may be filled with mercy, according to the flesh, that he may know according to the flesh how to succor his people according to their infirmities." (Alma 7:11-12) I had read these scriptures time and time again, but they had taken on a new meaning to me. Clearly, I was gaining a testimony of His healing power and love for us. He had to experience what we did in order to know how to comfort us.

"He that ascended up on high, as also he descended below all things, in that he comprehendeth all things, that he might be in all and through all things, the light of truth; Which truth shineth. This is the light of Christ." (D&C88:6) His atonement gave Him the capacity to experience all feelings and experiences, making Him understand us all on a personal level. Without experiencing all things, He could not comfort us. He could not comfort me. *The Holy Spirit testified to me that this scripture means there is no depth of despair that the light of Christ cannot comfort.* There is no level of hate that He cannot convert into charity. He comprehends us perfectly and personally. He knows our very thoughts and doubts, and by His willing, atoning sacrifice, we can see the light that will lead the way and relieve our personal sufferings.

Having the Holy Spirit bear testimony that these things are true filled my heart with love beyond measure. I came to love the Savior who willingly cleared the path for me to return to Heavenly Father. His suffering was immeasurable compared to mine. I suffered for my own abuse, but He suffered and experienced the suffering of *all mankind*. "Surely he hath borne our griefs, and carried our sorrows. But he was wounded for our transgressions, he was bruised for our iniquities: the chastisement of our peace was upon him; and with his stripes we are healed." (Isaiah. 53:4-5)

With this understanding of His willingness to endure his own suffering as well as the world's I realized I had a choice like He did. His work would not be finished if He did not atone for our sins, bear our griefs, willingly die and ascend on high for all of mankind. My work would not be done until I had forgiven. My strengthened testimony of the gospel made me want to experience the healing power of the atonement on a daily basis. I was understanding the value of each and every soul, even my parents. Although they would be accountable for their own transgressions, I realized that, in order to make the atonement real in my life, I had to forgive.

Even if my father repented of his many sins, he could not give back that which he took from me. The damage he inflicted on me was severe and unbearable at times. He could not make restitution. This is the very essence of the atonement. The Lord will mend that which my father cannot, even if my father repents. My father cannot give back that which he took, my sacred innocence. Although my father has never made an attempt to make peace with me, I still have the power of the atonement to make up for what was taken from me by His Almighty Grace. The Lord fills the gaps of pain with His love and restores that which was broken and replaces that which was taken.

How could I have an understanding of the atonement and not forgive? Forgiveness begins with a change in attitude, a strengthened testimony and a desire to be like Him. I love the story in Matthew 18:21 where Peter asks the Lord, "How oft shall my brother sin against me, and I forgive him? till

289

seven times? Jesus saith unto him, I say not unto thee, until seven times: but, until seventy times seven." I took this to mean there is nothing we cannot forgive through the Lord. There is no numerical limit on forgiving. No matter what the offense. "For with what judgment ye judge, ye shall be judged: and with what measure ye mete, it shall be measured to you again." (Matt. 7:2)

I did not expect to reach the place I did. I now knew I would be able to forgive, but I did not expect love to be associated with it. I reflected on the many blessings in my life and was most grateful for the gospel. My greatest blessings were spiritual in nature. I realized that my parents did not have the gospel in their lives. I did not expect them to apologize to me and, more importantly, I did not need them to in order to heal. They were not going to accept responsibility for their actions. They had their free agency. But having the gospel in my life, I needed to accept responsibility for mine. The Lord asks us to forgive. I would show an ungrateful heart if I did not forgive after receiving all my spiritual insight.

I read Matthew Chapter 5 over and over again. "An eye for an eye, and a tooth for a tooth" was the Mosaic law. But when Jesus came, the carnal law was replaced. "Love your enemies, bless them that curse you, do good to them that hate you, and pray for them which despitefully use you, and persecute you; That ye may be the children of your Father which is in heaven: for he maketh this sun to rise on the evil and on the good, and sendeth rain on the just and on the unjust. For if ye love them which love you, what reward have ye?"

This scripture was all encompassing. It not only challenged my feelings towards my family, it guided my feelings towards those who had hurt me. The phrase that touched me most was, "That ye may be the children of your Father which is in Heaven." By trying to forgive, I was experiencing His love more and more on a daily basis. I was letting Him in and trusting Him. My heart was changing. I was learning it was more important to become like Heavenly Father than to hate those who had hurt me. When we are bound by the powers of darkness, we cannot have the faith that precedes the miracle.

The growth that occurred took me further in a shorter amount of time than any other method of healing. As I read the words of the scriptures, their impact took me to new heights within the gospel I never experienced before.

Why else should I forgive? To show the Lord I understand His gospel, and that it is the only way I can try to pay the debt I owe Him for what He has done for me. Who was I that He worked so hard to help me heal? I was the "little one" He speaks about in Matthew 18. "But whoso shall offend one of these "little ones" which believe in me, it were better for him that a millstone were hanged about his neck, and that he were drowned in the depth of the sea. Woe unto the world because of offences! For it must needs be that offences come; but woe to that man by whom the offence cometh! Take heed that ye despise not one of these little ones; for I say unto you, That in heaven their angels do always behold the face of my Father which is in heaven. For the Son of man is come to save that which was lost." There is no doubt that Jesus Christ restored my worth and saved me from a life of repeated abuse. I no longer felt flawed or damaged, but rather whole, fulfilled and restored. The void I felt inside my whole life was gone.

My debt to Him is great. In Matthew 18, Jesus Christ shares a parable likening the kingdom of heaven to a certain king. A servant was in great debt to the king and when it came time to pay him back, he could not. Upon the king's judgment, the servant begged for forgiveness and asked that the king have patience with him, for surely he would pay the debt back in full. The king not only found compassion in his heart but forgave the servant his debt. Then the servant left and found someone who owed him money. But he refused to show the same kind of compassion. He had his debtor cast into prison until he should pay the debt. The king, hearing of this, was wroth with the servant. He chided, "I forgave thee all that debt, because thou desiredst me. Shouldest not thou also have had compassion on thy fellow servant, even as I had pity on thee?" Jesus ended the parable with this—"So likewise my Heavenly Father will do also unto you, if ye from your hearts forgive not every one his brother their trespasses."

In John 4:18-20, it states "There is no fear in love; but perfect love casteth out fear: because fear hath torment...If a man say, I love God, and hateth his brother, he is a liar: for he that loveth not his brother whom he hath seen, how can he love God whom he hath not seen? And this commandment have we from him, That he who loveth God love his brother also?" This is a very hard commandment to obey when others have hurt us.

Regarding my family, I had personally received a confirmation that the Lord had forgiven my great sins. I *had* to forgive my parents or I would be just like the ungrateful servant who asked for forgiveness and compassion but was not willing to give it himself. I knew I would always be in debt for what the Lord had done for me. Forgiving my parents would not pay the debt, but it would prove my attempts at living the gospel to my greatest capacity.

Love. At one time, this was such a hard word to associate with my parents. I felt loving them would make me weak and vulnerable. On my journey, I questioned why some are not given an opportunity to feel loved as a child.

I had to reflect again on my father's life, not through my own eyes, but how Jesus Christ might see him. I imagined my father's life as a young boy. I do not know if he was ever held in loving arms. He was taken from a home where he was neglected and put into an orphanage. There he was beaten, abused and scared. He was only eighteen months old when he was put into that orphanage. I could imagine how alone he felt and how confused he was as to why he was not treated better. I pulled out a picture of him when he was young. He could not have been more than five. I suddenly had compassion on this little boy. He looked so happy, even though I knew what type of life he had experienced by the time he was five. In this picture, my father was not an abuser, but rather, he was the abused.

During his teenage years, he was taken back to his birth mother where severe abuse continued. He must have been confused as to why life was so hard; or by this time, perhaps he stopped questioning and just tried to survive. He was not groomed or guided. I also had compassion on that teenage boy.

As a single adult, he had no guidance regarding life and relationships. I know all too well now that we mimic what we have been taught. I understood his mistakes of getting two women pregnant before marriage and had compassion on this young man.

Thinking of him as a father, it got harder to have compassion. I had compassion on my father for the physical and emotional abuse he inflicted on me because it was all he knew. But I could not have compassion for molesting his own child. Nor do I still. Those deeds were too evil. I could not have compassion on him for molesting me, but I could forgive him.

293

Instead of praying for vengeance against my father, I prayed to the Lord to have compassion on him, for his life was not fair. He was also a child who had been offended. That picture of him when he was five years old reminded me of the sacred duty of parenting–the important role we have as parents and the great influence we have on our children. He had only experienced darkness in this life. It started when he was so young. I prayed that Heavenly Father would embrace my father someday and let him experience what real love is and take his childhood pain away. I knew my father would be held accountable for his sins against me, and that was out of my hands. I just asked the Lord to let him experience the love he did not feel in this life. When my father was that little boy, he would never have dreamed of growing up to be what he became. After receiving the gospel in my life, how I wished he would have experienced what I had before he became what he did! Going through this very sacred experience, my heart had changed. Forgiveness suddenly made sense. I felt such a weight leave me as I experienced love for a father who had abused me! I had experienced that which seemed unobtainable. *I realized without a doubt that love and forgiveness are inseparable.* The love came from understanding the Savior's love for me, then passing it onto my father.

Forgiveness did not diminish my understanding that my father could still harm me or my children–I still chose to not have a relationship with him. But it helped me to be free of my hate towards him. Forgiving him seemed such a small thing to ask after experiencing it myself. Especially after considering what Jesus Christ had done for me. I realized that the Lord wanted me to experience it because it brought me closer to Him and to His ways. Forgiving gave me a glimpse of the tender mercies and grace the Lord shows us.

I could not believe the weight that was lifted from me. My focus had changed from my pains that bound me to forgiving that freed me.

Forgiving my mother did not come at the same time. I did not understand why, but it took longer to forgive her than my father. I guess she was harder to understand. Being the abuser was horrible, but being the person allowing it to happen was incomprehensible to me. I went through much of the same process as I did with my father, replaying her life in my mind and trying to have compassion on her.

What I discovered was that I had loved her the whole time and her betrayal of me still hurt. That is why it was harder to forgive her. My heart was broken that my mother could reject me so easily. I needed to forgive her for her actions. Even after I thought of the life she had experienced it was hard to forgive her. The reality was that I knew I could not have a relationship with her while she was still with my father–they were not good together. I had to trust in the Lord and where forgiveness would take me.

It is hard to love someone who does not love you back or just cannot. But, she too had a hard life. I prayed for my heart to change towards my mother. It took quite some time. I read scriptures and came across the story of Job once again. In Job, Chapter 42:2, he prays to the Lord and says "I know that thou canst do everything." In this scripture Job prayed for his friends who doubted and because Job held strong to his testimony the Lord blessed his later life more abundantly than his beginning. I knew the Lord could change my heart. I knew the Lord could help me love someone who could not love me. I also knew I could not do it alone.

Finally, I prayed to the Lord to love my mother, and like my father, embrace her with a love she was deserving to experience in this lifetime. I felt sorry for her. She deserved a better life and a better husband. Her trials kept her from being a better person. I understand what she was going through. It was hard for me to become a better person. It was hard to hate her anymore when my perspective had been changed by the Holy Spirit. Instead of looking at all her mean deeds, I could see her through spiritual eyes and hoped her soul would heal also. My mother's hard life had put a wall around her and like so many who have been abused it is hard to penetrate. It is hard to trust in the Lord because when we have been through so many bad experiences, we let our guard down only a little. Securing that no one will hurt us again. The wall, unfortunately, that is supposed to protect us from pain also keeps love out. I had to let down another wall to love my mother. I was still trying to protect myself from her. I remember crying and releasing the pain and fear I had held onto, to protect myself. I had reached a point where my trust in the Lord allowed me to do this. I had to trust that forgiving her would free me from getting hurt again.

I also decided that while she was still with my father, for my own safety as well as for my family, I would not contact her. I felt at peace. I was able to love my mother and hope that someday she would experience the joy I had.

I realized that my journey to forgiving my greatest trespassers helped me to forgive others who had hurt me. I was able to look past weaknesses of others and move on. I also realized that I did not need to place myself in situations where people are demeaning to me and that I had a choice to walk away. I realized it was okay to set boundaries.

It is empowering to be able to say I was molested as a child and do not hate my abusers! There is something so freeing in this statement! I could not have done it without the Lord and I am forever indebted to Him.

A peace had come to me that did not go away. "But the Comforter, which is the Holy Ghost, whom the Father will send in my name, he shall teach you all things, and bring all things to your remembrance, whatsoever I have said unto you. Peace I leave with you, my peace I give unto you: not as the world giveth, give I unto you. Let not your heart be troubled, neither let it be afraid." My path had led me to Jesus Christ and His love.

As horrible as my memories were, and though my soul was wrenched with pain through this trial, I had reached a point where the love I felt from the Lord and the peace He brought to me made it all worthwhile. I had never experienced such fullness in my life.

I can only testify that the Lord can heal all wounds. It is through the atonement that He provided the succor I needed to be healed–after I did my part. My part involved laying a strong foundation in the gospel and constantly strengthening my testimony. I had to believe that, through faith in Jesus Christ and His power and understanding the atonement, He could heal the spiritual wounds my father and mother had inflicted deep inside of me. I had to listen to the promptings of the Holy Spirit to finish my journey. My life may have started out with abuse, but now I know it does not have to end with it. **There is life after abuse!**

As I reflect back on this journey, it is amazing to me that it took almost ten years. I suffered needlessly during these years. The last two years I gained more insight and experienced the miracle of healing and forgiveness. I grew more the last two years than during any other time of my life.

How grateful I am for the Master's plan! Understanding and embracing the gospel has been the greatest blessing in my life. My journey does not stop here, though. There are many other things I need to work on. I look forward to these challenges because now I know without a doubt there is nothing I cannot overcome. Many of these challenges seem so small compared to what I have already overcome. I now understand where to find the secret of strength–the gospel.

In John 16:21-22, Jesus is sharing a parable about a woman who is delivering a baby. It is written "A woman when she is in travail hath sorrow, because her hour is come: but as soon as she is delivered of the child, she remembereth no more the anguish, for joy that a man is born into the world. And ye now therefore have sorrow: but I will see you again, and your heart shall rejoice, and your joy no man taketh from you." I have personally experienced the sorrow and anguish that comes with a journey like this. And like the woman, because I was delivered of this trial I, "remembereth no more the anguish." My memories are still there, but at a distance, and there is no pain associated with them. And just as Jesus Christ promised, my heart is full and no one can take the joy I now feel away. I knew moving past the pain of abuse would take a miracle, and, well, that's exactly what happened to me.

There is Life After Abuse

My life seems so different now that my trial has passed. I am able to focus on my family needs. I laugh more. I experience joy more. I have not experienced depression since healing. I have found new meaning to life. My marriage has been strengthened and I am able to look to the needs of keeping our relationship strong.

My most important goal was to enjoy my children. I felt shut down emotionally with my children after healing. I could see a barrier I had put up. I am now able to capture those special little moments with my children that seemed to escape my attention before. A special memory that always brings a smile to my face was when we were having a discussion on "choosing the right" at a Sunday dinner. We were giving examples and talking about how important it was to choose the right. My sweet five-year old daughter asked seriously, "Momma, what if we choose the left?" All of us silently looked around the table and then broke into laughter. My daughter seemed a little confused as I responded, "Well, that wouldn't be a good thing."

Real joy comes from within our home. It really is a refuge, or can be, from the world. It seems nothing compares to the experiences within the home. Children remember feelings in the home more than at school or church or any other experiences they can have. My focus for the past while has been to help make the home a more peaceful place. I do not expect perfection and by peaceful I do not mean quiet. A family of seven can get quite loud. What I mean is to keep the gospel centered in our home and a little more light heartedness towards each other brings peace. I want to be more nurturing and tap into that part of womanhood.

I also have been able to cherish my relationship with my husband more. We go out on dates more often now and I like to use those times to remind him I will always support him as he works on those things I need him to. He loves it when I do that. Actually, our dates are simple and just a time to enjoy each other alone.

At this time in my life, I have returned to school and I am attending the University of Utah to finish what I started twenty years ago. I am getting my degree in psychology. I have wanted to go back to school for so long and I am enjoying what I am learning. I seem to be older than everyone in the classes I take. My first teacher was 17 years younger than me with a master's degree. I was actually placed on probation at the school my first semester because I was on probation twenty years ago. That was hard to explain to admissions. My husband thought it hilarious as I proudly expressed I was probation free as I now have an "A" average.

Life is sacred. The life we give our children is precious. Our relationships within our home are vital to the gospel. I am so grateful for eternal families. I am grateful for the counsel of modern-day prophets. Listen to their counsel, read their talks. I especially found comfort in Elder Richard Scott's talks. It was through my healing process that I realized just how sacred innocence was. Sacred Innocence meaning our children. Our relationship with them is vital to our happiness on earth. We must protect them, love them, and enjoy them. *Life after abuse is captured in the home where the true essence of life is experienced.* It is my hope that by sharing my story you will turn to your Heavenly Father. It is never too late to heal or ask for help. There is always a point of return. He knows what you have been through and He can heal you.

FOR MORE INFORMATION

Wendy M. Johnson is an inspiring speaker on many subjects. Wendy uses personal experiences with humor and grace as she talks on more serious topics of healing. She is a motivational speaker as she helps her listeners move towards action. Her topics can cover Overcoming abuse, The Healing powers of Jesus Christ, Forgiveness and the Atonement. Tapping into the Atonement to help you heal...

Contact Information:

Wendy@livinglegacypublishing.com

Discounts given to quantity orders by calling (801)510-8764.